instant JAVA™

John A. Pew

SunSoft Press
A Prentice Hall Title

The publisher offers discounts on this book when ordered in bulk quantities.
For more information, contact Corporate Sales Department, Prentice Hall PTR ,
One Lake Street, Upper Saddle River, NJ 07458. Phone: 800-382-3419; FAX: 201- 236-7141.
E-mail: corpsales@prenhall.com.

Editorial/production supervision: *Joanne Anzalone*
Cover design director: *Jerry Votta*
Cover designer: *Anthony Gemellaro*
Cover illustration: *Karen Streleck*
Manufacturing manager: *Alexis R. Heydt*
Acquisitions editor: *Gregory G. Doench*
SunSoft Press publisher: *Rachel Borden*

10 9 8 7 6 5 4 3 2

ISBN 0-13-565821-7

SunSoft Press
A Prentice Hall Title

Contents

Chapter 2

Fundamental Applets, 11

Chapter 3

Text Applets, 47

Preface

Why I Wrote Instant Java

The first time I saw a Java applet running on a Web page I said to myself: "I've got to do that!" I started looking at some Java code and reading up on how to program in Java. I began to realize that there were many things that Java could do, but the first thing I wanted to try was some simple animation.

As I began to understand the requirements of the Java code, I began to consider what it was that I was going to animate. This turned out to be a challenging task. I'm not an artist, and even though I own both Adobe Illustrator and Adobe Photoshop I'm an expert in neither. What was I to use for images to animate? I had access to a fair number of digital images such as photos of my children, my company logo, and plenty of other stuff that I had gathered from the net, but animation requires a series of images that, when shown in rapid succession, give the appearance of an animate object. These, I did not have!

Who Should Use Instant Java

As I began organizing and designing this book, I wondered how many other people were like me: wanting to create animation with Java, but unable to do so because they lack access to, or the skills to create, a series of images for an animation sequence. I also wondered how many would want to use animation on their Web pages but not have the programming skills required to write the necessary Java code. If you fit into either or both of these categories, this book is for you!

Instant Java is written primarily for HTML authors who want to include Java applets on their Web pages. I have tried to create useful, general purpose applets that will appeal to the majority of Web authors. Since most Web pages are composed of text and images, I have concentrated on developing applets that display these in interesting ways.

Instant Java is also for people who don't have access to the tools that can create animation, or who don't have the skills needed to create images for an animation sequence. While I am not an artist and would be hard-pressed to create images that would look good in animation, I have discovered that there are many interesting things that can be done using just text or a single image. Many people have access to a single digital image, such as a company logo or scanned photograph. Using the applets in this book, you will be able to easily create your own interesting and provocative animation sequences.

Java Programming

One of the reasons the Web has been so successful is the ease with which programmers and non-programmers have been able to create and maintain Web pages. HTML is a truly simple language and almost anyone can learn the basics in a couple of hours.

While Java is often described as "simple", this is really true only from the point of view of a C or C++ programmer. If you are not a programmer, you'll find Java to be orders of magnitude more complex than HTML. It is a full-blown high level programming language that requires considerable programming experience.

If you are already a programmer, you may want to become familiar with Java programming so that you can develop your own customized applets. Though *Instant Java* does not actually teach Java programming, you may find it useful to study the source code in the appendix and on the CD. Furthermore, you can extend the existing Java code by writing your own text generating or image processing filters, as described in the Tips For Programmers sections that end Chapters 3 and 4.

Instant Java Updates

Java is still evolving and there are certain to be changes as well as bug fixes. Sun Microsystems already posts a list of known Java bugs on their Java Web site (http://www.javasoft.com). I have also come across a number of bugs in the course of development for this book. I am confident that these problems will be worked out in future versions of Java.

Though I'd like to think that my code is bug free, I'm sure it is not perfect. If you have a problem with an applet in this book, you should first try to isolate it by replacing an image or an audio file or some parameter in the HTML file. You will also want to check the Instant Java Web site at:

```
http://www.vivids.com
```

I will post known problems, bug fixes, and new versions at this site that you may freely download. If you cannot find an answer there and are convinced that you have discovered a bug, send a complete description (including the HTML code) to:

```
pew@vivids.com
```

Bug fixes and code updates will be posted to the Web site on an ongoing basis.

You may also want to check the Web site to find additional Instant Java applet samples, tips on creating audio files, and other useful information.

A Note About Performance

In building these Java applets I have tried to be as creative and far-ranging as possible. But it is worth bearing in mind that the more complex an applet is, the longer it takes to execute. When deciding which applets to install on your Web pages, you should always consider this tradeoff between complexity and performance.

Remember also that on any given visitor's machine, an applet might run more slowly than it does on yours; even if you find its performance acceptable it may not be so on your visitor's. This depends in large part, of course, on the speed and power of the system on which you construct and test your applets.

Images in particular present performance concerns. The larger the image file, the greater the processing time required. Often you can speed execution considerably by choosing smaller images for your applets.

Acknowledgements

First and foremost, my deepest gratitude to my wife, Renée, and to each of our children for their support. I nearly abandoned them for a period of about two months in order to write this book. They quietly sustained and encouraged me throughout this project. Though none of them contributed to the book directly, their support was crucial. I couldn't have done it without them. Thank you family!

A very big thanks to Bob Binstock, the developmental editor for this book. Bob's editorial suggestions and comments greatly influenced my writing style and the content and tone of the book. I also appreciate the contributions and professionalism of the Prentice Hall staff, especially Greg Doench, Joanne Anzalone, and Leabe Berman.

I want to thank my brother Steve for his involvement in testing the applets and reading the manuscript. He helped me find and solve some bugs in my code; his PC experience was extremely helpful to me at a critical time during development.

Thanks to Eric Smith, my business associate, for relieving me of some business commitments. Eric filled in for me on more than one occasion, freeing me to work on the book.

Chris Scott developed much of the artwork in the book. His expertise is Adobe Illustrator and Photoshop, and his creative design work contributed substantially to the book. Thanks, Chris.

I also want to thank Kimball Ungerman and Mike Macias for filling in for me in some of my non-professional commitments. These friends relieved me of some responsibilities that allowed me to meet some critical deadlines.

Rachel Borden, the SunSoft Press Publisher, and Karin Ellison, her predecessor, deserve most of the credit for the idea behind this book. Despite my insistence that I didn't want to write another book, they persisted and convinced me to do it. Thanks for believing in me.

CHAPTER

1

Introducing
Java Applets

Java and the Web

The World Wide Web is rapidly gaining popularity as a way of sharing information. Its appeal is due largely to the ease with which that information, usually in the form of text and graphics, can be retrieved by any user from anywhere in the world. As exciting as the Web is, however, it has always been limited by the one-way nature of Web pages, which have provided only unchanging words and images.

Java™ is an indispensable tool for creating dynamic Web pages. *Instant Java* helps you create dynamic Web pages as quickly and easily as possible.

With Java you can bring life to otherwise static Web pages. As a programming language specifically designed to work with HTML and the Web, Java allows you to insert programs in a Web page that are automatically executed on the machine of any user who visits the page. Through this feature you can animate your Web pages and even make them interactive.

When you load a Web page that contains a Java reference, you are downloading a small program, called a Java applet, that is then executed within your browser. The ability to provide "executable content" is one of Java's most exciting features.

Using Java Applets

Java applets can do all sorts of things. Rather than simply displaying a still image, for example, you can use Java to display consecutive images, producing live animation. Java applets can also be fully interactive; a Java calculator applet might perform mathematical calculations and graphs the results.

Java's capabilities are very broad, but this book concentrates on the fundamental tasks of every Web page: displaying text and graphics, loading Uniform Resource Locators (URLs), and playing audio files in interesting, animated, interactive ways.

Instant Java

This book provides and describes a collection of general purpose applets that anyone can use. These applet are ready as is; they are off-the-shelf programs that you can use in your Web pages right away. Just specify the text or image you want to display and customize the settings, if you wish, and the applet does the rest.

The applets in this book are designed to be as flexible as possible. You can customize as few or as many settings as you like. Just flip through the book to find the applet that does what you want, insert it into your Web page, set the parameters, and begin using it. With very little effort you can create applets that are both personal and unique.

For example, perhaps you'd like to animate your company logo where it appears in the corner of your home page. Or maybe you want an eye-catching title that flashes or changes colors. These types of tasks, and many more, are easily accomplished with these applets.

Java and HTML

It will help if you are already familiar with basic HTML, but you don't need to be an expert to use these applets. Each applet's description provides HTML code samples which show you exactly how to use it.

Which Browser?

In order to run a Java applet, you (or any Web user) must have a Java-enabled browser. Bear in mind that as of this writing (February, 1996) only Netscape Navigator™ 2.0 from Netscape Communications Corporation™ supports Java. Because of Java's tremendous popularity and acceptance in the market, other commercial producers have already announced plans to add Java support to their browsers.

The Instant Java CD

The CD that came with this book includes all source and the compiled code for the applets described. You can easily install this code on your system and use the applets without having to modify or compile any programs.

The CD also contains the Java Developer's Kit (JDK) and Café Lite from Symantec Corporation. The JDK contains the Java run-time environment, the appletviewer, and some popular Java demo applets. Café Lite is a Java development tools for Windows 95. Refer to Appendix C for complete installation instructions.

Using This Book

The rest of this book contains applet descriptions. Each chapter covers a set of related applets.

You do *not* need to read the book sequentially. You might want to begin by looking through the chapters to get a feeling for the kinds of things the applets can do.

Each applet description contains the following:

- One or more pictures of what the applet looks like

- A description of what the applet does

- Sample HTML code that you can use as a model for your own HTML code

- A description of the applet's customization settings, or parameters

Most of the descriptions are self-contained. However, the applets have been written in such a way that they can be used together. For example, you can use the features of several different applets to display text that has been rotated, slanted, embossed, and made transparent. To learn how this is done you may want to read the beginning of Chapter 4.

You might also want to read the beginning of Chapter 5 to learn how to do animation. You can create animation by supplying a series of images that are shown in rapid succession. One way to create such a series is to begin with a single image and manipulate it—move it, rotate it, change its color—many times. In fact, you can even use this technique to animate text!

Java Programming

If you're already a Java programmer, or want to learn to program in Java, you can refer to the Java source code on the CD, with selected files listed in Appendix A. This book was not designed to be a programmer's guide, but looking at working code can be very instructive.

Chapters 3 and 4 each include a **Tips for Programmers** section. Read these sections if you are a Java programmer and want to write Java code that will extend the functionality of applets described in these two chapters.

What's Next?

The rest of this chapter describes how to get started using the applets in this book. You can skip these instructions for now if you want; you can always come back to them later, when you are ready to use an applet in a Web page.

The Instant Java Tutorial

The rest of this chapter tells you exactly how to use the applets in this book.

Your first task is to get your Java environment set up on your computer. Once this is taken care of, you won't need to repeat it. It includes the following steps:

1. Loading the CD onto your computer's hard drive

2. Installing the Java Developers Kit

When you have set up your Java environment you are ready to run a Java applet. For each applet you will need to take the following steps:

1. Add the applet to an HTML file

2. Customize the applet settings

3. Run the applet using either the appletviewer or Netscape Navigator 2.0

Installing the Java Developers Kit

While you don't need the Java Developers Kit (JDK) to use Java applets and view them with Netscape Navigator 2.0, installing it is a very good idea. It includes the appletviewer, demonstration applets, the Java compiler, and other useful tools. The details of the installation are included in Appendix C.

Adding an Applet to an HTML file

Adding an applet to a Web page is very simple. The HTML applet start tag is **<applet>**; the end tag is **</applet>**. Between these two tags you must specify the name of the applet and its dimensions, as in this basic example:

```
<applet code=BasicText.class width=200 height=200>
</applet>
```

In addition to the start and end tags, three parameters (another word for settings) are required when specifying an applet in an HTML file.

- **code=<appletname>.class**
  The **code** parameter specifies the name of the applet. Compiled applet program names usually end with **.class**.

- **width=<size in pixels>**
  The **width** parameter specifies the width of the applet.

- **height=<size in pixels>**
  The **height** parameter specifies the height of the applet.

Note that while the **code** parameter specifies the primary applet file, most applets require other **.class** files in the same directory.

In addition to these required parameters, there is an optional parameter called **codebase**. The **codebase** parameter specifies a directory in which to find the applet program files, or **.class** files. By default, the **.class** file specified by the **code** parameter is assumed to be in the same directory as the HTML file. You can choose to put the **.class** file in another directory by using the **codebase** parameter. If you wanted to keep your Java **.class** file in a subdirectory named **javadir**, for example, you would use the following code:

```
<applet codebase=javadir code=BasicText.class width=200 height=200>
</applet>
```

You can put more than one applet in an HTML document. In fact, there is no limit to the number of applets that can reside on one Web page. Java applets are positioned in the same manner as any other component of a page.

Customizing Applet Settings

In order to customize an applet you must provide it with operating information. This is done by setting parameters with the optional **<param>** tag, the only HTML tag that Java recognizes.

To use the **<param>** tag, just specify a parameter name and value. To specify a value of 10 for the **XOffset** parameter of the **BasicText** applet, for example, you would use the following lines:

```
<applet code=BasicText.class width=200 height=200>
<param name=XOffset value=10>
</applet>
```

To specify several parameters, include a **<param>** tag for each. To set both the **XOffset** and the **YOffset** parameters, for example, you would use the following lines:

```
<applet code=BasicText.class width=200 height=200>
<param name=XOffset value=10>
<param name=YOffset value=25>
</applet>
```

Some parameter values contain more than one word. When a value contains one or more spaces, you must enclose the value in double quotes. To set the **Text** parameter to **Hello Web!**, for example, you would enclose **Hello Web!** in double quotes, as shown in the following lines:

```
<applet code=BasicText.class width=200 height=200>
<param name=Text value="Hello Web!">
<param name=XOffset value=10>
<param name=YOffset value=25>
</applet>
```

You may include a comment line in the parameter list by using the standard comment tag, **<!>**.

```
<applet code=BasicText.class width=200 height=200>
<param name=Text value="Hello Web!">
<! These next two parameters set the X and Y offsets>
<param name=XOffset value=10>
<param name=YOffset value=25>
</applet>
```

Don't forget to include the closing angle bracket on a parameter; if you leave it out, or forget the closing double quote, your results will be unpredictable and your applet probably won't run.

Using the Appletviewer

The appletviewer is a program included in the JDK that runs applets but does not interpret any HTML commands.

To use the appletviewer, you must specify an HTML file that includes an applet. You may use an existing HTML file or create a new one. Any standard HTML commands in the file are completely ignored by the appletviewer; only references to applets are executed.

If an HTML file contains multiple applets, the appletviewer creates a window for each.

The appletviewer also works across the net. You can specify a URL that represents an HTML file anywhere on the Internet and, assuming you're connected to the Internet, the appletviewer will load it and run any Java applets it contains.

Running Applets in Netscape (Windows 95)

Running an applet in Netscape Navigator 2.0 is very simple. Just drag an HTML file containing an applet from Windows Explorer and drop it on Netscape Navigator, as follows:

1. Bring up Windows Explorer

2. Bring up Netscape Navigator

3. Use Explorer to find the HTML file to load

4. Drag the HTML file from Explorer and drop it on Navigator

Another method is to enter the complete path of the HTML file in the **Location** field of Netscape Navigator.

Running Applets in Netscape (Solaris)

Under Solaris, there is no way to drag HTML files to Netscape Navigator. You must enter the path of the HTML file in the **Location** field of Navigator. For example, if you loaded the contents of the Instant Java CD in **/usr/instantjava**, you could load the file **BasicText.html** with the following path name:

```
file:/usr/instantjava/fund/BasicText.html
```

Planning for Users Without Java-enabled Browsers

It's important to remember that not everyone on the Web has a browser that supports Java. At the time of this writing, Netscape Navigator 2.0 is the only Java-enabled browser.

In order to make your Web pages work reasonably well on browsers that do not support Java, you must include standard HTML commands between the applet start and applet end tags. Since Java recognizes only the **<param>** tags, it will ignore these HTML commands. And since most browsers ignore HTML tags they don't understand, non Java-enabled browsers will ignore the **<param>** tags and execute the standard HTML commands, while Java-enabled browsers will recognize the **<param>** tags and execute the Java applet.

Here's an example:

```
<HTML>
<title>Vivid Solutions Home Page</title>
<BODY BGCOLOR=#cecece>

<Center>
<! Here's the Java applet that displays an image>
<applet codebase=classes code=BasicImage.class width=187 height=288>
<param name=Image value=vivid9.gif>

<! Here's the HTML code for non-Java-enabled browsers>
<! Java applets will ignore the <IMG SRC=..> line>
<! Browsers that don't support Java will use the <IMG SRC=..> line>
<IMG SRC="vivid9.gif" ALT="Vivid Solutions Corporation">
<P>
You are running a <I>Java-challenged</I> browser.
<br>
```

```
<A HREF="http://home.netscape.com/comprod/mirror/index.html">
Download</A>
Netscape Navigator Now!
<br>
<br>
<A HREF="http://home.netscape.com/comprod/mirror/index.html">
<IMG SRC="http://home.netscape.com/comprod/mirror/images/now8.gif"
ALIGN=CENTER>
</A>
</applet>
<br>
<applet codebase=classes code=Text.class width=300 height=150>
<param name=AppBGColor value=#cecece>
<param name=Text value="Java-enabled!">
<param name=TxPointSize value=36>
<param name=TxFilter value="depthshade 25 -25 yellow|waveimage 30 30">
</applet>
</Center>
</BODY>
</HTML>
```

Note that between the applet start and end tags are commands to display some text, an image, and a hyperlink. The Java applet may produce some animation which would be visible only to a Java-enabled browser. The non-Java-enabled browser would see a single non-animated image with the text about downloading Netscape Navigator. Here's what the page would look like in the two different browsers:

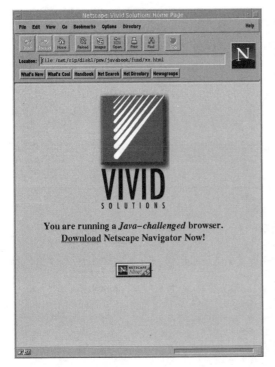

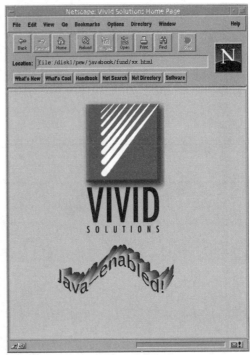

Browser without
Java support

Netscape 2.0
or other Java-enabled
browser

CHAPTER
2

Fundamental Applets

T his chapter introduces some fundamental applets. Each performs a basic function such as displaying text, displaying an image, playing an audio file, or loading a Uniform Resource Locator (URL). These functions are also combined in applets that perform complex actions such as displaying an image, playing an audio file when the pointer enters the image, and loading a URL when any mouse button is pressed.

Much of what these applets do is not unique to Java. You could easily write HTML code to do similar things. Subsequent chapters build on these applets to perform more interesting tasks that only Java can accomplish.

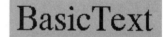

BasicText

Displays a string of characters

Description

The **BasicText** applet is the most basic applet in this book. It simply displays a string of characters. This may be centered or colored and used as a heading or title, or wherever text is used on a Web page.

There are a few advantages to using **BasicText** over the standard text that can be created with HTML. One is that it allows the explicit selection of the font, style, size, and color of the text. This ensures that the text will appear on the visitor's screen exactly as it appears on yours. HTML text, on the other hand, may be set to various fonts or sizes based on preferences selected for the user's particular browser. Another advantage of **BasicText** is that a border and frame can be drawn around the text.

Using BasicText in HTML Code

The following HTML code uses the **BasicText** applet to display the string *Welcome!* enclosed in a **ShadowEtchedOut** frame:

```
<applet code=BasicText.class width=300 height=80>
<param name=Text value=Welcome!>
<param name=TxFont value=Helvetica>
<param name=TxPointSize value=40>
<param name=TxHorizCenter value=true>
<param name=TxVertCenter value=true>
<param name=TxFrameThickness value=2>
<param name=TxFrameType value=ShadowEtchedOut>
<param name=TxFrameMargin value=5>
</applet>
```

Settings

Use the parameters to set the color of the text and the background, the position of the text including centering, the font, an optional border or frame, and of course the text itself. You can also create a border or frame around the entire applet.

Note that colors can be set in one of two ways: by the color name or by a hexadecimal value. The color names are limited to those that are listed in Appendix B on page 309. This includes over 130 color names.

Specifying a color by a hexadecimal value by using a pound sign (#) followed by six hexadecimal digits as shown here:

```
#FA8072
```

The first two digits (FA) represent the red content, the next two digits (80) represent the green content, and the final two digits (72) represent the blue content. Each pair of digits must be a value between 0 and 255 (FF).

Throughout this book parameters that apply to an entire applet begin with **App**, parameters that apply to text begin with **Tx**, and parameters that apply to images begin with **Img**.

Name	Description	Default
Text	The string of characters to display	(none)
TxColor	The text color	Set by browser
TxYOffset	The vertical distance (in pixels) from the top of the applet to the lower left corner of the text	The height of the text
TxXOffset	The horizontal distance (in pixels) from the left side of the applet to the text	0
TxHorizCenter	If true, the text is horizontally centered	false
TxVertCenter	If true, the text is vertically centered	false
TxFont	The font of the text: **TimesRoman**, **Helvetica**, **Courier**, **Dialog**, **DialogInput**, or **ZapfDingbats**	**Dialog**
TxStyle	The style of the font: **Plain**, **Bold**, **Italic**, or **BoldItalic**	**Plain**
TxPointSize	The size of the font in points	10
TxUnderLine	If true, the text is underlined	false
TxBorderWidth	The width of the text border (must be greater than 0 in order for a border to be drawn)	0
TxBorderColor	The color of the text border	black
TxBorderMargin	The distance (in pixels) from the text border to the text on all sides	0
TxFrameThickness	The thickness of the text frame (must be greater than 0 in order for a frame to be drawn)	0
TxFrameType	The type of text frame: **ShadowIn**, **ShadowOut**, **ShadowEtchedIn**, or **ShadowEtchedOut**	**ShadowIn**
TxFrameMargin	The distance (in pixels) from the text frame to the text	0
AppBGColor	The background color of the applet	Set by browser

Name	Description	Default
AppBorderWidth	The width of the applet border (must be greater than 0 in order for a border to be drawn)	0
AppBorderColor	The color of the applet border	black
AppFrameThickness	The thickness of the applet frame (must be greater than 0 in order for a frame to be drawn)	0
AppFrameType	The type of applet frame: **ShadowIn**, **ShadowOut**, **ShadowEtchedIn**, or **ShadowEtchedOut**	**ShadowIn**

Using the **AppBGColor** parameter to set the background color of the applet can be particularly useful if you use the HTML **<BODY BGCOLOR=*color*>** tag in a Web page to force a background color. By using the same color for **AppBGColor** and **<BODY BGCOLOR>**, you can ensure that the entire page has the same background color. If you want a Web page that contains the **BasicText** applet to have its entire background color set to #FA8072 (salmon), for example, you would use the following code:

```
<Title>Text Applet<Title>
<BODY BGCOLOR=#FA8072>
<applet code=BasicText.class width=300 height=80>
<param name=Text value=Welcome!>
<param name=AppBGColor value=#FA8072>
</applet>
```

The frame and border parameters allow you to draw a frame or border around the text and the entire applet. Since these parameters are available for almost every applet in this book, let's take a closer look at them.

Frames come in four types: **ShadowIn**, **ShadowOut**, **ShadowEtchedIn**, and **ShadowEtchedOut**. Each of these is shown in the following figures:

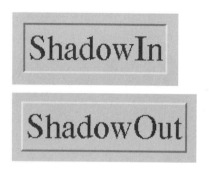
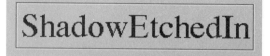

Setting the **TxFrameType** to one of these four values, and setting the **TxFrameThickness** parameter to some value other than the default, 0, draws a frame of the specified type directly around the text, regardless of the size of the applet. The **TxFrameThickness** parameter changes the thickness of the frame, while the **TxFrameMargin** parameter sets the distance from the text at which the frame is drawn. The following figures shows a **ShadowEtchedOut** frame with a **TxFrameThickness** of 4 and a **TxFrameMargin** of 5:

Borders work in much the same way. Specify a **TxBorderWidth** greater than 0 and a border is drawn around the text. You can also specify a color for the border. The following figure shows a border drawn around text with a **TxBorderWidth** of 1.

In addition to borders and frames around text, you can also draw a border or frame around the entire applet. The following figure displays a **ShadowIn** frame around the text, and a **ShadowEtchedOut** frame around the applet:

You can combine frames and borders in anyway you like. The following figure displays text drawn with a **ShadowEtchedIn** frame with thickness 4, within an applet that has a **App-BorderWidth** of 2:

The **TxHorizCenter** and **TxVertCenter** parameters take precedence over the **TxXOffset** and **TxYOffset** parameters. The **TxBorderColor** and **TxBorderMargin** parameters have no effect unless a **TxBorderWidth** is set. Likewise, the **TxFrameType** and **TxFrameMargin** have no effect unless a **TxFrameThickness** is set. The same is true for the applet border and frame settings.

See Also

URL for **BasicText**:   `http://www.vivids.com/java/fund/BasicText.html`

Pages for source code: **BasicText.java** on page 230

BasicImage

Displays an image and a string of characters

Description

The **BasicImage** applet displays a single static image. The image source must be in either GIF or JPEG format.

BasicImage is derived from **BasicText**. This means that all the parameters that available for **BasicText** are also available for **BasicImage**.

Setting the **Text** parameter allows you to include text with your image. You specify the text's position, color, font, and so forth exactly as you would for the **BasicText** applet.

You must leave enough space for the text and the image to be displayed. If you position the text or the image partially or completely outside the applet, you'll be able to see only the portion that is within the boundaries of the applet.

Using BasicImage in HTML Code

The following HTML code uses the **BasicImage** applet to display the Doutone image enclosed in a border with a margin of 34. Notice that the text positioning is identical to that in the **BasicText** example.

```
<applet code=BasicImage.class width=550 height=160>
<param name=Image value=../images/duotone.gif>
<param name=Text value="Doutone">
<param name=TxHorizCenter value=true>
<param name=TxYOffset value=142>
<param name=TxFont value=Dialog>
<param name=TxPointSize value=22>
<param name=ImgVertCenter value=true>
<param name=ImgHorizCenter value=true>
<param name=ImgBorderMargin value=34>
<param name=ImgBorderWidth value=2>
</applet>
```

Settings

The parameters relate to both the image and the text. You must specify the image that is to be displayed, its location, and whether you want to display the image as it is loaded or wait until the entire image is available before displaying it.

Name	Description	Default
Image	The image to display	(none)
ImgLoadWait	If true, the image is not displayed until it is completely loaded	false
ImgXOffset	The horizontal distance (in pixels) from the left side of the applet to the image	0
ImgYOffset	The vertical distance (in pixels) from the top of the applet to the image	0
ImgHorizCenter	If true, the image is horizontally centered	false
ImgVertCenter	If true, the image is vertically centered	false
ImgBorderWidth	The width of the image border (must be greater than 0 in order for a border to be drawn)	0
ImgBorderColor	The color of the image border	Set by browser
ImgBorderMargin	The distance (in pixels) from the image border to the image on all sides	0
ImgFrameThickness	The thickness of the image frame (must be greater than 0 in order for a frame to be drawn)	0
ImgFrameType	The type of image frame: **ShadowIn**, **ShadowOut**, **ShadowEtchedIn**, or **ShadowEtchedOut**	**ShadowIn**
ImgFrameMargin	The distance (in pixels) from the image frame to the image	0
TxColor	The text color	Set by browser
TxYOffset	The vertical distance (in pixels) from the top of the applet to the lower left corner of the text	The height of the text
TxXOffset	The horizontal distance (in pixels) from the left side of the applet to the text	0

Name	Description	Default
TxHorizCenter	If true, the text is horizontally centered	false
TxVertCenter	If true, the text is vertically centered	false
TxFont	The font of the text: **TimesRoman, Helvetica, Courier, Dialog, DialogInput,** or **ZapfDingbats**	**Dialog**
TxStyle	The style of the font: **Plain, Bold, Italic,** or **BoldItalic**	**Plain**
TxPointSize	The size of the font in points	10
TxUnderLine	If true, the text is underlined	false
TxBorderWidth	The width of the text border (must be greater than 0 in order for a border to be drawn)	0
TxBorderColor	The color of the text border	black
TxBorderMargin	The distance (in pixels) from the text border to the text on all sides	0
TxFrameThickness	The thickness of the text frame (must be greater than 0 in order for a frame to be drawn)	0
TxFrameType	The type of text frame: **ShadowIn, ShadowOut, ShadowEtchedIn,** or **ShadowEtchedOut**	**ShadowIn**
TxFrameMargin	The distance (in pixels) from the text frame to the text	0
AppBGColor	The background color of the applet	Set by browser
AppBorderWidth	The width of the applet border (must be greater than 0 in order for a border to be drawn)	0
AppBorderColor	The color of the applet border	black
AppFrameThickness	The thickness of the applet frame (must be greater than 0 in order for a frame to be drawn)	0
AppFrameType	The type of applet frame: **ShadowIn, ShadowOut, ShadowEtchedIn,** or **ShadowEtchedOut**	**ShadowIn**

See Also

Related applets:	**BasicText** on page 12
URL for **BasicImage**:	`http://www.vivids.com/java/fund/BasicImage.html`
Pages for source code:	**BasicText.java** on page 230

Audio
Plays an audio file when the page is visited

Description

The **Audio** applet plays an audio file when the page containing it is visited. There is no associated text or image. The audio source must be in **au** format.

This applet is useful if you want a particular audio file played every time a page is visited. For example, you may want to play a greeting when your home page is loaded.

You can specify that the file is to be played repeatedly; you can even play your file in a loop, in which case it will repeat indefinitely. You should be cautious, however, about using lengthy or repetitive audio, so as not to annoy your visitor.

A loop can include a fixed delay between repetitions, which is suitable for a greeting message that would repeat once in a while–say every 60 seconds or so. That way, the visitor is not deluged with audio information, but only occasionally reminded of the page's purpose or other information.

To ensure that this applet does not use any display space on the page, specify 0 for the **width** and **height**.

Using Audio in HTML Code

The following HTML code uses the **Audio** applet to play the **welcome.au** audio file.

```
<applet code=Audio.class width=0 height=0>
<param name=audio value=welcome.au>
<param name=PlayDelay value=60>
<param name=Loop value=true>
</applet>
```

Settings

The **Audio** applet has just three parameters. The **Audio** parameter specifies the audio source file. If you want the audio to play in a continuous loop, set the **Loop** parameter, and use the **PlayDelay** parameter to specify the delay between repetitions.

Name	Description	Default
Audio	The audio file to play	(none)
PlayDelay	The delay in seconds between repetitions (valid if **Loop** is true)	0
Loop	If true, the audio file is played continuously (repetitions are separated by **PlayDelay** seconds)	false

Since the only purpose of the **Audio** applet is to play an audio file, failing to specify the **Audio** parameter results in an error.

At the time of publication the only audio format supported by Java is 8-bit u-law 8kHz mono channel audio. This is the format commonly used on Sun workstations. Files containing audio data in this format generally have the **.au** suffix.

See Also

URL for **Audio**:   `http://www.vivids.com/java/fund/Audio.html`

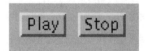

Plays an audio file when the Play button is
pressed
Stops playing when the Stop button is pressed

Description

The **AudioButton** applet provides two buttons and a label. One button plays the audio file
and the other stops it. The buttons are labeled *Play* and *Stop* by default, but you can rename
them with parameters.

Pressing *Play* starts the audio at the beginning; pressing *Stop* halts it. The audio always starts
at the beginning, even if *Play* is pressed while it is already playing.

If you set a button label to a value other than the default, the size of the button changes to
accommodate the size of the label.

Using AudioButton in HTML Code

The following HTML code uses the **AudioButton** applet
to label the two buttons *Play it!* and *Halt*. The label is
specified as *Press for Audio*.

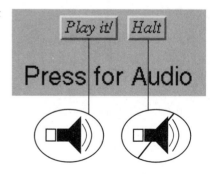

```
<applet code=AudioButton.class width=200
height=80>
<param name=audio value=audio/whistle.au>
<param name=label value="Press for Audio">
<param name=PlayLabel value="Play it!">
<param name=StopLabel value=Halt>
<param name=Font value=Helvetica>
<param name=PointSize value=24>
<param name=ButtonFont value=TimesRoman>
<param name=ButtonStyle value=Italic>
<param name=ButtonPointSize value=16>
</applet>
```

Settings

Use the parameters to specify the audio file to play and the text and display information for the buttons and label.

Name	Description	Default
Audio	The audio file to play	(none)
BGColor	The background color	Set by browser
FGColor	The foreground color	Set by browser
PlayLabel	The Play button label	Play
StopLabel	The Stop button label	Stop
Label	The label displayed beneath the buttons	(none)
Font	The font for the main label	**Dialog**
Style	The style of the main label font: **Plain**, **Bold**, **Italic**, or **BoldItalic**	**Plain**
PointSize	The size of the main label font in points	10
ButtonFont	The font for the button labels	**Dialog**
ButtonStyle	The style of the button label font: **Plain**, **Bold**, **Italic**, or **BoldItalic**	**Plain**
ButtonPointSize	The size of the button label font in points	10

See Also

Related applets: **Audio** on page 20

URL for **AudioButton**: `http://www.vivids.com/java/fund/AudioButton.html`

AudioText

Displays a string of characters
Plays an audio file when the pointer enters the text

Description

The **AudioText** applet is derived from the **BasicText** on page 12. In addition to displaying text, **AudioText** plays an audio file when the pointer enters the text. The text region is defined by a rectangle that encloses the string. You can make this region visible by specifying a one pixel border with a **TxBorderMargin** of 1.

When the pointer enters the text area the audio plays to completion, unless the pointer leaves the text, at which point the audio stops. If the pointer reenters the text, the audio plays again from the beginning.

Using AudioText in HTML Code

The following HTML code uses the **AudioText** applet to display the string *Move pointer here for sound!* When the pointer enters the text region, the **wind.au** audio file is played.

```
<applet code=AudioText.class width=400 height=100>
<param name=TxAudio value=audio/wind.au>
<param name=Text value="Move pointer here for sound!">
<param name=TxFont value=Helvetica>
<param name=TxStyle value=BoldItalic>
<param name=AppBGColor value=black>
<param name=TxColor value=white>
<param name=TxPointSize value=22>
<param name=TxXOffset value=35>
<param name=TxYOffset value=35>
<param name=TxBorderWidth value=1>
<param name=TxBorderColor value=white>
<param name=TxBorderMargin value=2>
</applet>
```

Move pointer here for sound!

Settings

The **AudioText** parameters are identical to the **BasicText** parameters with the addition of the **TxAudio** parameter, which specifies the audio file to play.

Name	Description	Default
TxAudio	The audio file to play	(none)
Text	The string of characters to display	(none)
TxColor	The text color	Set by browser
TxYOffset	The vertical distance (in pixels) from the top of the applet to the lower left corner of the text	The height of the text
TxXOffset	The horizontal distance (in pixels) from the left side of the applet to the text	0
TxHorizCenter	If true, the text is horizontally centered	false
TxVertCenter	If true, the text is vertically centered	false
TxFont	The font of the text: **TimesRoman, Helvetica, Courier, Dialog, DialogInput, or ZapfDingbats**	**Dialog**
TxStyle	The style of the font: **Plain, Bold, Italic,** or **BoldItalic**	**Plain**
TxPointSize	The size of the font in points	10
TxUnderLine	If true, the text is underlined	false
TxBorderWidth	The width of the text border (must be greater than 0 in order for a border to be drawn)	0
TxBorderColor	The color of the text border	black
TxBorderMargin	The distance (in pixels) from the text border to the text on all sides	0
TxFrameThickness	The thickness of the text frame (must be greater than 0 in order for a frame to be drawn)	0
TxFrameType	The type of text frame: **ShadowIn, ShadowOut, ShadowEtchedIn, or ShadowEtchedOut**	**ShadowIn**
TxFrameMargin	The distance (in pixels) from the text frame to the text	0
AppBGColor	The background color of the applet	Set by browser
AppBorderWidth	The width of the applet border (must be greater than 0 in order for a border to be drawn)	0
AppBorderColor	The color of the applet border	black
AppFrameThickness	The thickness of the applet frame (must be greater than 0 in order for a frame to be drawn)	0
AppFrameType	The type of applet frame: **ShadowIn, ShadowOut, ShadowEtchedIn,** or **ShadowEtchedOut**	**ShadowIn**

See Also

Related applets: **BasicText** on page 12

                                                                      Audio on page 20

URL for **AudioText**:   `http://www.vivids.com/java/fund/AudioText.html`

Pages for source code: **AudioText.java** on page 238

AudioImageText

Displays an image
Displays a string of characters
Plays an audio file when the pointer enters the text
Plays an audio file when the pointer enters the image

Description

The **AudioImageText** applet is derived from **BasicImage** on page 17. In addition to displaying an image and text, **AudioImageText** plays one audio file when the pointer enters the image and another when it enters the text. You can, of course, specify the same audio file for the image and the text.

The audio plays to completion unless the pointer leaves the image or text, at which point the audio stops. If the pointer reenters the image or text, the audio plays again from the beginning.

Using AudioImageText in HTML Code

The following HTML code uses the **AudioImageText** applet to display an image and text. Separate audio files are specified for the image and the text. Because the image and text overlap, positioning the pointer over the area that contains both text and image results in both audio files playing simultaneously.

```
<applet code=AudioImageText.class width=290 height=220>
<param name=AppBGColor value=white>
<! Text parameters>
<param name=Text value="Check This Out!">
<param name=TxAudio
value=audio/rooster.au>
<param name=TxPointSize value=18>
<param name=TxXOffset value=134>
<param name=TxYOffset value=150>
<param name=TxBorderWidth value=1>
<param name=TxBorderMargin value=3>
<! Image parameters>
<param name=ImgAudio
value=audio/welcome.au>
<param name=Image
value="../images/vivid.gif">
<param name=ImgHorizCenter value=true>
```

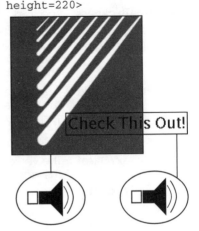

```
<param name=ImgYOffset value=20>
<param name=ImgBorderWidth value=1>
</applet>
```

Settings

The **AudioImageText** parameters are identical to the **BasicImage** parameters with the addition of the **TxAudio** and **ImgAudio** parameters, which specify the audio files to play.

Name	Description	Default
TxAudio	The audio file to play when the pointer enters the text	(none)
ImgAudio	The audio file to play when the pointer enters the image	(none)
Image	The image to display	(none)
ImgLoadWait	If true, the image is not displayed until it is completely loaded	false
ImgXOffset	The horizontal distance (in pixels) from the left side of the applet to the image	0
ImgYOffset	The vertical distance (in pixels) from the top of the applet to the image	0
ImgHorizCenter	If true, the image is horizontally centered	false
ImgVertCenter	If true, the image is vertically centered	false
ImgBorderWidth	The width of the image border (must be greater than 0 in order for a border to be drawn)	0
ImgBorderColor	The color of the image border	Set by browser
ImgBorderMargin	The distance (in pixels) from the image border to the image on all sides	0
ImgFrameThickness	The thickness of the image frame (must be greater than 0 in order for a frame to be drawn)	0
ImgFrameType	The type of image frame: **ShadowIn**, **ShadowOut**, **ShadowEtchedIn**, or **ShadowEtchedOut**	**ShadowIn**
ImgFrameMargin	The distance (in pixels) from the image frame to the image	0
Text	The string of characters to display	(none)
TxColor	The text color	Set by browser
TxYOffset	The vertical distance (in pixels) from the top of the applet to the lower left corner of the text	The height of the text
TxXOffset	The horizontal distance (in pixels) from the left side of the applet to the text	0
TxHorizCenter	If true, the text is horizontally centered	false
TxVertCenter	If true, the text is vertically centered	false

Name	Description	Default
TxFont	The font of the text: **TimesRoman, Helvetica, Courier, Dialog, DialogInput,** or **ZapfDingbats**	**Dialog**
TxStyle	The style of the font: **Plain, Bold, Italic,** or **BoldItalic**	**Plain**
TxPointSize	The size of the font in points	10
TxUnderLine	If true, the text is underlined	false
TxBorderWidth	The width of the text border (must be greater than 0 in order for a border to be drawn)	0
TxBorderColor	The color of the text border	black
TxBorderMargin	The distance (in pixels) from the text border to the text on all sides	0
TxFrameThickness	The thickness of the text frame (must be greater than 0 in order for a frame to be drawn)	0
TxFrameType	The type of text frame: **ShadowIn, ShadowOut, ShadowEtchedIn,** or **ShadowEtchedOut**	**ShadowIn**
TxFrameMargin	The distance (in pixels) from the text frame to the text	0
AppBGColor	The background color of the applet	Set by browser
AppBorderWidth	The width of the applet border (must be greater than 0 in order for a border to be drawn)	0
AppBorderColor	The color of the applet border	black
AppFrameThickness	The thickness of the applet frame (must be greater than 0 in order for a frame to be drawn)	0
AppFrameType	The type of applet frame: **ShadowIn, ShadowOut, ShadowEtchedIn,** or **ShadowEtchedOut**	**ShadowIn**

If the text and image overlap, you will hear both audio files play when the pointer is within the overlapped region.

See Also

Related applets:

BasicImage on page 17
BasicText on page 12

URL for **AudioImageText**:   http://www.vivids.com/java/fund/AudioImageText.html

 # URLButton

 http://java.sun.com

Loads the specified URL when the button is pressed

Description

The **URLButton** applet displays a button with a label that you specify. When the button is pressed, the specified URL is loaded into the visitor's browser.

Using URLButton in HTML Code

The **URLButton** applet might be used to let the visitor load the next page in a sequence of pages. By using the **ZapfDingbats** font, you can display an arrow on the button. When the visitor presses the button, the specified URL is loaded.

```
<applet code=URLButton.class width=400 height=60>
<param name=URL value=http://java.sun.com>
<param name=ButtonFont value=ZapfDingbats>
<param name=ButtonPointSize value=36>
<param name=Label value=\137>
</applet>
```

Settings

Specify the URL to load with the **URL** parameter. Other parameters set the button label text, font, and color.

Name	Description	Default
URL	The URL to load when the button is pressed	(none)
BGColor	The background color	From browser
FGColor	The foreground color of the text	From browser
Label	The button labe	(none)
ButtonFont	The font of the button label	**Dialog**
ButtonStyle	The style of the button label font, e.g. **Plain, Bold, Italic, BoldItalic**	**Plain**
ButtonPointSize	The size of the button font in points	10

See Also

URL for **URLButton**:   http://www.vivids.com/java/fund/URLButton.html

URLAudImgTxt

Displays an image
Displays a string of characters
Plays an audio file when the pointer enters the text
Plays an audio file when the pointer enters the image
Loads the specified URL when any mouse button is pressed

Description

The **URLAudImgTxt** applet is derived from the **AudioImageText** on page 27. It has the same characteristics as **AudioImageText**, with the additional feature that if the user presses any mouse button while the pointer is within the image or text, the specified URL is loaded into the browser.

You can specify separate URLs for the text and the image. If the image and text overlap, the URL specified for the text takes precedence in the overlapping region.

When the pointer is within the text region or image region, the specified URL (if any) is displayed in the browser's status line.

Using URLAudImgTxt in HTML Code

The following HTML code uses the **URLAudImgTxt** applet to display an image and text. When the pointer moves within the image the specified URL (http://www.powertr.com) is displayed in the browser's status line. When the user presses any mouse button, the URL is loaded.

This example specifies only one URL, but you can specify separate URLs for both the text and the image.

```
<applet code=URLAudImgTxt.class width=600 height=150>
<param name=Image value=../images/powertr.gif>
<param name=ImgURL value=http://www.powertr.com>
<param name=ImgAudio value=audio/powertr.au>
<param name=ImgHorizCenter value=true>
<param name=ImgYOffset value=10>
<param name=ImgFrameThickness value=4>
<param name=ImgFrameType value=ShadowEtchedOut>
<param name=ImgFrameMargin value=4>
<param name=Text value="Power Trac">
<param name=TxPointSize value=24>
<param name=TxHorizCenter value=true>
<param name=TxYOffset value=115>
</applet>
```

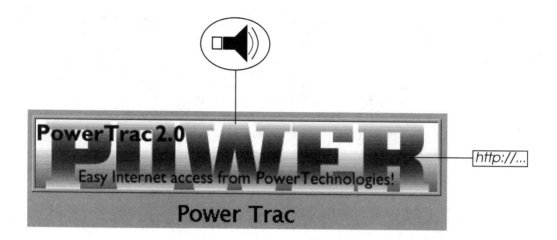

Settings

The parameters are identical to those for **AudioImageText** with the addition of the **TxURL** and **ImgURL** parameters, which specify the URLs to load when the user presses any mouse button while the pointer is within the text or image area.

Name	Description	Default
TxURL	The URL to load when the pointer is within the text and any mouse button is pressed	(none)
ImgURL	The URL to load when the pointer is within the image and any mouse button is pressed	(none)
TxAudio	The audio file to play when the pointer enters the text	(none)
ImgAudio	The audio file to play when the pointer enters the image	(none)
Image	The image to display	(none)
ImgLoadWait	If true, the image is not displayed until it is completely loaded	false
ImgXOffset	The horizontal distance (in pixels) from the left side of the applet to the image	0
ImgYOffset	The vertical distance (in pixels) from the top of the applet to the image	0
ImgHorizCenter	If true, the image is horizontally centered	false
ImgVertCenter	If true, the image is vertically centered	false
ImgBorderWidth	The width of the image border (must be greater than 0 in order for a border to be drawn)	0
ImgBorderColor	The color of the image border	Set by browser

Name	Description	Default
ImgBorderMargin	The distance (in pixels) from the image border to the image on all sides	0
ImgFrameThickness	The thickness of the image frame (must be greater than 0 in order for a frame to be drawn)	0
ImgFrameType	The type of image frame: **ShadowIn**, **ShadowOut**, **ShadowEtchedIn**, or **ShadowEtchedOut**	**ShadowIn**
ImgFrameMargin	The distance (in pixels) from the image frame to the image	0
Text	The string of characters to display	(none)
TxColor	The text color	Set by browser
TxYOffset	The vertical distance (in pixels) from the top of the applet to the lower left corner of the text	The height of the text
TxXOffset	The horizontal distance (in pixels) from the left side of the applet to the text	0
TxHorizCenter	If true, the text is horizontally centered	false
TxVertCenter	If true, the text is vertically centered	false
TxFont	The font of the text: **TimesRoman**, **Helvetica**, **Courier**, **Dialog**, **DialogInput**, or **ZapfDingbats**	**Dialog**
TxStyle	The style of the font: **Plain**, **Bold**, **Italic**, or **BoldItalic**	**Plain**
TxPointSize	The size of the font in points	10
TxUnderLine	If true, the text is underlined	false
TxBorderWidth	The width of the text border (must be greater than 0 in order for a border to be drawn)	0
TxBorderColor	The color of the text border	black
TxBorderMargin	The distance (in pixels) from the text border to the text on all sides	0
TxFrameThickness	The thickness of the text frame (must be greater than 0 in order for a frame to be drawn)	0
TxFrameType	The type of text frame: **ShadowIn**, **ShadowOut**, **ShadowEtchedIn**, or **ShadowEtchedOut**	**ShadowIn**
TxFrameMargin	The distance (in pixels) from the text frame to the text	0
AppBGColor	The background color of the applet	Set by browser
AppBorderWidth	The width of the applet border (must be greater than 0 in order for a border to be drawn)	0

Name	Description	Default
AppBorderColor	The color of the applet border	black
AppFrameThickness	The thickness of the applet frame (must be greater than 0 in order for a frame to be drawn)	0
AppFrameType	The type of applet frame: **ShadowIn**, **ShadowOut**, **ShadowEtchedIn**, or **ShadowEtchedOut**	**ShadowIn**

See Also

Related applets:

AudioImageText on page 27
BasicImage on page 17
BasicText on page 12

URL for **URLAudImgTxt**: `http://www.vivids.com/java/fund/URLAudImgTxt.html`

URLAudImgTxtBG

Displays an image
Displays a string of characters
Plays an audio file when the pointer enters the
text
Plays an audio file when the pointer enters the image
Loads the specified URL when any mouse button is pressed
Displays a background image which can be tiled

Description

The **URLAudImgTxtBG** applet is derived from the **URLAudImgTxt** on page 31. It has all the same characteristics as **URLAudImgTxt**, which means that it can display text and an image, play an audio file, and load URLs.

In addition, you can specify a background image. The text and image overlie the background image. The background image can be *tiled*. This means that it is repeated so that it fills the entire applet area.

Using URLAudImgTxtBG in HTML Code

The following HTML code uses the **URLAudImgTxtBG** applet to display an image and text against a tiled background image. When the pointer enters the text area, the wel-come.au audio file is played. When the pointer moves within the image, the specified URL (http://www.powertr.com) is displayed in the browser's status line; when the visitor presses any mouse button, the URL is loaded.

```
<BODY BACKGROUND=../images/plaid.gif>
<applet code=URLAudImgTxtBG.class width=300 height=180>
<param name=TxURL value=http://www.vivids.com>
<param name=Text value="Welcome!">
<param name=TxAudio value=audio/welcome.au>
<param name=TxPointSize value=36>
<param name=TxFont value=Helvetica>
<param name=TxStyle value=BoldItalic>
<param name=TxColor value=white>
<param name=TxYOffset value=110>
<param name=TxXOffset value=120>
<param name=Image value="../images/vivid.gif">
<param name=ImgYOffset value=10>
<param name=ImgXOffset value=15>
<param name=AppBGImage value=../images/plaid.gif>
<param name=AppBGImageXOffset value=2>
```

```
<param name=AppBGImageYOffset value=2>
<param name=AppTile value=true>
</applet>
```

Settings

The parameters are identical to those for **URLAudImgTxt** with the addition of the parameters that specify the background image, the background image offsets, and the tiling. Since the background image applies to the entire applet, the parameters begin with the **App** prefix.

Name	Description	Default
AppBGImage	The background image	(none)
AppBGImageXOffset	The horizontal offset at which to position the background image	0
AppBGImageYOffset	The vertical offset at which to position the background image	0
AppTile	If true, tile the background image	false
TxURL	The URL to load when the pointer is within the text and any mouse button is pressed	(none)
ImgURL	The URL to load when the pointer is within the image and any mouse button is pressed	(none)
TxAudio	The audio file to play when the pointer enters the text	(none)
ImgAudio	The audio file to play when the pointer enters the image	(none)
Image	The image to display	(none)
ImgLoadWait	If true, the image is not displayed until it is completely loaded	false
ImgXOffset	The horizontal distance (in pixels) from the left side of the applet to the image	0

Name	Description	Default
ImgYOffset	The vertical distance (in pixels) from the top of the applet to the image	0
ImgHorizCenter	If true, the image is horizontally centered	false
ImgVertCenter	If true, the image is vertically centered	false
ImgBorderWidth	The width of the image border (must be greater than 0 in order for a border to be drawn)	0
ImgBorderColor	The color of the image border	Set by browser
ImgBorderMargin	The distance (in pixels) from the image border to the image on all sides	0
ImgFrameThickness	The thickness of the image frame (must be greater than 0 in order for a frame to be drawn)	0
ImgFrameType	The type of image frame: **ShadowIn**, **ShadowOut**, **ShadowEtchedIn**, or **ShadowEtchedOut**	**ShadowIn**
ImgFrameMargin	The distance (in pixels) from the image frame to the image	0
Text	The string of characters to display	(none)
TxColor	The text color	Set by browser
TxYOffset	The vertical distance (in pixels) from the top of the applet to the lower left corner of the text	The height of the text
TxXOffset	The horizontal distance (in pixels) from the left side of the applet to the text	0
TxHorizCenter	If true, the text is horizontally centered	false
TxVertCenter	If true, the text is vertically centered	false
TxFont	The font of the text: **TimesRoman**, **Helvetica**, **Courier**, **Dialog**, **DialogInput**, or **ZapfDingbats**	**Dialog**
TxStyle	The style of the font: **Plain**, **Bold**, **Italic**, or **BoldItalic**	**Plain**
TxPointSize	The size of the font in points	10
TxUnderLine	If true, the text is underlined	false
TxBorderWidth	The width of the text border (must be greater than 0 in order for a border to be drawn)	0
TxBorderColor	The color of the text border	black
TxBorderMargin	The distance (in pixels) from the text border to the text on all sides	0
TxFrameThickness	The thickness of the text frame (must be greater than 0 in order for a frame to be drawn)	0

Name	Description	Default
TxFrameType	The type of text frame: **ShadowIn**, **ShadowOut**, **ShadowEtchedIn**, or **ShadowEtchedOut**	**ShadowIn**
TxFrameMargin	The distance (in pixels) from the text frame to the text	0
AppBGColor	The background color of the applet	Set by browser
AppBorderWidth	The width of the applet border (must be greater than 0 in order for a border to be drawn)	0
AppBorderColor	The color of the applet border	black
AppFrameThickness	The thickness of the applet frame (must be greater than 0 in order for a frame to be drawn)	0
AppFrameType	The type of applet frame: **ShadowIn**, **ShadowOut**, **ShadowEtchedIn**, or **ShadowEtchedOut**	**ShadowIn**

Applets do not use the background image of the Web page; they overwrite the background image with a solid background color. By using the same background color or image for the Web page and the applet, you can create a uniform background. If the applet background and the page background contain a repeating pattern, use the **BGImageXOffset** and **BGImageYOffset** parameters to align the applet background with the page background. This may require some experimentation.

The following illustration shows the sample **URLAudImgTxtBG** on page 35 applet on a Web page with the same tiled background image:

Unfortunately, there is no way to make sure that an applet background image will line up with the page background image in precisely the same way for all browsers on all platforms.

See Also

Related applets:

URLAudImgTxt on page 31
AudioImageText on page 27
BasicImage on page 17
BasicText on page 12

URL for **URLAudImgTxtBG**: `http://www.vivids.com/java/fund/URLAudImgTxtBG.html`

ImageMap

Displays an image
Displays a string of characters
Plays an audio file when the pointer enters the text
Plays an audio file when the pointer enters the image
Loads the specified URL when any mouse button is pressed
Displays a background image which can be tiled
Loads the specified URL based on image maps

Description

The **ImageMap** applet is derived from the **URLAudImgTxtBG** on page 35. It has all the same characteristics as **URLAudImgTxtBG**, with the additional feature that image maps can be specified to associate a URL with a given rectangular region of the applet. URLs specified by image maps take precedence over URLs specified for the image or text.

Image maps are useful when you have a single image with graphics that indicate various URLs. For example, a single image might have the appearance of multiple buttons. You could in this case map the area of each button to a particular URL.

Using ImageMap in HTML Code

The following HTML code uses the **ImageMap** applet to display an image containing four image maps. The image displays four button on a control strip. A URL is specified for each image map; each image map corresponds to one of the four buttons in the image.

In the map parameter settings the number immediately following **Map** indicates the image map number. **X** and **Y** indicate horizontal and vertical coordinates, and **1** and **2** specify left and right or top and bottom, respectively. To specify the left horizontal coordinate for image map 2, for example, you use **Map2_X1**. To specify the bottom vertical coordinate for image map 3 you use **Map3_Y2**.

```
<applet code=ImageMap.class width=561 height=132>
<param name=Map1_URL
value=http://www.vivids.com/java/instant/index.html>
<param name=Map2_URL
value=http://www.vivids.com/java/training/index.html>
<param name=Map3_URL value=http://www.vivids.com/fontmaker/index.html>
<param name=Map4_URL value=http://www.vivids.com/services/index.html>
<! Maps >
<param name=AppNumMaps value=4>
<param name=Map1_X1 value=66>
<param name=Map1_Y1 value=20>
```

```
<param name=Map1_X2 value=152>
<param name=Map1_Y2 value=100>

<param name=Map2_X1 value=192>
<param name=Map2_Y1 value=20>
<param name=Map2_X2 value=275>
<param name=Map2_Y2 value=100>

<param name=Map3_X1 value=314>
<param name=Map3_Y1 value=20>
<param name=Map3_X2 value=397>
<param name=Map3_Y2 value=100>

<param name=Map4_X1 value=432>
<param name=Map4_Y1 value=20>
<param name=Map4_X2 value=507>
<param name=Map4_Y2 value=100>

<param name=Image value="stripcmp.gif">
<!param name=TestMode value=true>
<param name=ImgURL value="http://java.sun.com">

<param name=ImgXOffset value=20>
<param name=ImgYOffset value=20>
</applet>
```

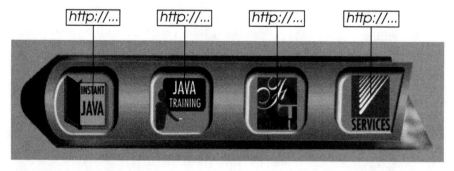

The **AppNumMaps** parameter specifies the number of image maps that the applet contains. The default for **AppNumMaps** is 0, so if you forget to set it none of the image maps you specify will be observed.

The **TestMode** parameter is used to help you determine the horizontal and vertical coordinates of the image map. When you set **TestMode** to **true**, the browser's status line displays the horizontal and vertical coordinates of the pointer as you move it across the applet. This should help you identity the exact coordinates that you want for your image map settings.

Settings

The parameters are identical to those for **URLAudImgTxtBG** with the addition of the parameters that specify the image maps.

Name	Description	Default
AppNumMaps	The number of image maps (must be set to use image maps)	0
MapN_X1	The left horizontal coordinate for map N	0
MapN_Y1	The top vertical coordinate for map N	0
MapN_X2	The right horizontal coordinate for map N	0
MapN_Y2	The bottom vertical coordinate for map N	0
MapN_URL	The URL for map N	(none)
TestMode	If true, the pointer position is displayed in the status line	false
AppBGImage	The background image	(none)
AppBGImageXOffset	The horizontal offset at which to position the background image	0
AppBGImageYOffset	The vertical offset at which to position the background image	0
AppTile	If true, tile the background image	false
TxURL	The URL to load when the pointer is within the text and any mouse button is pressed	(none)
ImgURL	The URL to load when the pointer is within the image and any mouse button is pressed	(none)
TxAudio	The audio file to play when the pointer enters the text	(none)
ImgAudio	The audio file to play when the pointer enters the image	(none)
Image	The image to display	(none)
ImgLoadWait	If true, the image is not displayed until it is completely loaded	false
ImgXOffset	The horizontal distance (in pixels) from the left side of the applet to the image	0
ImgYOffset	The vertical distance (in pixels) from the top of the applet to the image	0
ImgHorizCenter	If true, the image is horizontally centered	false

Name	Description	Default
ImgVertCenter	If true, the image is vertically centered	false
ImgBorderWidth	The width of the image border (must be greater than 0 in order for a border to be drawn)	0
ImgBorderColor	The color of the image border	Set by browser
ImgBorderMargin	The distance (in pixels) from the image border to the image on all sides	0
ImgFrameThickness	The thickness of the image frame (must be greater than 0 in order for a frame to be drawn)	0
ImgFrameType	The type of image frame: **ShadowIn**, **ShadowOut**, **ShadowEtchedIn**, or **ShadowEtchedOut**	**ShadowIn**
ImgFrameMargin	The distance (in pixels) from the image frame to the image	0
Text	The string of characters to display	(none)
TxColor	The text color	Set by browser
TxYOffset	The vertical distance (in pixels) from the top of the applet to the lower left corner of the text	The height of the text
TxXOffset	The horizontal distance (in pixels) from the left side of the applet to the text	0
TxHorizCenter	If true, the text is horizontally centered	false
TxVertCenter	If true, the text is vertically centered	false
TxFont	The font of the text: **TimesRoman, Helvetica, Courier, Dialog, DialogInput,** or **ZapfDingbats**	**Dialog**
TxStyle	The style of the font: **Plain, Bold, Italic,** or **BoldItalic**	**Plain**
TxPointSize	The size of the font in points	10
TxUnderLine	If true, the text is underlined	false
TxBorderWidth	The width of the text border (must be greater than 0 in order for a border to be drawn)	0
TxBorderColor	The color of the text border	black
TxBorderMargin	The distance (in pixels) from the text border to the text on all sides	0
TxFrameThickness	The thickness of the text frame (must be greater than 0 in order for a frame to be drawn)	0
TxFrameType	The type of text frame: **ShadowIn, ShadowOut, ShadowEtchedIn,** or **ShadowEtchedOut**	**ShadowIn**
TxFrameMargin	The distance (in pixels) from the text frame to the text	0

Name	Description	Default
AppBGColor	The background color of the applet	Set by browser
AppBorderWidth	The width of the applet border (must be greater than 0 in order for a border to be drawn)	0
AppBorderColor	The color of the applet border	black
AppFrameThickness	The thickness of the applet frame (must be greater than 0 in order for a frame to be drawn)	0
AppFrameType	The type of applet frame: **ShadowIn**, **ShadowOut**, **ShadowEtchedIn**, or **ShadowEtchedOut**	**ShadowIn**

See Also

Related applets:

URLAudImgTxtBG on page 35
URLAudImgTxt on page 31
AudioImageText on page 27
BasicImage on page 17
BasicText on page 12

URL for **ImageMap**:

`http://www.vivids.com/java/fund/ImageMap.html`

CHAPTER
3

Text
Applets

A Web page conveys information. That information can be displayed in many ways, but one of the most common and useful is through text—characters, words, titles, paragraphs and so forth.

In this chapter we introduce some new and interesting ways to display text that will grab the attention of your visitor. Using the applets in this chapter, you will be able to create text with shadows and depth as well as characters that are embossed, engraved, or transparent.

All the applets in this chapter are derived from the **ImageMap** applet described in the previous chapter. This means that all the **ImageMap** parameters are inherited by these applets. If you want to play an audio file when the pointer enters the text of any of the applets in this chapter, use the **TxAudio** parameter; if you want to load a URL when the user presses a mouse button, use the **TxURL** parameter; if you want a background image displayed beneath the text you are displaying, use the **AppBGImage** parameter; if you want to draw a border or frame, use the **TxFrameThickness** or **TxBorderWidth** parameters; if you want image maps, use the **MapN_** parameters.

Common Settings

The following table show parameters that are is common to all the applets in this chapter.

Name	Description	Default
AppNumMaps	The number of image maps (must be set to use image maps)	0
MapN_X1	The left horizontal coordinate for map N	0
MapN_Y1	The top vertical coordinate for map N	0
MapN_X2	The right horizontal coordinate for map N	0
MapN_Y2	The bottom vertical coordinate for map N	0
MapN_URL	The URL for map N	(none)
TestMode	If true, the pointer position is displayed in the status line	false
AppBGImage	The background image	(none)
AppBGImageXOffset	The horizontal offset at which to position the background image	0
AppBGImageYOffset	The vertical offset at which to position the background image	0
AppTile	If true, tile the background image	false
TxURL	The URL to load when the pointer is within the text and any mouse button is pressed	(none)
ImgURL	The URL to load when the pointer is within the image and any mouse button is pressed	(none)
TxAudio	The audio file to play when the pointer enters the text	(none)
ImgAudio	The audio file to play when the pointer enters the image	(none)
Image	The image to display	(none)
ImgLoadWait	If true, the image is not displayed until it is completely loaded	false
ImgXOffset	The horizontal distance (in pixels) from the left side of the applet to the image	0
ImgYOffset	The vertical distance (in pixels) from the top of the applet to the image	0
ImgHorizCenter	If true, the image is horizontally centered	false
ImgVertCenter	If true, the image is vertically centered	false
ImgBorderWidth	The width of the image border (must be greater than 0 in order for a border to be drawn)	0
ImgBorderColor	The color of the image border	Set by browser
ImgBorderMargin	The distance (in pixels) from the image border to the image on all sides	0

Name	Description	Default
ImgFrameThickness	The thickness of the image frame (must be greater than 0 in order for a frame to be drawn)	0
ImgFrameType	The type of image frame: **ShadowIn**, **ShadowOut**, **ShadowEtchedIn**, or **ShadowEtchedOut**	**ShadowIn**
ImgFrameMargin	The distance (in pixels) from the image frame to the image	0
Text	The string of characters to display	(none)
TxColor	The text color	Set by browser
TxBGColor	The text background color	transparent
TxYOffset	The vertical distance (in pixels) from the top of the applet to the lower left corner of the text	The height of the text
TxXOffset	The horizontal distance (in pixels) from the left side of the applet to the text	0
TxHorizCenter	If true, the text is horizontally centered	false
TxVertCenter	If true, the text is vertically centered	false
TxFont	The font of the text: **TimesRoman**, **Helvetica**, **Courier**, **Dialog**, **DialogInput**, or **ZapfDingbats**	**Dialog**
TxStyle	The style of the font: **Plain**, **Bold**, **Italic**, or **BoldItalic**	**Plain**
TxPointSize	The size of the font in points	10
TxUnderLine	If true, the text is underlined	false
TxBorderWidth	The width of the text border (must be greater than 0 in order for a border to be drawn)	0
TxBorderColor	The color of the text border	black
TxBorderMargin	The distance (in pixels) from the text border to the text on all sides	0
TxFrameThickness	The thickness of the text frame (must be greater than 0 in order for a frame to be drawn)	0
TxFrameType	The type of text frame: **ShadowIn**, **ShadowOut**, **ShadowEtchedIn**, or **ShadowEtchedOut**	**ShadowIn**
TxFrameMargin	The distance (in pixels) from the text frame to the text	0
AppBGColor	The background color of the applet	Set by browser
AppBorderWidth	The width of the applet border (must be greater than 0 in order for a border to be drawn)	0

Name	Description	Default
AppBorderColor	The color of the applet border	black
AppFrameThickness	The thickness of the applet frame (must be greater than 0 in order for a frame to be drawn)	0
AppFrameType	The type of applet frame: **ShadowIn, ShadowOut, ShadowEtchedIn**, or **ShadowEtchedOut**	**ShadowIn**

The only new parameter is **TxBGColor**. This parameter is needed because the applets in this chapter use a different mechanism to draw characters on the screen.

When you use these applets, the characters are actually drawn into a rectangular image; this image is then displayed on the screen with a transparent background, allowing the background color (**AppBGColor**) or image (**AppBGImage**) to show through. This produces the same effect that we saw in the previous chapter.

It is possible to make the text background non-transparent, however. When you specify **TxBGColor**, the text's background is the color you specify, rather than being transparent.

 *Text*

Displays a string of characters

Description

The **Text** applet displays a string of characters.

This applet may appear to be just like the **BasicText** on page 12. It is implemented differently, however, and will be useful later in the book when filters are used.

Using Text in HTML Code

The following HTML code uses the **Text** applet to display the string *Enter Here* in blue characters with a **ShadowEtchedIn** frame:

```
<applet code=Text.class width=300 height=100>
<param name=Text value="Enter Here">
<param name=TxPointSize value=48>
<param name=TxColor value=blue>
<param name=TxFont value=Helvetica>
<param name=TxHorizCenter value=true>
<param name=TxVertCenter value=true>
<param name=TxFrameThickness value=2>
<param name=TxFrameMargin value=4>
<param name=TxFrameType value=ShadowEtchedIn>
</applet>
```

Settings

The common settings described on page 48 all apply to the **Text** applet. Remember that they always allow you to play an audio file, load a URL, and use a background image, among other things.

See Also

URL for **Text**:   http://www.vivids.com/java/text/Text.html

Shadow

Adds a shadow to a string of characters

Description

The **Shadow** applet displays a string of characters with a shadow behind it. The offset or position of the shadow can be controlled using parameters. The position of the shadow creates the impression of illumination from a particular direction.

Using Shadow in HTML Code

The following HTML code uses the **Shadow** applet to display the string *Members Only!* with a border against a tiled background:

```
<applet code=Shadow.class width=400 height=160>
<param name=Text value="Members Only!">
<param name=TxPointSize value=48>
<param name=TxFont value=TimesRoman>
<param name=TxHorizCenter value=true>
<param name=TxVertCenter value=true>
<param name=ShadowXOffset value=-3>
<param name=ShadowYOffset value=3>
<param name=AppBgImage value=../images/pattern.gif>
<param name=AppTile value=true>
<param name=TxBorderWidth value=2>
<param name=TxBorderMargin value=4>
</applet>
```

Here's another example that uses **Shadow** to display the string *Camping Season* against a background image of mountains and trees.

```
<applet code=Shadow.class width=312 height=179>
<param name=text value="Camping Season">
<param name=Txstyle value=bold>
<param name=TxPointSize value=24>
<param name=ShadowXOffset value=4>
<param name=ShadowYOffset value=-3>
<param name=TxHorizCenter value=true>
<param name=TxYOffset value=120>
<param name=TxXOffset value=170>
<param name=ShadowColor value=black>
<param name=TxColor value=white>
<param name=AppBGImage value=../images/forest.gif>
</applet>
```

Settings

The common settings described on page 48 all apply to the **Shadow** applet. Remember that they always allow you to play an audio file, load a URL, and use a background image, among other things. Three additional parameters set the color and offset of the shadow.

Name	Description	Default
ShadowXOffset	The horizontal offset (in pixels) of the shadow	2
ShadowYOffset	The vertical offset (in pixels) of the shadow	2
ShadowColor	The color of the shadow	gray (#646464)

See Also

Related applets: **SoftShadow** on page 54

URL for **Shadow**:   `http://www.vivids.com/java/text/Shadow.html`

SoftShadow

Adds a soft shadow to a string of characters

Description

The **SoftShadow** applet displays a string of characters with a soft shadow behind it. The soft shadow differs from that produced by the **Shadow** applet in that its outline is less well-defined. This effect is produced by using more than one color to draw the shadow; a lighter shade is used around the edges.

The offset, or position, of the shadow can be controlled using parameters. The position creates the impression of illumination from a particular direction and of distance between the text and the background.

Using SoftShadow in HTML Code

The following HTML code uses the **SoftShadow** applet to display the string *Sale!* against a white background. The **ShadowXOffset** and **ShadowYOffset** parameters are used to make the characters appear to be illuminated from the lower right.

```
<applet code=SoftShadow.class width=430 height=120>
<param name=text value="Sale!">
<param name=AppBGColor value=#ffffff>
<param name=Txstyle value=bold>
<param name=TxPointSize value=72>
<param name=ShadowYOffset value=-6>
<param name=ShadowXOffset value=-6>
<param name=SoftThickness value=4>
<param name=TxHorizCenter value=True>
</applet>
```

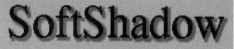

Settings

The common settings described on page 48 apply to the **SoftShadow** applet. Remember that they always allow you to play an audio file, load a URL, and use a background image, among other things. Four additional parameters set the color and offset of the shadow as seen previously with the **Shadow** applet.

The **SoftThickness** parameter determines the softness of the shadow. The greater the value, the softer (or blurrier) the shadow appears to be.

Name	Description	Default
ShadowXOffset	The horizontal offset (in pixels) of the shadow	2
ShadowYOffset	The vertical offset (in pixels) of the shadow	2
ShadowColor	The color of the shadow	gray (#646464)
SoftThickness	The size (in pixels) of the blurring used to create the soft shadow effect	2

The **SoftThickness** parameter should be adjusted based on the size of the text displayed. For small text, you should probably set **SoftThickness** to 1. For very large text, you may want **SoftThickness** to be greater than the default of 2.

See Also

Related applets: **Shadow** on page 52

URL for **SoftShadow**:   `http://www.vivids.com/java/text/SoftShadow.html`

Pages for source code: **SoftShadow.java** on page 257
fsoftshadow.java on page 224

56

SmoothText

Smooths a string of characters

Description

The **SmoothText** applet displays a string of characters which have been *anti-aliased*. Anti-aliasing removes the jagged appearance of lines and characters that appear on the computer screen.

To understand the need for anti-aliasing, look at the following uppercase A, which has been magnified many times:

The jagged appearance of the character is due to the fact that computer displays have limited resolution. Lines that are not perfectly vertical or horizontal exhibit this effect. Anti-aliasing is a technique that replaces the pixels along the edges with various shades of color to make the edge look smoother. Here is the same character after it has been anti-aliased:

Although the anti-aliased character looks a little fuzzy at this magnification, its appearance is clean and smooth when viewed at regular size.

The different shades of color that are used to create the smoothing effect are based on the foreground and the background colors. Even if you specify a background image with this applet, the shades used are based on the background color you specify, not on the background image. (If you do not specify a background color, the default background color is used.)

If the color of the background image is very different from the specified background color, the characters may appear to have a slight outline or ghost around them. For this reason, if you do place anti-aliased text on a background image you will probably want to pick a background color that matches the color of your image.

Using SmoothText in HTML Code

It's difficult to fully appreciate the anti-aliased effect on the printed page because printed resolution is so much greater than that on the screen. The effects are, however, quite noticeable when viewed on your computer display.

The following HTML code uses the **SmoothText** applet to display the string *JAVA!* against a white background.

```
<applet code=SmootTexth.class width=250 height=120>
<param name=Text value=JAVA!>
<param name=TxPointSize value=72>
<param name=TxFont value=Helvetica>
<param name=TxStyle value=Bold>
<param name=AppBGColor value=#ffffff>
<param name=TxVertCenter value=true>
<param name=TxHorizCenter value=true>
<param name=TxBorderWidth value=2>
<param name=TxBorderMargin value=2>
</applet>
```

Settings

All settings for **SmoothText** are included in the settings described on page 48. Remember that they always allow you to play an audio file, load a URL, and use a background image, among other things.

See Also

URL for **SmoothText**:   http://www.vivids.com/java/text/SmoothText.html

WaveText

Arranges a string of characters in a sine wave

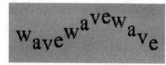

Description

The **WaveText** applet displays a string of characters arranged in a sine wave. Adjust the **Amplitude** and **WaveLength** parameters to determine the exact shape of the wave.

Using WaveText in HTML Code

The following HTML code uses the **WaveText** applet to display the string *Life has its little ups and downs*. The amplitude and wavelength are set to place the word *ups* at the top of the wave and the word *downs* toward the bottom.

```
<applet code=WaveText.class width=250 height=100>
<param name=Text value="Life has its little ups and downs">
<param name=TxPointSize value=18>
<param name=TxFont value=TimesRoman>
<param name=TxHorizCenter value=true>
<param name=TxVertCenter value=true>
<param name=Amplitude value=25>
<param name=WaveTextLength value=30>
</applet>
```

Here's another example using the **WaveText** applet. This time we set the **BeginRange** and **EndRange** parameters so that the wave pattern appears only on the characters within the range specified.

```
<applet code=WaveText.class width=350 height=120>
<param name=Text value="Life has its little ups and downs, doesn't it?">
<param name=TxPointSize value=18>
<param name=TxFont value=TimesRoman>
<param name=TxHorizCenter value=true>
<param name=TxVertCenter value=true>
<param name=Amplitude value=25>
<param name=WaveTextLength value=20>
<param name=BeginRange value=15>
```

```
<param name=EndRange value=31>
<param name=XTranslate value=30>
</applet>
```

Life has its little ups a n d dow n s, doesn't it?

Settings

The common settings described on page 48 all apply to the **WaveText** applet. Remember that they always allow you to play an audio file, load a URL, and use a background image, among other things. Six additional parameters set the wave's characteristics.

The **Amplitude** parameter sets the height of the wave. The **WaveLength** parameter sets the horizontal length of the wave. The **XTranslate** and **YTranslate** parameters translate the wave in the horizontal and vertical directions respectively. The **BeginRange** and **EndRange** parameters set the range of characters to which the wave function applies.

Name	Description	Default
Amplitude	The amplitude of the wave	10
WaveLength	The wavelength of the wave	10
XTranslate	The horizontal translation of the wave	0
YTranslate	The vertical translation of the wave	0
BeginRange	The character with which to begin the wave	Beginning of line
EngRange	The character with which to end the wave	End of line

See Also

URL for **WaveText**:   `http://www.vivids.com/java/text/WaveText.html`

Depth

Adds 3-dimensional depth to a string of characters

Description

The **Depth** applet displays a string of characters that appear to have 3-dimensional depth. The depth can be set to any reasonable degree.

Using Depth in HTML Code

The following HTML code uses the **Depth** applet to display the string *Enter Here* with green text, purple background, and black depth.

```
<applet code=Depth.class width=400 height=160>
<param name=Text value="Enter Here">
<param name=AppBGColor value=#ff00ff>
<param name=TxPointSize value=72>
<param name=TxColor value=#00ff00>
<param name=TxFont value=Dialog>
<param name=TxHorizCenter value=true>
<param name=TxVertCenter value=true>
<param name=DepthColor value=#000000>
<param name=DepthXOffset value=10>
<param name=DepthYOffset value=-10>
</applet>
```

Here's one more example of the **Depth** applet. It displays the string *WOW!!* in white against a black background, with depth offsets of –20.

```
<applet code=Depth.class width=300 height=120>
<param name=Text value="WOW!!">
<param name=TxPointSize value=48>
<param name=TxColor value=#ffffff>
<param name=AppBGColor value=#000000>
<param name=TxFont value=TimesRoman>
<param name=TxHorizCenter value=true>
```

```
<param name=TxVertCenter value=true>
<param name=DepthXOffset value=-20>
<param name=DepthYOffset value=-20>
</applet>
```

Settings

The common settings described on page 48 all apply to the **Depth** applet. Remember that they always allow you to play an audio file, load a URL, and use a background image, among other things. Three additional parameters set the color of the depth, and the horizontal and vertical offsets of the depth.

Name	Description	Default
DepthXOffset	The horizontal offset (in pixels) of the depth	-10
DepthYOffset	The vertical offset (in pixels) of the depth	-10
DepthColor	The color of the depth	The text color darkened by 50%

The **DepthColor** defaults to a shade of the text color that is 50% darker. Thus, if the foreground color is black, the depth color will also be black. You will probably want to explicitly select another color for the depth if you are using black or any other dark color as your foreground.

See Also

Related applets: **DepthFade** on page 62
                          DepthShade on page 64

URL for **Depth**:   `http://www.vivids.com/java/text/Depth.html`

Adds fading 3-dimensional depth to a string of characters

Description

The **DepthFade** applet displays a string of characters that appear to have 3-dimensional depth, fading into the background. By default the depth fades from the foreground color to the background color. You can also specify a contrasting outline for the characters themselves, which is sometimes helpful in distinguishing between the characters and their depth.

Using DepthFade in HTML Code

The following HTML code uses the **DepthFade** applet to display the string *WOW!!* with a **FGColor** of white and a **BGColor** of black.

```
<applet code=DepthFade.class width=300 height=120>
<param name=Text value="WOW!!">
<param name=TxPointSize value=48>
<param name=TxColor value=#ffffff>
<param name=AppBGColor value=#000000>
<param name=TxFont value=TimesRoman>
<param name=TxHorizCenter value=true>
<param name=TxVertCenter value=true>
<param name=DepthXOffset value=-20>
<param name=DepthYOffset value=-20>
</applet>
```

You may prefer to add an outline. If so, set the **OutlineColor** parameter. The following code adds the **OutlineColor** parameter to set the outline to black.

```
<applet code=DepthFade.class width=300 height=120>
<param name=Text value="WOW!!">
<param name=TxPointSize value=48>
<param name=TxColor value=#ffffff>
<param name=AppBGColor value=#000000>
<param name=TxFont value=TimesRoman>
<param name=TxHorizCenter value=true>
<param name=TxVertCenter value=true>
<param name=DepthXOffset value=-20>
<param name=DepthYOffset value=-20>
<param name=OutlineColor value=#000000>
</applet>
```

You can do some interesting things by changing the **DepthColor** parameter. The next example uses the default background color (gray in this case), a black foreground, and a yellow **DepthColor**. The effect is much more dramatic on a color display.

```
<applet code=DepthFade.class width=800 height=160>
<param name=Text value="Acme Tools">
<param name=TxPointSize value=48>
<param name=TxColor value=#000000>
<param name=DepthColor value=#ffff00>
<param name=TxHorizCenter value=true>
<param name=TxVertCenter value=true>
<param name=DepthXOffset value=30>
<param name=DepthYOffset value=-30>
</applet>
```

Settings

The common settings described on page 48 all apply to the **DepthFade** applet. Remember that they always allow you to play an audio file, load a URL, and use a background image, among other things. Four additional parameters set the color of the depth, the outline color, and the horizontal and vertical offsets of the depth.

Name	Description	Default
DepthXOffset	The horizontal offset (in pixels) of the depth	-10
DepthYOffset	The vertical offset (in pixels) of the depth	-10
DepthColor	The color of the depth	**AppBGColor**
OutlineColor	The color of the outline	(none)

The depth changes gradually from the text color (**TxColor**) to the depth color (**DepthColor**). **DepthColor** defaults to the background color (**AppBGColor**), so if you do not explicitly specify **DepthColor** the depth fades directory from the text color to the background color.

See Also

Related applets: **Depth** on page 60
Depth on page 60
DepthShade on page 64

URL for **DepthFade**:   http://www.vivids.com/java/text/DepthFade.html

 # DepthShade

Adds a 3-dimensional shadow
that fades toward a string of
characters

Description

The **DepthShade** applet, like the **DepthFade** applet, displays a string of characters that
appear to be 3-dimensional. The difference, however, is that the depth of the characters
fades in the reverse direction, from the background color to the foreground color, producing an effect of shadowed depth.

Using DepthShade in HTML Code

The following HTML code uses the **DepthShade** applet to display the string *WOW!!* with a
FGColor of white and a **BGColor** of black.

```
<applet code=DepthShade.class width=300 height=120>
<param name=Text value="WOW!!">
<param name=TxPointSize value=48>
<param name=TxColor value=white>
<param name=AppBGColor value=black>
<param name=TxFont value=TimesRoman>
<param name=TxHorizCenter value=true>
<param name=TxVertCenter value=true>
<param name=DepthXOffset value=-20>
<param name=DepthYOffset value=-20>
</applet>
```

Here's the Acme Tools example from the **DepthFade** applet using **DepthShade** instead.
Compare it with the earlier version.

```
<applet code=DepthShade.class width=340 height=120>
<param name=Text value="Acme Tools">
<param name=TxPointSize value=48>
<param name=TxColor value=#000000>
<param name=DepthColor value=#ffff00>
<param name=TxHorizCenter value=true>
<param name=TxVertCenter value=true>
<param name=DepthXOffset value=30>
<param name=DepthYOffset value=-30>
</applet>
```

Settings

The common settings described on page 48 all apply to the **DepthShade** applet. Remember that they always allow you to play an audio file, load a URL, and use a background image, among other things. Three additional parameters set the color of the depth, and the horizontal and vertical offsets of the depth.

Name	Description	Default
DepthXOffset	The horizontal offset (in pixels) of the depth	-10
DepthYOffset	The vertical offset (in pixels) of the depth	-10
DepthColor	The color of the depth	**AppBGColor**

See Also

Related applets: **Depth** on page 60
DepthFade on page 62

URL for **DepthShade**:   http://www.vivids.com/java/text/DepthShade.html

Emboss

Embosses a string of characters on the background

Description

The **Emboss** applet displays a string of characters that appear to be embossed on the background. By default, the background is a solid color.

Using Emboss in HTML Code

The following HTML code uses the **Emboss** applet to display the string *Back to Home Page* against a gray background. The characters are displayed with an intensity of 75. The **Contrast** parameter determines the shades of color that are used to create the embossed look.

```
<applet code=Emboss.class width=300 height=100>
<param name=text value="Back to Home Page">
<param name=Txstyle value=bold>
<param name=TxPointSize value=24>
<param name=TxFont value=Dialog>
<param name=TxFrameThickness value=2>
<param name=TxFrameType value=ShadowEtchedOut>
<param name=TxFrameMargin value=5>
<param name=TxHorizCenter value=true>
<param name=TxVertCenter value=true>
<param name=Contrast value=75>
</applet>
```

If you plan to emboss text that is displayed over a background image, remember that the specified background color, not the colors in the background image, is used to create the embossed look—even if the background is completely obscured by the background image. You may be able to select a background color that matches your background image to create a reasonable embossed effect.

The following example displays the string *Cruise, Anyone?* against a background image of some sailboats. The color specified as the **AppBGColor** closely matches the color of the sky, allowing the embossed effect to succeed.

```
<applet code=Emboss.class width=336 height=226>
<param name=text value="Cruise, Anyone?">
<param name=Txstyle value=bold>
<param name=AppBGImage value=../images/sailboat.gif>
<param name=AppBGColor value=#a5d6f7>
<param name=TxPointSize value=24>
<param name=Depth value=1>
<param name=TxFont value=Dialog>
<param name=TxHorizCenter value=true>
<param name=TxYOffset value=82>
<param name=Contrast value=75>
</applet>
```

Settings

The common settings described on page 48 all apply to the **Emboss** applet. Remember that they always allow you to play an audio file, load a URL, and use a background image, among other things. Two additional parameter set the intensity and the depth of the embossed look.

Name	Description	Default
Depth	The depth of the embossing	1
Contrast	The contrast of the colors used to create the embossed effect	50

Contrast can be any value between 0 and 100. The stronger the contrast, the greater the contrast in the colors that are used to produce the embossed effect, and the more intense the effect itself.

Embossing a string on a very dark or very light background may produce poor results.

See Also

Related applets:

Engrave on page 69
EmbossImage on page 103

URL for **Emboss**:

http://www.vivids.com/java/text/Emboss.html

 *Engrave*

Engraves a string of characters into the
background image

Description

The **Engrave** applet displays a string of characters that appear to be engraved into the background. By default, the background is a solid color.

Using Engrave in HTML Code

The following HTML code uses the **Engrave** applet to display the string *Congratulations*
against a gray background. The characters are displayed using a **Contrast** of 90 and are
enclosed in a **ShadowOut** frame.

```
<applet code=Engrave.class width=400 height=160>
<param name=text value="Congratulations">
<param name=Txstyle value=BoldItalic>
<param name=TxPointSize value=48>
<param name=TxFont value=Helvetica>
<param name=TxFrameThickness value=1>
<param name=TxFrameMargin value=6>
<param name=TxFrameType value=ShadowOut>
<param name=TxHorizCenter value=true>
<param name=TxVertCenter value=true>
<param name=Contrast value=90>
</applet>
```

Congratulations

Engraving text over an image poses the same problem as with embossed text: you must
choose a background color that matches the color of your image. Finding the right color can
be challenging. However, if you are able to select a background color that closely matches
the color of your image, the results can be satisfying, as shown in the next example.

```
<applet code=Engrave.class width=336 height=226>
<param name=text value="Cruise, Anyone?">
<param name=Txstyle value=bold>
```

```
<param name=AppBGImage value=../images/sailboat.gif>
<param name=AppBGColor value=#a5d6f7>
<param name=TxPointSize value=24>
<param name=Depth value=1>
<param name=TxFont value=Dialog>
<param name=TxHorizCenter value=true>
<param name=TxYOffset value=82>
</applet>
```

Settings

The common settings described on page 48 all apply to the **Engrave** applet. Remember that they always allow you to play an audio file, load a URL, and use a background image, among other things. Two additional parameters set the contrast and the depth of the engraved look.

Name	Description	Default
Depth	The depth of the engraving	1
Contrast	The intensity of the engraving	50

Contrast can be any value between 0 and 100. The stronger the intensity, the greater the contrast in the colors that are used to produce the engraved effect, and the more intense the effect itself.

Engraving a string into a very dark or very light background may produce poor results.

See Also

Related applets: **Emboss** on page 66

URL for **Engrave**: `http://www.vivids.com/java/text/Engrave.html`

Stencil

Draws a string of characters using the background image

Stencil

Description

The **Stencil** applet displays a string of characters that are drawn using the background image rather than a text color and thus appear to be transparent.

Using the **Stencil** applet without a background image produces text which cannot be seen.

Using Stencil in HTML Code

The following HTML code uses the **Stencil** applet to display the string *Money* against a background image of currency:

```
<applet code=Stencil.class width=400 height=100>
<param name=text value=" MONEY   ">
<param name=Txstyle value=bold>
<param name=TxFont value=Helvetica>
<param name=AppBGImage value=../images/money.gif>
<param name=AppTile value=true>
<param name=TxPointSize value=96>
<param name=AppBGColor value=black>
<param name=TxColor value=white>
<param name=TxVertCenter value=true>
</applet>
```

Although the text color is not displayed by the **Stencil** applet, it must be different from the background color. If you specify a black background, for example, and leave the foreground color to default to black, only the background image displays.

Settings

All settings for **Stencil** are included in the settings described at the beginning of this chapter on page 48. Remember that they always allow you to play an audio file, load a URL, and use a background image, among other things.

See Also

Related applets: **TransColor** on page 105
                      Transparent on page 111

URL for **Stencil**:   `http://www.vivids.com/java/text/Stencil.html`

MultiColor

Draws a string of characters using different colors

Description

The **MultiColor** applet displays a string of characters in which each character is a different color. You may specify one or more colors to be used in succession to color the characters. If you specify fewer colors than there are characters, the colors are reused, starting with the first one specified.

Using MultiColor in HTML Code

The following HTML code uses the **MultiColor** applet to display the string *Colorful* using red, yellow, and blue. The characters are enclosed in a **ShadowEtchedOut** frame and drawn against a tiled background. Note that the colors repeat, starting with the fourth character.

```
<applet code=MultiColor.class width=400 height=300>
<param name=AppBgImage value=../images/pattern.gif>
<param name=AppTile value=true>
<param name=Text value="Colorful">
<param name=TxPointSize value=72>
<param name=Colors value="red yellow blue">
<param name=TxFont value=Helvetica>
<param name=TxStyle value=Bold>
<param name=TxHorizCenter value=true>
<param name=TxVertCenter value=true>
<param name=TxFrameThickness value=4>
<param name=TxFrameMargin value=12>
<param name=TxFrameType value=ShadowEtchedOut>
</applet>
```

Settings

The common settings described on page 48 all apply to the **MultiColor** applet. Remember that they always allow you to play an audio file, load a URL, and use a background image, among other things. One additional parameter sets the colors used to draw the characters.

Name	Description	Default
Colors	The colors to use for the characters	black

To set the **Colors** parameter, enclose a list of all the colors you want to use in double quotes, separated by spaces. This is shown in the sixth line of the sample HTML code.

See Also

URL for **MultiColor**:   `http://www.vivids.com/java/text/MultiColor.html`

MultiText

Draws multiple strings of characters

String One
String Two

Description

The **MultiText** applet displays multiple strings of characters. Each string may be displayed using any of the techniques seen in this chapter. You could, for example, display three strings: one multicolored, one embossed, and one with a shadow.

Each string has its own characteristics, such as font, pointsize, offsets, border, frame, audio file, URL and so forth. For each string you can specify any of the parameters that are used in this chapter.

All the parameters that begin with **Tx** can be specified independently for each string. Each **Tx** parameter must instead begin with **Tx*N***, however, where ***N*** is the number that identifies the text string. For example, to set the font for string 2 to TimesRoman, use **Tx2Font**. To set the horizontal offset for string 1 use **Tx1XOffset**.

Using MultiText in HTML Code

To display multiple strings you must specify the **TxCount** parameter, which specifies the number of strings to be displayed. To display three strings, set **TxCount** as follows:

```
<param name=TxCount value=3>
```

To draw a string using one of the techniques discussed in the chapter, use the **Tx*N*Filter** parameter. You will learn more about **Tx*N*Filter** in Chapter 4. The **Tx*N*Filter** parameter can be used to manipulate string and images in many interesting ways. For now, you will use it to invoke one of the string display techniques that have been introduced in this chapter.

Suppose that you wanted the first string to be drawn with a shadow and the second to be drawn with an engraved look. You would specify the **Tx*N*Filter** parameter as follows:

```
<param name=Tx1Filter value=shadow>
<param name=Tx2Filter value=engrave>
```

By default, this would display the first string with the default values for the three shadow parameters—**ShadowXOffset**, **ShadowYOffset**, and **ShadowColor** (see **Shadow** on page 54). To set one or more of these parameters, supply arguments to the **Tx1Filter** value. For example, to display a shadow with a horizontal offset of -4, a vertical offset of 3, and a shadow color of green, use the following parameter settings:

```
<param name=Tx1Filter value="shadow -4 3 green">
```

The arguments must be specified in the exact order in which they were described in the Settings section for the applet that corresponds to the filter you are calling.

To set the engraved depth and intensity of the second string to 1 and 90, respectively, use the following settings:

```
<param name=Tx2Filter value="engrave 1 90">
```

Note that you must specify the **Depth** value first and then the **Contrast** value, as indicated for **Engrave** on page 69.

The following HTML code uses the **MultiText** applet to display three strings, each drawn using a different filter. The first string is drawn using **engrave**, the second is drawn using **multicolor**, and the third uses **stencil**.

```
<applet code=MultiTxt.class width=320 height=240>
<param name=AppTile value=true>
<param name=AppBgImage value=pattern.gif>

<param name=TxCount value=3>

<param name=Text1 value="Engraved Text">
<param name=Tx1PointSize value=48>
<param name=Tx1Font value=TimesRoman>
<param name=Tx1Style value=BoldItalic>
<param name=Tx1XOffset value=20>
<param name=Tx1YOffset value=10>
<param name=Tx1Filter value="engrave 1 90">
<param name=Tx1Audio value=../fund/sam.au>
<param name=Tx1URL value=http://www.sun.com>

<param name=Text2 value="Colorful">
<param name=Tx2PointSize value=48>
<param name=Tx2Font value=Helvetica>
<param name=Tx2Style value=Bold>
<param name=Tx2XOffset value=20>
<param name=Tx2YOffset value=80>
<param name=Tx2FrameThickness value=4>
<param name=Tx2FrameMargin value=12>
<param name=Tx2FrameType value=ShadowEtchedOut>
<param name=Tx2Filter value="multicolor yellow green blue black white red">
<param name=Tx2Audio value=../fund/sun.au>
<param name=Tx2URL value=http://www.vivids.com>

<param name=Text3 value="Transparent">
<param name=Tx3PointSize value=48>
<param name=Tx3Font value=TimesRoman>
<param name=Tx3Style value=Bold>
```

```
<param name=Tx3XOffset value=20>
<param name=Tx3YOffset value=160>
<param name=Tx3BorderWidth value=1>
<param name=Tx3BGColor value=black>
<param name=Tx3Color value=white>
<param name=Tx3Underline value=true>
<param name=Tx3Filter value="stencil">
<param name=Tx3Audio value=../fund/pledge.au>
<param name=Tx3URL value=http://www.adobe.com>
</applet>
```

Settings

The common settings described on page 48 all apply to the **MultiText** applet. However, the parameters that begin with **Tx** must instead begin with **Tx*N***, where ***N*** specifies the string involved. The **Tx*N*Filter** parameter is used to specify the program (or filter) that is used to draw the string. In addition, the **TxCount** parameter must be specified to indicate the number of strings to display.

Name	Description	Default
TxCount	The number of text strings to display	0
Tx*N*Filter	The program to use to generate the *N*th string	0

Remember that the common settings always allow you to play an audio file, load a URL, and use a background image, among other things.

See Also

URL for **MultiText**:   http://www.vivids.com/java/text/MultiText.html

Tips for Programmers

The applets in this chapter are implemented by extending the **ImgFilt** class defined in the classes directory. The **ImgFilt** class is an abstract class that requires any subclass to supply a `filter` method. To create a text generating filter (like the ones discussed in this chapter), you create a class that subclasses **ImgFilt** and write the `filter` method that creates the text.

We'll go over the steps in detail and show an example. The benefit of following this procedure is that you can create your own text generating filter that will work with the rest of the applets and filters described in this book.

To begin, let's look at the source code for the **shadow** filter. The filter naming convention is to prepend a lower-case 'f', so the **shadow** filter is in a file named **fshadow.java**, and the name of the class is **fshadow**:

```
1    import java.awt.*;
2    import java.awt.image.*;
3
4    class fshadow extends ImgFilt {
5        int shadow_xoffset = 2;
6        int shadow_yoffset = 2;
7        Color shadow_color = new Color(100, 100, 100);
8
9        public void setparameter(String str, int i) {
10           switch(i) {
11           case 0:
12               shadow_xoffset = Integer.parseInt(str);
13               break;
14           case 1:
15               shadow_yoffset = Integer.parseInt(str);
16               break;
17           case 2:
18               shadow_color = String2Color(str);
19               break;
20           }
21       }
22
23       public int[] filter(int[] p1, int w, int h) {
24           int x, y;
25           Image image;
26           Graphics g;
27           int ascent, descent;
28           FontMetrics fontmetrics;
29           int pixels[];
30           boolean retval;
31           ftransp tp;
```

```
32
33          // Ignore p1, w, and h
34
35          fontmetrics = applet.getFontMetrics(font);
36          ascent = fontmetrics.getAscent();
37          descent = fontmetrics.getDescent();
38          new_width = fontmetrics.stringWidth(tx) +
39                                          Math.abs(shadow_xoffset);
40          new_height = fontmetrics.getHeight() +
41                                          Math.abs(shadow_yoffset);
42
43          image = applet.createImage(new_width, new_height);
44          g = image.getGraphics();
45          g.setFont(font);
46          g.setColor(bg);
47          g.fillRect(0, 0, new_width, new_height);
48
49          x = (shadow_xoffset < 0) ? Math.abs(shadow_xoffset) : 0;
50          y = (shadow_yoffset < 0) ? Math.abs(shadow_yoffset) : 0;
51
52          // Draw text in shadow color offset by xoffset, yoffset
53          g.setColor(shadow_color);
54          g.drawString(tx, x+shadow_xoffset,
55                          y+ascent+shadow_yoffset);
56          drawUnderline(g, fontmetrics, x+shadow_xoffset,
57                          y+ascent+shadow_yoffset+
58                          Math.max(1, (descent/4)),
59                          new_width, shadow_color);
60
61          // Now draw the main foreground text
62          g.setColor(fg);
63          g.drawString(tx, x, y+ascent);
64          drawUnderline(g, fontmetrics, x,
65                          y+ascent+Math.max(1, (descent/4)),
66                          new_width, fg);
67
68          // Grab the pixels
69          pixels = ImgGetr.getPixels(image, applet);
70          if(transparent) {
71              tp = new ftransp();
72              tp.setTransparentColor(bg);
73              pixels = tp.filter(pixels, new_width, new_height);
74          }
75          return pixels;
76      }
77  }
```

All text generating filters draw text into an off-screen image, retrieve the array of pixels that represent the image, and return the array to the calling object. Here is a list of requirements for filters that are to work in this environment:

- The `filter` method must return an array of pixels which represent the image
- The filter must set the `new_width` instance variable to the width of the image
- The filter must set the `new_height` instance variable to the height of the image

In addition, the filter may also elect to do the following:

- Define a `setparameter` method to set customizable options

The **fshadow** filter demonstrates each of these features.

The setparameter method

On line 9 the `setparameter` method is declared. The setparameter method is automatically called when the filter is specified as a **TxFilter**. For each argument specified in the HTML file, the `setparameter` method is called. The `i` parameter specifies the position at which the argument was supplied. If, for example, the HTML file includes this line,

```
<param name=TxFilter value="shadow 2 -2 green">
```

then `setparameter` is called three times because there are three arguments to shadow. The first time it is called, the `str` parameter is 2 (the first argument to shadow) and the `i` parameter is 0 (representing the first parameter). The second time, the `str` parameter is –2 and the `i` parameter is 1. The third time, the `str` parameter is `green` and the `i` parameter is 2.

The code in the `setparameter` method sets the appropriate variables that correspond to the filter parameter being set. In this example the horizontal shadow offset is 2, the vertical shadow offset is –2, and the shadow color is green. It is important to specify default values in case the HTML author does not specify an argument.

The filter method

The `filter` method contains the code that generates the text. The arguments passed to the `filter` method are ignored for all text generating filters. The arguments are used when manipulating an image, as seen in Chapter 4. None of the filters is this chapter, however, use the filter arguments.

Variables

After the parameters are set, the `filter` method is called. This is where the real work of generating the text is done. There are several instance variables defined in `ImgFilt` that are set automatically (when invoked using the **TxFilter** parameter). You can use these variables within your filter method:

`bg`	A Color object. The background color.
`fg`	A Color object. The foreground color.
`font`	A Font object. The specified font.
`tx`	A String object. The specified text.
`applet`	An Applet object. The current applet.
`underline`	A boolean variable. If true, underline the text.
`transparent`	A boolean variable. If true, make the background transparent.

Exactly what you do in the `filter` method will be up to you, but here is a general outline for a generic text generating filter:

- Determine the dimensions that the text will require

- Create an image

- Retrieve the `Graphics` context for the image

- Draw the text into the image using the `Graphics` context

- Get the array of integers representing the pixels of the image

- Set the `new_width` and `new_height` variables

- If specified, make the background transparent

- Return the pixel array

Let's look at each of these steps in the code example shown above.

Determine the dimensions that the text will require

On lines 35 through 37 the `FontMetrics` class is used to determine the size of the string based on the font. Because this code draws a shadow, we must allow some extra horizontal and vertical space for the shadow, as shown on lines 38 through 41:

```
35          fontmetrics = applet.getFontMetrics(font);
36          ascent = fontmetrics.getAscent();
37          descent = fontmetrics.getDescent();
38          new_width = fontmetrics.stringWidth(tx) +
39                                      Math.abs(shadow_xoffset);
40          new_height = fontmetrics.getHeight() +
41                                      Math.abs(shadow_yoffset);
```

Create an image

This step will probably be the same for most filters. Use the width and height that you calculated for your image and call `createImage` to create a new, empty image of the specified dimensions. Line 43 of the example performs this step.

```
43              image = applet.createImage(new_width, new_height);
```

Retrieve the `Graphics` context for the image

Simply call the `getGraphics` method of the image object to retrieve the `Graphics` object as shown on line 44.

```
44              g = image.getGraphics();
```

Draw the text into the image using the `Graphics` context

You will probably want to set the font and fill the background with the background color before drawing into the image, as shown on lines 45 and 46.

```
45              g.setFont(font);
46              g.setColor(bg);
47              g.fillRect(0, 0, new_width, new_height);
```

Then perform the filter specific tasks. In this case we will draw the string once in the shadow color with the appropriate offset, and again in the foreground color.

```
49              x = (shadow_xoffset < 0) ? Math.abs(shadow_xoffset) : 0;
50              y = (shadow_yoffset < 0) ? Math.abs(shadow_yoffset) : 0;
51
52              // Draw text in shadow color offset by xoffset, yoffset
53              g.setColor(shadow_color);
54              g.drawString(tx, x+shadow_xoffset,
55                              y+ascent+shadow_yoffset);
56              drawUnderline(g, fontmetrics, x+shadow_xoffset,
57                              y+ascent+shadow_yoffset+
58                              Math.max(1, (descent/4)),
59                              new_width, shadow_color);
60
61              // Now draw the main foreground text
62              g.setColor(fg);
63              g.drawString(tx, x, y+ascent);
64              drawUnderline(g, fontmetrics, x,
65                              y+ascent+Math.max(1, (descent/4)),
66                              new_width, fg);
```

Get the array of integers representing the pixels of the image

Simply call the getPixels method from the ImgGetr class. The getPixels method is static so you don't need to worry about instantiating ImgGetr.

```
69              pixels = ImgGetr.getPixels(image, applet);
```

Set the new_width and new_height variables

We already took care of this step when we calculated the dimensions of the image, back on lines 38 through 41.

```
38              new_width = fontmetrics.stringWidth(tx) +
39                                          Math.abs(shadow_xoffset);
40              new_height = fontmetrics.getHeight() +
41                                          Math.abs(shadow_yoffset);
```

If specified, make the background transparent

Most text generating filters will have the transparent variable set to true unless the user explicitly specified a text background color using the **TxBGColor** parameter. Check the transparent variable to determine if the background should be made transparent. For most cases you can simply use these lines of code:

```
70              if(transparent) {
71                  tp = new ftransp();
72                  tp.setTransparentColor(bg);
73                  pixels = tp.filter(pixels, new_width, new_height);
74              }
```

These lines invoke the ftransp filter, which makes transparent all pixels that match the color specified as the argument to setTransparentColor.

Return the pixel array

Finally, return the array of pixels.

```
75              return pixels;
```

What's Next?

Now you're ready to compile and install your filter. After you compile it, just put it in the same directory as the other filters. There is no other action required. The class loader will automatically find the filter at run time. If you're interested in how the filter is loaded, check out the Filter class in Appendix A on page 209.

CHAPTER
4

Image
Applets

Text and images are the two most common components of any Web page. Chapter 3 covered text; this chapter covers images. The techniques developed in the last chapter applied specifically to text. In this chapter we develop new techniques to apply to images, but these can also be applied to text.

All the applets in this chapter are intended to display a single image. They are all derived from the applets in the **Fundamental Applets** and the **Text Applets** chapters. This allows you to do all the things you have learned about, including playing audio, loading URLs, using image maps, and displaying a background image behind your primary image. Even though this chapter focuses on manipulating images, you can always include an audio file that is played when the pointer enters the applet, or a URL that is loaded when the mouse button is pressed while the pointer is within the text or image.

When you are done with this chapter you will be able to display both images and text in a variety of ways, including rotated, mirrored, slanted, waved, blurred, or embossed effects. In addition to using these individual techniques, you will be able to combine most of them to produce interesting and useful results. Remember that the text capabilities of the previous chapter are all still available when displaying images.

Common Settings

The following parameters are common to all the applets in this chapter.

Name	Description	Default
AppNumMaps	The number of image maps (must be set to use image maps)	0
Map$N$_X1	The left horizontal coordinate for map N	0
Map$N$_Y1	The top vertical coordinate for map N	0
Map$N$_X2	The right horizontal coordinate for map N	0
Map$N$_Y2	The bottom vertical coordinate for map N	0
Map$N$_URL	The URL for map N	(none)
TestMode	If true, the pointer position is displayed in the status line	false
AppBGImage	The background image	(none)
AppBGImageXOffset	The horizontal offset at which to position the background image	0
AppBGImageYOffset	The vertical offset at which to position the background image	0
AppTile	If true, tile the background image	false
ImgFilter	The programs to use to manipulate the image	(none)
TxFilter	The programs to use to generate and manipulate the string	(none)
TxURL	The URL to load when the pointer is within the text and any mouse button is pressed	(none)
ImgURL	The URL to load when the pointer is within the image and any mouse button is pressed	(none)
TxAudio	The audio file to play when the pointer enters the text	(none)
ImgAudio	The audio file to play when the pointer enters the image	(none)
Image	The image to display	(none)
ImgLoadWait	If true, the image is not displayed until it is completely loaded	false
ImgXOffset	The horizontal distance (in pixels) from the left side of the applet to the image	0
ImgYOffset	The vertical distance (in pixels) from the top of the applet to the image	0
ImgHorizCenter	If true, the image is horizontally centered	false
ImgVertCenter	If true, the image is vertically centered	false
ImgBorderWidth	The width of the image border (must be greater than 0 in order for a border to be drawn)	0

Name	Description	Default
ImgBorderColor	The color of the image border	Set by browser
ImgBorderMargin	The distance (in pixels) from the image border to the image on all sides	0
ImgFrameThickness	The thickness of the image frame (must be greater than 0 in order for a frame to be drawn)	0
ImgFrameType	The type of image frame: **ShadowIn**, **ShadowOut**, **ShadowEtchedIn**, or **ShadowEtchedOut**	**ShadowIn**
ImgFrameMargin	The distance (in pixels) from the image frame to the image	0
Text	The string of characters to display	(none)
TxColor	The text color	Set by browser
TxBGColor	The text background color	transparent
TxYOffset	The vertical distance (in pixels) from the top of the applet to the lower left corner of the text	The height of the text
TxXOffset	The horizontal distance (in pixels) from the left side of the applet to the text	0
TxHorizCenter	If true, the text is horizontally centered	false
TxVertCenter	If true, the text is vertically centered	false
TxFont	The font of the text: **TimesRoman**, **Helvetica**, **Courier**, **Dialog**, **DialogInput**, or **ZapfDingbats**	**Dialog**
TxStyle	The style of the font: **Plain**, **Bold**, **Italic**, or **BoldItalic**	**Plain**
TxPointSize	The size of the font in points	10
TxUnderLine	If true, the text is underlined	false
TxBorderWidth	The width of the text border (must be greater than 0 in order for a border to be drawn)	0
TxBorderColor	The color of the text border	black
TxBorderMargin	The distance (in pixels) from the text border to the text on all sides	0
TxFrameThickness	The thickness of the text frame (must be greater than 0 in order for a frame to be drawn)	0
TxFrameType	The type of text frame: **ShadowIn**, **ShadowOut**, **ShadowEtchedIn**, or **ShadowEtchedOut**	**ShadowIn**
TxFrameMargin	The distance (in pixels) from the text frame to the text	0
AppBGColor	The background color of the applet	Set by browser

Name	Description	Default
AppBorderWidth	The width of the applet border (must be greater than 0 in order for a border to be drawn)	0
AppBorderColor	The color of the applet border	black
AppFrameThickness	The thickness of the applet frame (must be greater than 0 in order for a frame to be drawn)	0
AppFrameType	The type of applet frame: **ShadowIn**, **ShadowOut**, **ShadowEtchedIn**, or **ShadowEtchedOut**	**ShadowIn**

Using Filters

In the last chapter, you learned about the **Tx***N***Filter** parameter in the description of the **MultiText** on page 75. The **Tx***N***Filter** parameter was used to specify which filter should be used to draw a particular string, so each string could be drawn uniquely. Most of the applets in this chapter display a single text and image, so the ***N*** is not needed in the parameter name. The **Tx***N***Filter** parameter will be used again in the **MultiImage** on page 124.

In this chapter we extend the definition and usage of the **TxFilter** parameter and introduce the **ImgFilter** parameter. Let's begin by defining what a filter is.

A filter is not actually an applet, although it corresponds to one; applets are self-contained programs that can run in a browser. The filters described in this book are actually just classes—that's objected oriented programming terminology meaning a piece of code that performs some function—that are the bases of the functional cores of applets. The applets in Chapter 3 and in this chapter are simple programs that actually just invoke a filter, which then does all the work.

In general, a filter takes an image and manipulates it in some way. Therefore, we can manipulate an image any number of times by invoking a series of filters on the same image. This is true of all the filters discussed in this chapter.

The filters introduced in the previous chapter, **Text Applets**, are slightly different in that they *generate* an image rather than manipulating an existing one. The filters introduced in this chapter require an image that already exists. In either case, the result is an image which can be further manipulated by invoking yet another filter.

To further understand this concept, suppose that you want to display smooth text that had been rotated some number of degrees. You would generate the text using the **smooth** filter and then invoke the **rotate** filter (**rotate** is introduced later in this chapter). Here's the HTML code:

```
<param name=Text value="Some smooth text">
<param name=TxPointSize value=36>
<param name=TxFilter value="smooth|rotate 45">
```

The **Text** parameter specifies the text to be displayed and **TxPointSize** specifies its size. The | (vertical bar) is used to join a sequence of filters, so the **TxFilter** value of `"smooth|rotate 45"` invokes the **smooth** filter, which generates text, and sends the output to the **rotate** filter. The result is smooth text that has been rotated 45 degrees.

Let's take this one step further. Suppose that you want the smoothed rotated text to also be slanted 28 degrees to the right and blurred. To accomplish all of this you would use the following **TxFilter** parameter:

```
<param name=TxFilter value="smooth|rotate 45|slantright 28|blur">
```

The **ImgFilter** parameter works the same way as **TxFilter**, except that it is used with images instead of text. The text generating filters described in Chapter 3 will not work with images; if you specify one of the text generating filters from Chapter 3 with an image, there is no result.

Most of the applets in this chapter automatically invoke one of the image filters. The **Mirror** applet, for example, displays the mirror image of the specified image; the **Scale** applet displays the image after scaling it horizontally and vertically.

All the applets in this chapter support text as well as images. In order to display text that appears over an image or background image, you must specify some **TxFilter**. If you want just plain text use the **Text** filter. If you do not specify a **TxFilter**, the text is displayed on a rectangular area the color of the background, which obscures the image.

Here's an example that displays an image that is slanted right 20 degrees with text that is embossed and mirrored:

```
<param name=Text value="Engraved & mirrored">
<param name=TxPointSize value=24>
<param name=TxFilter value="engrave|mirror">
<param name=Image value=sailboat.gif>
<param name=ImgFilter value="slantright 20">
```

Img

Displays an image

Description

The **Img** applet displays an unaltered image.

This applet may appear to be just like the **BasicImage** on page 17. It is implemented using filters, however, as described at the beginning of this chapter.

Using Img in HTML Code

The following HTML code display a company logo:

```
<applet code=Img.class width=179 height=179>
<param name=Image value=../images/vivid.gif>
<param name=AppBGColor value=white>
<param name=ImgXOffset value=10>
<param name=ImgYOffset value=10>
</applet>
```

Settings

All settings for **Img** are described at the beginning of this chapter, on page 86. Remember that they always allow you to play audio, load a URL, and display text or a background image, among other things.

See Also

URL for **Img**:   http://www.vivids.com/java/image/Img.html

Rotate

Rotates an image counter clockwise

Description

The **Rotate** applet rotates the image an arbitrary number of degrees counter clockwise.

Using Rotate in HTML Code

The following HTML code rotates the company logo –10 degrees against a background image.

```
<applet code=Rotate.class width=240 height=240>
<param name=Image value=../images/vivid.gif>
<param name=AppTile value=true>
<param name=AppBGImage
value=../images/pattern.gif>
<param name=Angle value=-10>
<param name=ImgVertCenter value=true>
<param name=ImgHorizCenter value=true>
</applet>
```

Settings

All settings for **Rotate** are described at the beginning of this chapter, on page 86. Remember that they always allow you to play audio, load a URL, and display text or a background image, among other things. One other parameter sets the degree of rotation.

Name	Description	Default
Degree	The degree of rotation	0

See Also

URL for **Rotate**: http://www.vivids.com/java/image/Rotate.html

Mirror

Mirrors an image

Description

The **Mirror** applet flips the image around its vertical center line.

Using Mirror in HTML Code

The following HTML code mirrors the company logo. The applet also displays the string *VIVID*, which is drawn using the **depthfade** text generating filter.

```
<applet code=Mirror.class width=220
height=220>
<param name=Image value=../images/vivid.gif>
<param name=ImgVertCenter value=true>
<param name=ImgHorizCenter value=true>
<param name=ImgAudio value=welcome.au>
<param name=AppBGColor value=white>
<param name=Text value="VIVID">
<param name=TxPointSize value=36>
<param name=TxStyle value=Bold>
<param name=TxXOffset value=10>
<param name=TxYOffset value=135>
<param name=TxColor value=black>
<param name=TxFilter value="depthfade 10 -10
#00849c">
</applet>
```

Settings

All settings for **Mirror** are described at the beginning of this chapter, on page 86. Remember that they always allow you to play audio, load a URL, and display text or a background image, among other things.

See Also

URL for **Mirror**:   http://www.vivids.com/java/image/Mirror.html

 # SlantRight

Slant an image to the right

Description

The **SlantRight** applet slants the image to the right.

Using SlantRight in HTML Code

The following HTML code slants the company logo 45 degrees.

```
<applet code=SlantRt.class width=440
height=200>
<param name=Image
value=../images/vivid.gif>
<param name=ImgVertCenter value=true>
<param name=ImgHorizCenter value=true>
<param name=AppBGColor value=white>
<param name=Angle value=45>
</applet>
```

Settings

The common settings described on page 86 all apply to the **SlantRight** applet. Remember that they always allow you to play audio, load a URL, and display text or a background image, among other things. One other parameter sets the slant angle.

Name	Description	Default
Angle	The slant angle	45

See Also

Related applets:

SlantLeft on page 95
SlantUp on page 97
SlantDown on page 98

URL for **SlantRight**:

`http://www.vivids.com/java/image/SlantRight.html`

SlantLeft

Slants an image to the left

Description

The **SlantLeft** applet slants the image to the left.

Using SlantLeft in HTML Code

The following HTML code slants the company logo
25 degrees. The image is enclosed in a
ShadowEtchedOut frame and displayed against a
background color that closely matches the background color of the image.

```
<applet code=SlantLeft.class width=350 height=200>
<param name=Image value=../images/vivid.gif>
<param name=ImgVertCenter value=true>
<param name=ImgHorizCenter value=true>
<param name=Angle value=25>
<param name=AppBGColor value=#00849c>
<param name=ImgFrameThickness value=6>
<param name=ImgFrameType value=ShadowEtchedIn>
<param name=ImgFrameMargin value=2>
</applet>
```

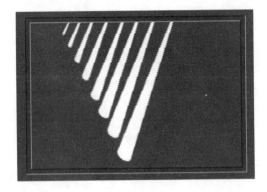

Note that the frame in the above example is not slanted. Frames and borders are drawn
independent of any image processing.

Settings

The common settings described on page 86 all apply to the **SlantLeft** applet. Remember that they always allow you to play audio, load a URL, and display text or a background image, among other things. One other parameter sets the slant angle.

Name	Description	Default
Angle	The slant angle	45

See Also

Related applets:

SlantRight on page 93
SlantUp on page 97
SlantDown on page 98

URL for **SlantLeft**:

`http://www.vivids.com/java/image/SlantLeft.html`

SlantUp

Slants an image up

Description

The **SlantUp** applet slants the image up.

Using SlantUp in HTML Code

The following HTML code slants the logo up 20 degrees and also slants it right 20 degrees.

```
<applet code=SlantUp.class width=220 height=300>
<param name=Image
value=../images/vivid.gif>
<param name=ImgVertCenter value=true>
<param name=ImgHorizCenter value=true>
<param name=Angle value=20>
<param name=AppBGColor value=#ffffff>
<param name=ImgFilter value="slantright
20">
</applet>
```

Settings

The common settings described on page 86 all apply to the **SlantUp** applet. Remember that they always allow you to play audio, load a URL, and display text or a background image, among other things. One other parameter sets the slant angle.

Name	Description	Default
Angle	The slant angle	45

See Also

Related applets:

SlantRight on page 93
SlantLeft on page 95
SlantDown on page 98

URL for **SlantUp**:

http://www.vivids.com/java/image/SlantUp.html

Slants an image down

Description

The **SlantDown** applet slants the image down.

Using SlantDown in HTML Code

The following HTML code slants the logo against a black background. The text has the same slant as the image. The horizontal and vertical offsets of the text result in the text overlapping the image and the background.

```
<applet code=SlantDown.class width=200
height=250>
<param name=Image value=../images/vivid.gif>
<param name=ImgXOffset value=20>
<param name=ImgYOffset value=20>
<param name=Angle value=10>
<param name=AppBGColor value=#000000>
<param name=TxColor value=#ffffff>
<param name=Text value=VIVID>
<param name=TxPointSize value=36>
<param name=TxFont value=Helvetica>
<param name=TxStyle value=Bold>
<param name=TxXOffset value=50>
<param name=TxYOffset value=168>
<param name=TxFilter value="text|slantdown
10">
</applet>
```

Settings

The common settings described on page 86 all apply to the **SlantDown** applet. Remember that they always allow you to play audio, load a URL, and display text or a background image, among other things. One other parameter sets the slant angle.

Name	Description	Default
Angle	The slant angle	45

See Also

Related applets: **SlantRight** on page 93
                        SlantLeft on page 95
                        SlantUp on page 97

URL for **SlantDown**:   `http://www.vivids.com/java/image/SlantDown.html`

Alters an image along a sine wave

Description

The **WaveImage** applet creates a sine wave pattern in the image. It is similar to the **WaveText** on page 58.

Using WaveImage in HTML Code

The following HTML code uses the **WaveImage** applet to distort the company logo by setting **Amplitude** to 35 and **WaveLength** to 8.

```
<applet code=WaveImage.class width=250
height=250>
<param name=Image value=../images/vivid.gif>
<param name=Amplitude value=35>
<param name=WaveLength value=8>
<param name=ImgXOffset value=20>
<param name=ImgYOffset value=20>
<param name=AppBGColor value=#00849c>
</applet>
```

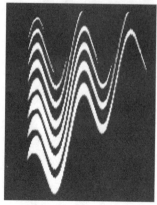

The following example uses the **BeginRange, EndRange,** and **XTranslate** parameters to create an ocean wave effect through part of an image of sailboats.

```
<applet code=WaveImage.class width=360 height=256>
<param name=Image value=../images/sailboat.gif>
<param name=Amplitude value=6>
<param name=WaveLength value=8>
<param name=ImgXOffset value=20>
<param name=ImgYOffset value=20>
<param name=BeginRange value=20>
<param name=EndRange value=200>
<param name=XTranslate value=-2>
<param name=AppBGColor value=#00849c>
</applet>
```

Settings

The common settings described on page 86 all apply to the **WaveImage** applet. Remember that they always allow you to play audio, load a URL, and display text or a background image, among other things. Six additional parameters set the amplitude, wavelength, horizontal and vertical translation, and the begin and end range.

Name	Description	Default
Amplitude	The amplitude of the wave (in pixels)	10
WaveLength	The wave length of the wave	10
XTranslate	The horizontal translation (in pixels)	0
YTranslate	The vertical translation (in pixels)	0
BeginRange	The pixel at which to begin the sinewave function	0
EngRange	The pixel at which to end the sinewave function	width of image

See Also

Related applets: **WaveText** on page 58

URL for **WaveImage**:   `http://www.vivids.com/java/image/WaveImage.html`

Blur

Blurs an image

Description

The **Blur** applet blurs the image by sampling surrounding pixels.

Using Blur in HTML Code

The following HTML code uses the **Blur** applet to blur the company logo four times in all. This produces an extremely blurred image.

```
<applet code=Blur.class width=300 height=200>
<param name=Image value=../images/vivid.gif>
<param name=ImgFilter value="blur|blur|blur">
</applet>
```

Settings

The common settings described on page 86 all apply to the **Blur** applet. Remember that they always allow you to play audio, load a URL, and display text or a background image, among other things. One additional parameter sets the blur amount.

Name	Description	Default
Blur	The amount of the blur	1

See Also

URL for **Blur**: http://www.vivids.com/java/image/Blur.html

EmbossImage

Creates an embossed effect in an image

Description

The **EmbossImage** applet displays the image with a directional edge enhancement for an embossed effect.

Using EmbossImage in HTML Code

The following HTML code uses the **EmbossImage** applet to emboss the image to the **NorthWest**:

```
<applet code=EmbossImage.class width=180
height=180>
<param name=Image value=../images/vivid.gif>
<param name=ImgVertCenter value=true>
<param name=ImgHorizCenter value=true>
<param name=AppBGColor value=#ffffff>
<param name=Direction value=NorthWest>
</applet>
```

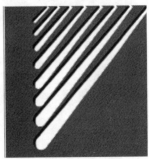

The next example displays the same image but sets the direction to **SouthWest**.

```
<applet code=EmbossImage.class width=180 height=180>
<param name=Image value=../images/vivid.gif>
<param name=ImgVertCenter value=true>
<param name=ImgHorizCenter value=true>
<param name=AppBGColor value=#ffffff>
<param name=Direction value=SouthEast>
</applet>
```

Settings

The common settings described on page 86 all apply to the **EmbossImage** applet. Remember that they always allow you to play audio, load a URL, and display text or a background image, among other things. One additional parameter sets the direction of the embossing.

Name	Description	Default
Direction	The direction of the embossing: **North, South, East, West, NorthWest, NorthEast, SouthWest, SouthEast**	**West**

See Also

Related applets: **Emboss** on page 66

URL for **EmbossImage**:   `http://www.vivids.com/java/image/EmbossImage.html`

TransColor

Makes one or more of an image's colors transparent

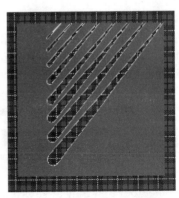

Description

The **TransColor** applet removes the specified colors from the image, creating transparency instead. There is no limit to the number of colors that can be made transparent.

Using TransColor in HTML Code

The following HTML code uses the **TransColor** applet to make the image partially transparent. The solid color in the logo is actually a composite of several colors. The **Colors** parameter includes several but not all of the colors which constitute the logo's background color, resulting in a partially transparent look.

```
<applet code=TransColor.class width=200 height=200>
<param name=Image value=../images/vivid.gif>
<param name=AppBGImage value=plaid.gif>
<param name=AppTile value=true>
<param name=ImgVertCenter value=true>
<param name=ImgHorizCenter value=true>
<param name=Colors value="#088ca5 #0884a5
#008ca5 #0084a5 #007b9c">
</applet>
```

The next example makes transparent all the colors in the logo's background. Only the white solids from the logo remain, displayed over the background image.

```
<applet code=TransColor.class width=200
height=200>
<param name=Image value=../images/vivid.gif>
<param name=BGImage value=plaid.gif>
<param name=Tile value=true>
<param name=VertCenter value=true>
<param name=HorizCenter value=true>
<param name=Colors value="#088ca5 #0884a5
#008ca5 #0084a5 #00849c #007b9c">
</applet>
```

Settings

The common settings described on page 86 all apply to the **TransColor** applet. Remember that they always allow you to play audio, load a URL, and display text or a background image, among other things. One additional parameter sets the colors that are to be made transparent. Each color in the list is separated by a space. The list of colors must be enclosed in double quotes, with spaces separating the colors.

Name	Description	Default
Colors	The colors to make transparent	(none)

Remember that they always allow you to play audio, load a URL, and display text or a background image, among other things.

See Also

Related applets: **Stencil** on page 71
                     Transparent on page 111

URL for **TransColor**:   `http://www.vivids.com/java/image/TransColor.html`

Scale

Alters the horizontal or vertical scale of an image

Description

The **Scale** applet horizontally or vertically scales an image. You can scale one or the other dimension, or both. You can scale one amount in one dimension and another in the other dimension. The picture at right is scaled 50% in the horizontal dimension only.

Using Scale in HTML Code

The following HTML code uses the **Scale** applet to rescale the logo 300% horizontally and 50% vertically.

```
<applet code=Scale.class width=500 height=100>
<param name=Image value=../images/vivid.gif>
<param name=ScaleX value=300>
<param name=ScaleY value=50>
</applet>
```

Settings

The common settings described on page 86 all apply to the **Scale** applet. Remember that they always allow you to play audio, load a URL, and display text or a background image, among other things. Three additional parameters set the scale factors.

Name	Description	Default
ScaleX	The percentage to rescale in the horizontal direction	100
ScaleY	The percentage to rescale in the vertical direction	100
Scale	The percentage to rescale in both directions (overrides **ScaleX** and **ScaleY)**	100

The **ScaleX** and **ScaleY** parameters are for setting the horizontal and vertical scale factors respectively. The scale factor is a percentage where 100 represents no rescaling, 50 represents half size, and 200 represents double size.

The **Scale** parameter overrides both the **ScaleX** and **ScaleY** parameters. Using **Scale** always preserves the original aspect ratio.

See Also

URL for **Scale**: http://www.vivids.com/java/image/Scale.html

Pages for source code: **Scale.java** on page 260
fscale.java on page 229

Negative

Displays an image with negative colors

Description

The **Negative** applet displays an image with negative colors. Each component (red, green, blue) of each color is subtracted from 255—the maximum color intensity—to produce the negative color. The effect is similar to that of looking at the negative of a color photograph.

Using Negative in HTML Code

The following HTML code uses the **Negative** applet to display the company logo with negative colors.

```
<applet code=Negative.class width=159 height=159>
<param name=Image value=vivid.gif>
</applet>
```

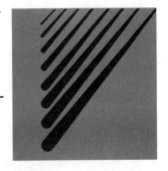

Settings

The common settings described on page 86 all apply to the **Negative** applet. Remember that they always allow you to play audio, load a URL, and display text or a background image, among other things. One additional parameter sets the number (default is 255) from which to subtract the color components.

Name	Description	Default
SubFrom	The number from which to subtract each color component	255

Setting the **SubFrom** parameter to 0 will produce the original unaltered image. **SubFrom** values greater than 255 produce unpredictable (though interesting) results.

See Also

URL for **Negative**:   http://www.vivids.com/java/image/Negative.html

Pages for source code: **Negative.java** on page 259
fnegative.java on page 228

Fade

Displays an image with faded colors

Description

The **Fade** applet fades an image. This fading is accomplished by altering the colors of the image toward one specific color. By default, the image is faded toward the background color. You can also specify another color to which the image is faded.

Using Fade in HTML Code

The following HTML code uses the **Fade** applet to fade the company logo 75 percent toward white. Note the washed out appearance.

```
<applet code=Fade.class width=159 height=159>
<param name=Image value=../images/vivid.gif>
<param name=Percent value=75>
<param name=FadeColor value=white>
</applet>
```

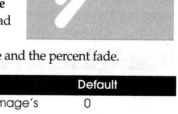

Settings

The common settings described on page 86 all apply to the **Fade** applet. Remember that they always allow you to play audio, load a URL, and display text or a background image, among other things. Two additional parameters set the color to which to fade and the percent fade.

Name	Description	Default
Percent	The percentage (0 to 100) to fades the image's colors	0
FadeToColor	The color to which the image is faded	AppBgColor

Fading an image 100% turns the image into a solid area of the **FadeToColor** specified. Fading 0% leaves the image unaltered.

See Also

Related applets: **SlideShowFade** on page 204

URL for **Fade**:   http://www.vivids.com/java/image/Fade.html

Transparent

Displays an image with a degree of transparency

Description

The **Transparent** applet displays an image with the specified percentage transparency. The higher the percentage transparency, the more transparent the image. A transparency of 100% will cause the image to completely disappear.

Using Transparent in HTML Code

The following HTML code uses the **Transparent** applet to display the company logo against a plaid background and with a yellow frame. The **Transparency** parameter is set to 40.

```
<applet code=Transparent.class width=200 height=200>
<param name=Image value=../images/vivid.gif>
<param name=Transparency value=40>
<param name=ImgHorizCenter value=true>
<param name=ImgVertCenter value=true>
<param name=ImgFrameThickness value=2>
<param name=ImgFrameType
value=ShadowEtchedOut>
<param name=ImgFrameMargin value=5>
<param name=AppBGImage
value=../images/plaid.gif>
<param name=AppBGColor value=yellow>
<param name=AppTile value=true>
</applet>
```

Settings

The common settings described on page 86 all apply to the **Transparent** applet. Remember that they always allow you to play audio, load a URL, and display text or a background image, among other things. One additional parameter sets the transparency percentage.

Name	Description	Default
Transparency	The percentage transparency	0

See Also

Related applets: **Stencil** on page 71
TransColor on page 105

URL for **Transparent**: `http://www.vivids.com/java/image/Transparent.html`

CropRectangle

Crops an image to a rectangular region

Description

The **CropRectangle** applet displays an image that has been cropped to fit the specified rectangular region. The image area outside the cropped region reveals the background color or image behind it.

Using CropRectangle in HTML Code

The following HTML code uses the **CropRectangle** applet to display the cropped company logo against a plaid background.

```
<applet code=CropRectangle.class width=159
height=159>
<param name=Image value=../images/vivid.gif>
<param name=CropXOffset value=25>
<param name=CropYOffset value=25>
<param name=CropWidth value=75>
<param name=CropHeight value=125>
<param name=AppBGImage
value=../images/plaid.gif>
<param name=AppTile value=true>
</applet>
```

Settings

The common settings described on page 86 all apply to the **CropRectangle** applet. Remember that they always allow you to play audio, load a URL, and display text or a background image, among other things. Four additional parameters set the horizontal and vertical position, and the width and height of the crop region.

Name	Description	Default
CropXOffset	The horizontal offset of the crop region (in pixels)	0
CropYOffset	The vertical offset of the crop region (in pixels)	0
CropWidth	The width of the crop region (in pixels)	The width of the image
CropHeight	The height of the crop region (in pixels)	The height of the image

See Also

Related applets:

RemoveRectangle on page 114
CropOval on page 116
RemoveOval on page 118
CropRoundRect on page 120
RemoveRoundRect on page 122

URL for **CropRectangle**:

`http://www.vivids.com/java/image/CropRectangle.html`

RemoveRectangle

Removes a rectangular region from an image

Description

The **RemoveRectangle** applet removes a rectangular region from an image. The removed part of the image reveals the background color or image behind it.

Using RemoveRectangle in HTML Code

The following HTML code uses the **RemoveRectangle** applet to display the altered company logo against a plaid background.

```
<applet code=RemoveRectangle.class width=159 height=159>
<param name=Image value=../images/vivid.gif>
<param name=CropXOffset value=25>
<param name=CropYOffset value=25>
<param name=CropWidth value=75>
<param name=CropHeight value=125>
<param name=AppBGImage value=../images/plaid.gif>
<param name=AppTile value=true>
</applet>
```

Settings

The common settings described on page 86 all apply to the **RemoveRectangle** applet. Remember that they always allow you to play audio, load a URL, and display text or a background image, among other things. Four additional parameters set the horizontal and vertical position, and the width and height of the crop region.

Name	Description	Default
CropXOffset	The horizontal offset of the crop region (in pixels)	0
CropYOffset	The vertical offset of the crop region (in pixels)	0
CropWidth	The width of the crop region (in pixels)	The width of the image
CropHeight	The height of the crop region (in pixels)	The height of the image

See Also

Related applets:

CropRectangle on page 112
CropOval on page 116
RemoveOval on page 118
CropRoundRect on page 120
RemoveRoundRect on page 122

URL for **RemoveRectangle**:   `http://www.vivids.com/java/image/RemoveRectangle.html`

CropOval

Crops an image to an oval region

Description

The **CropOval** applet displays an image that has been cropped to fit the specified oval region. The image area outside the cropped region reveals the background color or image behind it.

Using CropOval in HTML Code

The following HTML code uses the **CropOval** applet to display the cropped company logo against a plaid background.

```
<applet code=CropOval.class width=159 height=159>
<param name=Image value=../images/vivid.gif>
<param name=CropXOffset value=25>
<param name=CropYOffset value=25>
<param name=CropWidth value=75>
<param name=CropHeight value=125>
<param name=AppBGImage value=../images/plaid.gif>
<param name=AppTile value=true>
</applet>
```

Settings

The common settings described on page 86 all apply to the **CropRectangle** applet. Remember that they always allow you to play audio, load a URL, and display text or a background image, among other things. Four additional parameters set the horizontal and vertical position, and the width and height of the crop region.

Name	Description	Default
CropXOffset	The horizontal offset of the crop region (in pixels)	0
CropYOffset	The vertical offset of the crop region (in pixels)	0
CropWidth	The width of the crop region (in pixels)	The width of the image
CropHeight	The height of the crop region (in pixels)	The height of the image

If the **CropWidth** and **CropHeight** parameters are identical the cropped region will be a circle.

See Also

Related applets:

CropRectangle on page 112
RemoveRectangle on page 114
RemoveOval on page 118
CropRoundRect on page 120
RemoveRoundRect on page 122

URL for **CropOval**:

`http://www.vivids.com/java/image/CropOval.html`

RemoveOval

Removes an oval region from an image

Description

The **RemoveOval** applet removes an oval region from an image. The removed part of the image reveals the background color or image behind it.

Using RemoveOval in HTML Code

The following HTML code uses the **RemoveOval** applet to display the altered company logo against a plaid background.

```
<applet code=RemoveOval.class width=159 height=159>
<param name=Image value=../images/vivid.gif>
<param name=CropXOffset value=25>
<param name=CropYOffset value=25>
<param name=CropWidth value=75>
<param name=CropHeight value=125>
<param name=AppBGImage value=../images/plaid.gif>
<param name=AppTile value=true>
<param name=ImgYOffset value=2>
</applet>
```

Settings

The common settings described on page 86 all apply to the **CropOval** applet. Remember that they always allow you to play audio, load a URL, and display text or a background image, among other things. Four additional parameters set the horizontal and vertical position, and the width and height of the crop region.

Name	Description	Default
CropXOffset	The horizontal offset of the crop region (in pixels)	0
CropYOffset	The vertical offset of the crop region (in pixels)	0
CropWidth	The width of the crop region (in pixels)	The width of the image
CropHeight	The height of the crop region (in pixels)	The height of the image

If the **CropWidth** and **CropHeight** parameters are identical the cropped region will be a circle.

See Also

Related applets:

CropRectangle on page 112
RemoveRectangle on page 114
CropOval on page 116
CropRoundRect on page 120
RemoveRoundRect on page 122

URL for **RemoveOval**:

`http://www.vivids.com/java/image/RemoveOval.html`

Crops an image to a rounded rectangular region

Description

The **CropRoundRect** applet displays an image that has been cropped to fit the specified rounded rectangular region. The image area outside the cropped region reveals the background color or image behind it.

Using CropRoundRect in HTML Code

The following HTML code uses the **CropRoundRect** applet to display the cropped company logo against a plaid background.

```
<applet code=CropRoundRect.class width=159 height=159>
<param name=Image value=../images/vivid.gif>
<param name=CropXOffset value=25>
<param name=CropYOffset value=25>
<param name=CropWidth value=75>
<param name=CropHeight value=125>
<param name=ArcWidth value=20>
<param name=ArcHeight value=60>
<param name=AppBGImage value=../images/plaid.gif>
<param name=AppTile value=true>
</applet>
```

Settings

The common settings described on page 86 all apply to the **CropRoundRect** applet. Remember that they always allow you to play audio, load a URL, and display text or a background image, among other things. Six additional parameters set the horizontal and vertical position, the width and height of the crop region, and the horizontal and vertical diameters of the arcs at the four corners.

Name	Description	Default
CropXOffset	The horizontal offset of the crop region (in pixels)	0
CropYOffset	The vertical offset of the crop region (in pixels)	0
CropWidth	The width of the crop region (in pixels)	The width of the image

Name	Description	Default
CropHeight	The height of the crop region (in pixels)	The height of the image
ArcWidth	The horizontal diameter of the arc at the four corners (in pixels)	One half the width of the image
ArcHeight	The vertical diameter of the arc at the four corners (in pixels)	One half the height of the image

See Also

Related applets:

CropRectangle on page 112
RemoveRectangle on page 114
CropOval on page 116
RemoveOval on page 118
RemoveRoundRect on page 122

URL for **CropRoundRect**:   `http://www.vivids.com/java/image/CropRoundRect.html`

RemoveRoundRect

Removes a rounded rectangular region from an image

Description

The **RemoveRoundRect** applet removes a rounded rectangular region from an image. The removed part of the image reveals the background color or image behind it.

Using RemoveRoundRect in HTML Code

The following HTML code uses the **RemoveRoundRect** applet to display the altered company logo against a plaid background.

```
<applet code=RemoveRoundRect.class width=159 height=159>
<param name=Image value=../images/vivid.gif>
<param name=CropXOffset value=25>
<param name=CropYOffset value=25>
<param name=CropWidth value=75>
<param name=CropHeight value=125>
<param name=ArcWidth value=20>
<param name=ArcHeight value=60>
<param name=AppBGImage value=../images/plaid.gif>
<param name=AppTile value=true>
</applet>
```

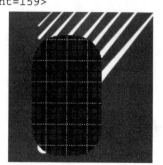

Settings

The common settings described on page 86 all apply to the **RemoveRoundRect** applet. Remember that they always allow you to play audio, load a URL, and display text or a background image, among other things. Six additional parameters set the horizontal and vertical position, the width and height of the crop region, and the horizontal and vertical diameters of the arcs at the four corners.

Name	Description	Default
CropXOffset	The horizontal offset of the crop region (in pixels)	0
CropYOffset	The vertical offset of the crop region (in pixels)	0
CropWidth	The width of the crop region (in pixels)	The width of the image

Name	Description	Default
CropHeight	The height of the crop region (in pixels)	The height of the image
ArcWidth	The horizontal diameter of the arc at the four corners (in pixels)	One half the width of the image
ArcHeight	The vertical diameter of the arc at the four corners (in pixels)	One half the height of the image

See Also

Related applets:

CropRectangle on page 112
RemoveRectangle on page 114
CropOval on page 116
RemoveOval on page 118
CropRoundRect on page 120

URL for **RemoveRoundRect**:

`http://www.vivids.com/java/image/RemoveRoundRect.html`

MultiImage

Displays multiple images

Description

The **MultiImage** applet displays more than one image. Each image may be displayed using any of the techniques seen in this chapter. Furthermore, one or more strings may also be displayed, as described for the **MultiText** applet on page 75.

Each image and string has its own characteristics that may be uniquely set. You can, for example, rotate one image, scale another, and slant and blur yet another. Use the filter technique described at the beginning of this chapter to manipulate the image or images as desired.

All parameters that begin with **Img** can be specified independently for each image. Each **Img** parameter must instead begin with **Img$N$**, however, where **N** is the number that identifies the image. For example, to scale the second image 50%, use the **Img2Filter** parameter and specify the **scale** filter as shown here:

```
<param name=Image2 value=bluejava.gif>
<param name Img2Filter value="scale 50 50">
```

Using MultiImage in HTML Code

You must specify the **ImgCount** parameter, which specifies the number of images the applet displays. To indicate three images, set **ImgCount** to 3:

```
<param name=ImgCount value=3>
```

The following HTML code uses the **MultiImage** applet to display three images.

```
<applet code=MultiImage.class width=400 height=420>
<param name=AppBGImage value=../images/pattern.gif>
<param name=AppTile value=true>

<param name=ImgCount value=3>
<param name=Image1 value=../images/pie.gif>
<param name=Img1XOffset value=160>
<param name=Img1YOffset value=240>
<param name=Img1Filter value="slantright 10">
```

```
<param name=Image2 value=../images/key.gif>
<param name=Img2XOffset value=20>
<param name=Img2YOffset value=130>

<param name=Image3 value=../images/wndlcup.gif>
<param name=Img3YOffset value=10>
<param name=Img3HorizCenter value=true>
<param name=Img3Filter value="scale 60 60">

</applet>
```

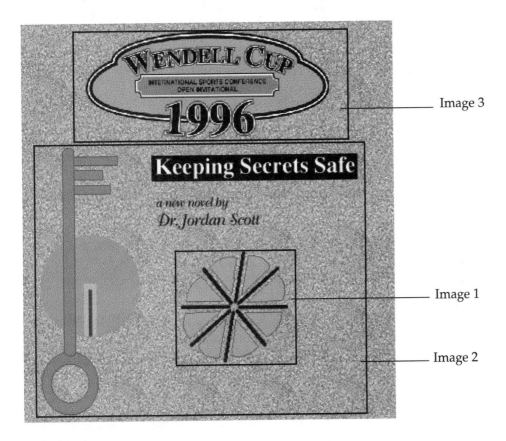

Settings

The common settings described on page 86 all apply to the **MultiImage** applet. Remember that the common settings always allow you to play audio, load a URL, and display text or a background image, among other things. However, the parameters that begin with **Img** must instead begin with **Img*N***, where **N** specifies the string involved. The **Img*N*Filter** parameter is used to specify the program (or filter) that is used to draw the string. In addition, the **ImgCount** parameter must be specified to indicate the number of strings to display.

Name	Description	Default
ImgCount	The number of images to display	0
Img/Filter	The filters for image *N*	0

See Also

Related applets: **MultiText** on page 75

URL for **MultiImage**: `http://www.vivids.com/java/image/MultiImage.html`

Tips for Programmers

The applets in this chapter are implemented by extending the **ImgFilt** class shown on page 215. The filters in this chapter each manipulate an image. The method is similar to that discussed in Chapter 3, except that rather than generating text you will be taking an existing image and processing it in some way.

You should become familiar with the Tips for Programmers section in Chapter 3 on page 78. The techniques for image manipulation have some similarities to text generating filters. You must, for example, return an array on integers which represent the image. You must also set the new_width and new_height variables.

To understand image filters let's look at the **negative** filter. The conventions for filter naming are identical to those discussed in Chapter 3. The **negative** filter is in a file named **fnegative.java**, and the name of the class is **fnegative**:

```
1    public class fnegative extends ImgFilt {
2        int subfrom = 255;
3
4        public void setparameter(String str, int i) {
5            switch(i) {
6            case 0:
7                subfrom = Integer.parseInt(str);
8                break;
9            }
10       }
11
12       public int[] filter(int[] p1, int w, int h) {
13           int x, y, i;
14           int index, new_index;
15           int alpha, red, green, blue;
16           int nalpha, nred, ngreen, nblue;
17
18           if(p1.length != (w*h)) {
19               System.out.println("negative filter: wrong size array");
20               System.out.println("p1.length = " + p1.length +
21                          " (w,h) = " + w + "," + h);
22               return null;
23           }
24
25           newpixels = new int[h * w];
26
27           new_index = 0;
28           for(y=0;y<h;y++) {
29               for(x=0;x<w;x++) {
30                   index = (y*w) + x;
```

```
31              alpha = (p1[index] & 0xff000000) >>> 24;
32              red   = (p1[index] & 0x00ff0000) >> 16;
33              green = (p1[index] & 0x0000ff00) >> 8;
34              blue  = (p1[index] & 0x000000ff);
35
36              nred   = Math.abs(subfrom - red);
37              ngreen = Math.abs(subfrom - green);
38              nblue  = Math.abs(subfrom - blue);
39              newpixels[new_index++] =
40                  (alpha << 24)|(nred << 16)|(ngreen << 8)|nblue;
41          }
42      }
43      new_width  = w;
44      new_height = h;
45      return newpixels;
46   }
47 }
```

Image filters have the same requirements as do text generating filters.

- The `filter` method must return an array of pixels which represent the image

- The filter must set the `new_width` instance variable to the width of the image

- The filter must set the `new_height` instance variable to the height of the image

In addition, the filter may also elect to do the following:

- Define a `setparameter` method to set customizable options

When image filters are invoked, an existing image is passed to the `filter` method. The first argument, p1, is the array of pixels containing the image. The two other arguments, w and h, represent the width and height of the image. The image may or may not have already passed through other image filters, or it may have been generated by a text generating filter. It doesn't matter where it came from; we simply treat it as an array of integers.

Image filters may have a `setparameter` method to set customizable features. Setting parameters for image filters is identical to setting parameters for text generating filters. For more information, see the discussion on page 78.

The setparameter method

The setparameter method for image filters is identical to that for text. The **negative** filter gets the `subfrom` variable from the setparameter method as shown here:

```
4       public void setparameter(String str, int i) {
5           switch(i) {
6           case 0:
7               subfrom = Integer.parseInt(str);
```

```
8                  break;
9              }
10     }
```

Basic Steps

The procedure for processing an image is even easier than that for generating text. Of course, the algorithm used to process the image may be more complex, but the procedure is very straightforward. Here are the steps:

- Verify the array size

- Determine the dimensions that your processed image will require

- Create an array of integers for the new image (optional)

- Process the image

- Set the new_width and new_height variables

- Return the pixel array

Let's look at each of these steps in the code example shown above.

Verify the array size

The first thing to check in the filter method is the size of the image. The size of the array should match the width multiplied by the height. If it doesn't, the image data has been corrupted.

```
18         if(p1.length != (w*h)) {
19             System.out.println("negative filter: wrong size array");
20             System.out.println("p1.length = " + p1.length +
21                         " (w,h) = " + w + "," + h);
22             return null;
23         }
```

Determine the dimensions that your text will require

The **negative** filter simply replaces the pixels in the image without changing the size. Therefore, we do not have to calculate new dimensions.

Create an array of integers for the new image

Depending on the type of image processing being done, you may need to create a new array in which to store the new image. This is particularly true if the size of the image is changing. If you are rotating the image, for example, you will probably end up with a new image size. So, before processing the image, create a new array:

```
25              newpixels = new int[h * w];
```

Process the image

This is where the real work gets done. Depending on the complexity of the image processing, this may be a few lines of code or several hundred. The **negative** filter simply calculates a new color value for each pixel based on the previous value.

```
27              new_index = 0;
28              for(y=0;y<h;y++) {
29                  for(x=0;x<w;x++) {
30                      index = (y*w) + x;
31                      alpha = (p1[index] & 0xff000000) >>> 24;
32                      red   = (p1[index] & 0x00ff0000) >> 16;
33                      green = (p1[index] & 0x0000ff00) >> 8;
34                      blue  = (p1[index] & 0x000000ff);
35
36                      nred   = Math.abs(subfrom - red);
37                      ngreen = Math.abs(subfrom - green);
38                      nblue  = Math.abs(subfrom - blue);
39                      newpixels[new_index++] =
40                          (alpha << 24)|(nred << 16)|(ngreen << 8)|nblue;
41                  }
42              }
```

Set the new_width and new_height variables

You must set the new_width and new_height variables to the new values of the width and height. Even if the width and height do not change, set the new_width and new_height variables.

```
43              new_width  = w;
44              new_height = h;
```

Return the pixel array

Finally, return the array of pixels.

```
45              return newpixels;
```

Array Format

It's essential to understand exactly how the array of integers is organized to represent the image. The array is a single dimensional array and images are two-dimensional entities. The array maintains the pixels of the image in row order. Each row of the image is placed in the image back-to-back. For example, an image that is 5 pixels in width by 3 pixels in length is be contained in an array of size 15. The first row of the image is contained in positions 0 through 4, the second row of the image is contained in array positions 5 through 9, and so on.

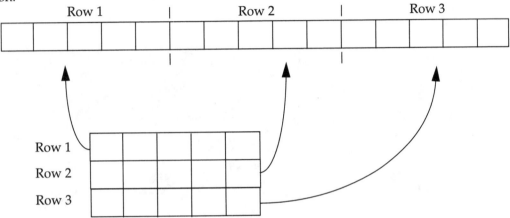

Pixel Format

To better understand the image processing capabilities, one needs to understand the pixel data and how it is used. Each integer (a 32-bit value) represents the red, green, and blue components of a single pixel in the image. The low order 8 bits represent blue, the next 8 bits represent green, and the next 8 bits represent red. The high order 8 pixels represent the alpha component of the color.

alpha	red	green	blue

The values of each of these color components can range from 0 to 255.

The red, green, and blue components of the pixel represent the intensity of the respective color in the pixel. The alpha component controls the transparency of the color. A value of 255 indicates that the pixel is fully opaque. A value of 0 indicates that the pixel is full transparent. Values between 0 and 255 represent a percentage of transparency.

CHAPTER
5

Animation Applets

I n Chapters 3 and 4 you learned many different techniques for displaying text and images. In this chapter you will use what you learned to produce animation.

Animation Defined

Let's begin with a definition. Animation is a series of images that are displayed in rapid succession to simulate live action. On television and in movies, this is accomplished by displaying many images per second.

Animation on a computer screen also involves a series of images displayed in rapid succession. The conventional method for creating computer animation is to use some independent means to generate the images required, and then use an animation application to display them.

Figure 5.1 illustrates a typical use of this sort of animation. Ten different images of a company logo are displayed in rapid sequence to produce an animated effect.

If you have or can make such a series of images, you can use the Java applets in this chapter to create animation by this familiar method.

You can also use them to create animation by another method, however, one that does not require you to start out with a prepared series of images.

133

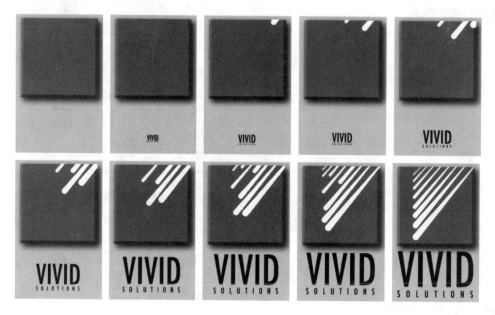

Figure 5.1 Vivid Solutions animated logo

How Do I Animate?

One of the challenges of traditional animation is that you must have some means of creating the series of images to be animated. If you are a graphic artist, or a whiz with an animation program, this may be easy for you. If you can afford a professional animator you will be able to come up with some dazzling animation sequences.

The rest of us are stuck wanting to create animation, but at a loss as to how to produce anything effective.

Self-Animation

To solve this problem, you are going to use the techniques for generating and displaying text and images introduced in Chapters 3 and 4 to create the needed series of images *on the fly*. This is called self-animation. In self-animation, a single image—or text that is generated and maintained as an image—is manipulated in any of a variety of ways to produce multiple images. These images are then displayed in sequence to create animation.

Suppose you have a single image of your company logo. You would like to create some kind of animation, but don't have the means to generate the sort of multiple images shown in the previous example.

Instead, you can use the filters you learned about in Chapter 4 to alter an image numerous times. For example, suppose you use the **scale** filter to produce a sequence of 10 images, each a different size. You could then display them in rapid succession to create the effect of a growing logo, as shown in Figure 5.2.

Figure 5.2 Self-animation by rescaling

You can apply several filters to an image to create more complex self-animation. Figure 5.3 both rescales and rotates the image in 10 steps.

Figure 5.3 Self-animation by rescaling and rotating

Animation Without Images

By using the text-generating techniques introduced in Chapter 3 you can even animate strings. You could use the **multicolor** filter, for example, to display a string of characters in which each character is a different color, changing the colors to create animated colored text like a neon sign, as shown in Figure 5.4.

Figure 5.4 Self-animation using Text only

Another example of text animation is embossed text with gradually increasing contrast, which creates an effect of characters emerging from the screen, as shown in Figure 5.5.

Figure 5.5 Self-animation using embossed text

In addition to using filters to manipulate text or images, you can also position each image in the animation sequence by specifying explicit horizontal and vertical coordinates. This allows you to animate with movement alone, or to combine image movement with other forms of self-animation.

Which Method to Use?

Remember that you can use the applets in this chapter to create either type of animation. If you have, or can create, a series of separate images, you can use these applets to produce conventional animation. But you can always take advantage of self-animation to create exciting animated effects.

The Animation Applets in this Chapter

There are seven applets in this chapter. The first six can display and animate one string and one image at the same time. These six applets share almost identical settings.

The last applet in this chapter can display multiple text and image animations simultaneously. Its settings are slightly expanded.

The first six applets each animate in a slightly different manner. Here is a list of those applets, with a brief description of what they do:

- **AnimateContinuous**

  Continuous animation in one direction. The images are displayed in order from first to last, at which time a specified pause may take effect. The animation then begins again with the first image.

- **AnimateTwoWay**

  Continuous animation in two directions. The images are displayed in order from first to last, at which time a specified pause may take effect. The animation then reverses itself, displaying the images from last to first.

- **AnimateOnButton**

  One forward animation when the visitor presses a mouse button within the image or text. If the visitor presses a mouse button again, the animation repeats.

- **AnimateOnButtonTwoWay**

  One forward or backward animation when the visitor presses a mouse button within the image or text. If the visitor presses a mouse button again, the animation reverses itself.

- **AnimateOnEntry**

  Continuous forward animation when the pointer enters the text or image area. The animation continues until the pointer leaves the area.

- **AnimateOnEntryTwoWay**

  One forward animation when the pointer enters the text or image area. When the pointer leaves the area, the animation reverses itself.

The settings for these applets are almost identical.

Using the Animation Applets in this Chapter

Before describing the settings for these applets, let's look at an example illustrating the fundamental concepts you will use throughout this chapter.

The basic idea is that you use parameters to specify the sources and filters that will generate a series of images for animation. These images will be displayed in succession, at a rate (the fixed delay between images) that you specify.

Let's begin with the applet settings that produced the animation shown in Figure 5.1. This was actually a series of 10 separate images; no filters were involved. Here is the HTML code:

```
<applet code=AnimateContinuous.class width=300 height=400>

<! Delay between images >
<param name=ImgDelayBetweenImages value=200>
```

```
<! Delay between runs >
<param name=ImgDelayBetweenRuns value=5000>

<param name=ImgNumImages value=10>
<param name=Image1 value=../images/vivid0.gif>
<param name=Image2 value=../images/vivid1.gif>
<param name=Image3 value=../images/vivid2.gif>
<param name=Image4 value=../images/vivid3.gif>
<param name=Image5 value=../images/vivid4.gif>
<param name=Image6 value=../images/vivid5.gif>
<param name=Image7 value=../images/vivid6.gif>
<param name=Image8 value=../images/vivid7.gif>
<param name=Image9 value=../images/vivid8.gif>
<param name=Image10 value=../images/vivid9.gif>
</applet>
```

The **ImgNumImages** parameter specifies the number of images included in the animation sequence. If you specify **ImgNumImages** to be less than the actual number of images you include in the code, only the number of images you specify is displayed. If you specify **ImgNumImages** to be greater than the actual number of images you have, the applet will not run.

The parameter for specifying the images is **ImageN**, where **N** represents the sequence number of the image. The images are displayed according to sequence number: **Image1** is first, **Image2** second, and so forth.

The **ImgDelayBetweenImages** parameter specifies the number of milliseconds between images. This controls the rate of animation. The **ImgDelayBetweenRuns** parameter specifies the number of milliseconds between animation runs. If you specify identical values for **ImgDelayBetweenRuns** and **ImgDelayBetweenImages**, the animation is continuous, with no discernible pause between runs.

Reusing an Image

You may want to use an image more than once in a given animation sequence. To do this you can specify the image repeatedly, but this means that Java will reload the image each time. This is unnecessary, and slows the animation. To reuse an image in an animation sequence, you can instead employ a special identifier when specifying the value for the **ImageN** parameter. To reuse **Image3** as the 7th image in the animation sequence, specify **$3** as the value for **Image7**:

```
<param name=Image7 value=$3>
```

This indicates "Reuse **Image3** as **Image7**."

To demonstrate the use of this feature, let's rewrite the previous example to display images 5, 6, and 7 a few extra times during the animation. By using the **$N** identifier, we avoid taking any time to reload the images. Here's the modified HTML code:

```
<applet code=AnimateContinuous.class width=300 height=400>

<! Delay between images >
<param name=ImgDelayBetweenImages value=200>
<! Delay between runs >
<param name=ImgDelayBetweenRuns value=5000>

<param name=ImgNumImages value=15>
<param name=Image1 value=../images/vivid0.gif>
<param name=Image2 value=../images/vivid1.gif>
<param name=Image3 value=../images/vivid2.gif>
<param name=Image4 value=../images/vivid3.gif>
<param name=Image5 value=../images/vivid4.gif>
<param name=Image6 value=../images/vivid5.gif>
<param name=Image7 value=../images/vivid6.gif>
<param name=Image8 value=$7>
<param name=Image9 value=$6>
<param name=Image10 value=$5>
<param name=Image11 value=$6>
<param name=Image12 value=$7>
<param name=Image13 value=../images/vivid7.gif>
<param name=Image14 value=../images/vivid8.gif>
<param name=Image15 value=../images/vivid9.gif>
</applet>
```

Note that while there are now 15 images in our sequence, we had to load only 10 unique image sources.

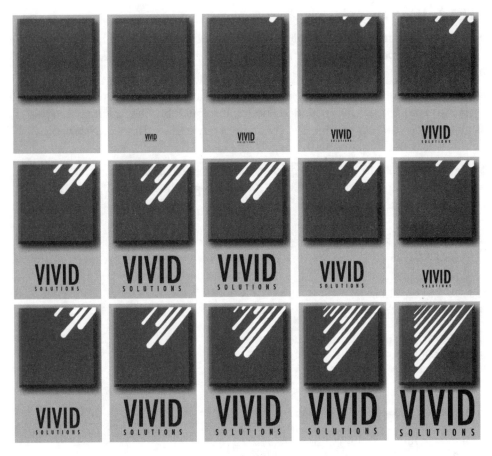

Figure 5.6 Reusing images in an animation sequence

Displaying an Image During Loading

It is often time consuming to load and manipulate multiple images. By default, the animation does not begin until all necessary images have been loaded and manipulated. You may, however, want to provide something for your viewer to look at while waiting for the animation to begin. You can use the **ImgDisplayFirst** parameter to specify that you want the initial image in the sequence to display while waiting for the rest to load. To activate this feature, set **ImgDisplayFirst** to true:

```
<param name=ImgDisplayFirst value=true>
```

Setting the Initial Image

The **ImgInitialImage** parameter is available to specify which image should begin the animation sequence. If you specify image 4 as the initial image, then images 1, 2, and 3 are not included in the sequence.

This feature is useful for several reasons. If, for example, you want to display an image while the animation sequence is being loaded and manipulated, but the first image in the sequence is not the one you want to display, you can specify image #1 as the **ImgDisplayFirst** image, but start your animation with image 2.

In the previous example, if you wanted to display the complete company logo (vivid9.gif) during load time, but have vivid0.gif begin the animation sequence, you would use the following HTML code:

```
<applet code=AnimateContinuous.class width=300 height=400>

<! Delay between images >
<param name=ImgDelayBetweenImages value=200>
<! Delay between runs >
<param name=ImgDelayBetweenRuns value=5000>

<param name=ImgDisplayFirst value=true>
<param name=ImgInitialImage value=2>
<param name=ImgNumImages value=11>
<param name=Image1 value=../images/vivid9.gif>
<param name=Image2 value=../images/vivid0.gif>
<param name=Image3 value=../images/vivid1.gif>
<param name=Image4 value=../images/vivid2.gif>
<param name=Image5 value=../images/vivid3.gif>
<param name=Image6 value=../images/vivid4.gif>
<param name=Image7 value=../images/vivid5.gif>
<param name=Image8 value=../images/vivid6.gif>
<param name=Image9 value=../images/vivid7.gif>
<param name=Image10 value=../images/vivid8.gif>
<param name=Image11 value=$1>
</applet>
```

Moving Images

One of the easiest ways to create animation is to move an image repeatedly. Such movement is independent of any other action being taken. Whether you are using multiple images or generating images by manipulation, you can create movement by specifying the horizontal and vertical positions of the images in your sequence.

The following example moves an image from right to left by changing the **ImgXOffsetN** parameter, where **N** represents the image sequence number.

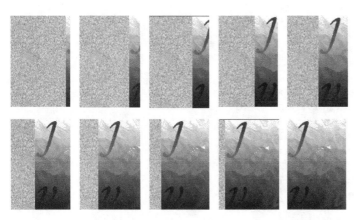

Figure 5.7 Moving an image

Note that the code specifies just one image and uses the **ImgXOffsetN** parameter to move it. You can also move an image vertically by using the **ImgYOffsetN** parameter.

```
<applet code=AnimateTowWay.class width=96 height=144>
<param name=AppBGImage value=../images/pattern.gif>
<Param name=AppTile value=true>

<param name=ImgDelayBetweenRuns value=2000>
<param name=ImgDelayBetweenImages value=200>

<param name=ImgNumImages value=11>
<param name=Image1 value=../images/bluejava.gif>
<param name=ImgXOffset1 value=100>
<param name=ImgXOffset2 value=90>
<param name=ImgXOffset3 value=80>
<param name=ImgXOffset4 value=70>
<param name=ImgXOffset5 value=60>
<param name=ImgXOffset6 value=50>
<param name=ImgXOffset7 value=40>
<param name=ImgXOffset8 value=30>
<param name=ImgXOffset9 value=20>
<param name=ImgXOffset10 value=10>
<param name=ImgXOffset11 value=0>
</applet>
```

Using Filters for Self-Animation

Now let's look at the HTML code that generated the animation sequence shown in Figure 5.2. This is the first self-animation example we've seen:

```
<applet code=AnimateContinuous.class width=300 height=500>
```

```
<param name=ImgDelayBetweenRuns value=2000>
<param name=ImgDelayBetweenImages value=200>
<param name=ImgVertCenter value=true>
<param name=ImgHorizCenter value=true>

<param name=ImgNumImages value=10>
<param name=Image1 value=../images/vivid9.gif>
<param name=ImgFilter1 value="scale 10 10">
<param name=ImgFilter2 value="scale 20 20">
<param name=ImgFilter3 value="scale 30 30">
<param name=ImgFilter4 value="scale 40 40">
<param name=ImgFilter5 value="scale 50 50">
<param name=ImgFilter6 value="scale 60 60">
<param name=ImgFilter7 value="scale 70 70">
<param name=ImgFilter8 value="scale 80 80">
<param name=ImgFilter9 value="scale 90 90">
<param name=ImgFilter10 value="scale 100 100">
</applet>
```

Only one image source (**Image1**) is specified, yet **ImgNumImages** is set to 10. This is because the example manipulates one image 10 times by using the **ImgFilterN** parameter. Since only one image is specified, the specified filters all must apply to that image. This is the filter rule:

Filters operate on the last specified image of the same or smaller sequence number.

In the example, all the filters apply to **Image1** because it is the last image specified and its number is the same as or smaller than those of the filter numbers. If another image had been specified as **Image5**, **ImgFilter1** through **ImgFilter4** would have manipulated **Image1**, and **ImgFilter5** through **ImgFilter10** would have manipulated **Image5**.

Animation with Multiple Filters

There is no limit to the number of filters you can specify for an image. Let's look at the HTML code that generated Figure 5.3, another example of self-animation. The same image is used as in the previous example; this time however, the image is sent through two filters, **scale** and **rotate**, to create a rotating, growing animation. Here's the HTML code:

```
<applet code=AnimateContinuous.class width=300 height=340>

<param name name=AppBGColor value=#cecece>
<param name=ImgDelayBetweenRuns value=2000>
<param name=ImgDelayBetweenImages value=200>
<param name=ImgVertCenter value=true>
<param name=ImgHorizCenter value=true>

<param name=ImgNumImages value=10>
```

```
<param name=Image1 value=../images/vivid9.gif>
<param name=ImgFilter1 value="scale 10 10|rotate 324">
<param name=ImgFilter2 value="scale 20 20|rotate 288">
<param name=ImgFilter3 value="scale 30 30|rotate 252">
<param name=ImgFilter4 value="scale 40 40|rotate 216">
<param name=ImgFilter5 value="scale 50 50|rotate 180">
<param name=ImgFilter6 value="scale 60 60|rotate 144">
<param name=ImgFilter7 value="scale 70 70|rotate 108">
<param name=ImgFilter8 value="scale 80 80|rotate 72">
<param name=ImgFilter9 value="scale 90 90|rotate 36">
<param name=ImgFilter10 value="scale 100 100">
</applet>
```

Reusing Filtered Images

Sometimes you may want to reuse an image after it has been processed through a filter. Just as you reused an image so that you did not have to reload it, you can also reuse an image after it has passed through filters so that you don't need to filter it again.

The following example uses the **removerectangle** filter to selectively remove rectangular regions of a photograph. By reusing the last image in the sequence each time, we can slowly make the image entirely disappear.

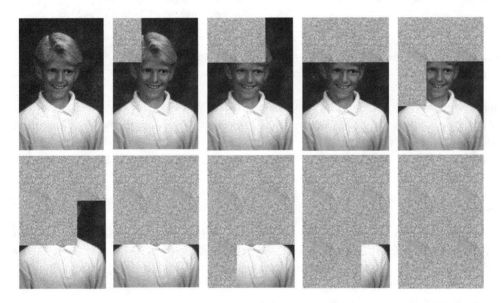

Figure 5.7 Reusing a filtered image

You have already seen how to reuse an unaltered image by specifying the **$N** identifier. It can be employed in just the same way to reuse a previously manipulated image—one that has already been filtered. For example, to reuse the 3rd filtered image for image number 7, use the following parameter setting:

```
<param name=ImgFilter7 value=$3>
```

Here's the HTML code used to generate the disappearing Jeffrey animation shown above:

```
<applet code=AnimateTwoWay.class width=140 height=209>
<param name=AppBGImage value=../images/pattern.gif>
<Param name=AppTile value=true>

<param name=ImgDelayBetweenRuns value=2000>
<param name=ImgDelayBetweenImages value=200>

<param name=ImgNumImages value=10>
<param name=Image1 value=../images/jeff.gif>
<param name=ImgFilter2 value="$1|removerectangle 0 0 47 70">
<param name=ImgFilter3 value="$2|removerectangle 47 0 47 70">
<param name=ImgFilter4 value="$3|removerectangle 94 0 47 70">
<param name=ImgFilter5 value="$4|removerectangle 0 70 47 70">
<param name=ImgFilter6 value="$5|removerectangle 47 70 47 70">
<param name=ImgFilter7 value="$6|removerectangle 94 70 47 70">
<param name=ImgFilter8 value="$7|removerectangle 0 140 47 70">
<param name=ImgFilter9 value="$8|removerectangle 47 140 47 70">
<param name=ImgFilter10 value="$9|removerectangle 94 140 47 70">
</applet>
```

If you reuse an image by specifying the value of **ImageN** as **$M**, you are reusing unaltered image **M**. If you reuse a filtered image by specifying the value of **ImgFilterN** as **$M**, you are reusing image **M** which has been filtered. If you reuse a filtered image by specifying the value of **ImageFilterN** as **$M**, and filter **M** has not been specified, then unaltered image **M** is reused instead.

Animating Text

The examples so far have shown image animation only. However, text animation is created in very similar fashion. You must, of course, specify a text generating filter as the primary (first) filter, because this generates the text that is then manipulated by any other filters you use. Most parameter settings are the same for text as for images, except that the parameter names begin with **Tx** rather than **Img**.

To demonstrate the use of self-animation with text, let's look at the HTML code that generated the animation shown in Figure 5.4. Here we use the **multicolor** text generating filter to produce three images:

```
<applet code=AnimateContinuous.class width=350 height=100>
<param name=AppBGImage value=../images/pattern.gif>
<Param name=AppTile value=true>

<param name=Text value="Color Flash">
<param name=TxFont value=Helvetica>
<param name=TxStyle value=Bold>
<param name=TxPointSize value=48>
<param name=TxDelayBetweenRuns value=200>
<param name=TxDelayBetweenImages value=200>
<param name=TxNumImages value=3>
<param name=TxFilter1 value="multicolor white blue red">
<param name=TxFilter2 value="multicolor blue red white">
<param name=TxFilter3 value="multicolor red white blue">
<param name=TxXOffset1 value=20>
<param name=TxYOffset1 value=20>
</applet>
```

There is no reason to limit ourselves to text filters with generated text. Let's expand the last example to add rotation to the flashing. In addition, we'll use some of the other techniques we've already learned about, such as setting the initial image and reusing filtered images.

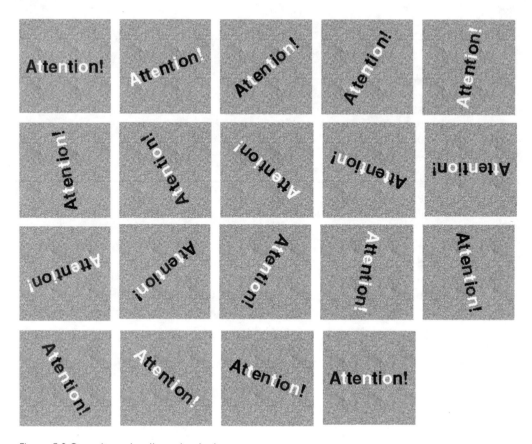

Figure 5.8 Complex animation using text

```
<applet code=AnimateContinuous.class width=200 height=200>
<param name=AppBGImage value=../images/pattern.gif>
<Param name=AppTile value=true>

<param name=Text value="Attention!">
<param name=TxFont value=Helvetica>
<param name=TxHorizCenter value=true>
<param name=TxVertCenter value=true>
<param name=TxStyle value=Bold>
<param name=TxPointSize value=36>
<param name=TxDelayBetweenRuns value=250>
<param name=TxDelayBetweenImages value=250>
<param name=TxNumImages value=21>
<param name=TxInitialImage value=4>
<param name=TxFilter1 value="multicolor white blue red">
<param name=TxFilter2 value="multicolor blue red white">
<param name=TxFilter3 value="multicolor red white blue">
```

```
<param name=TxFilter4 value="$1|rotate 20">
<param name=TxFilter5 value="$2|rotate 40">
<param name=TxFilter6 value="$3|rotate 60">
<param name=TxFilter7 value="$1|rotate 80">
<param name=TxFilter8 value="$2|rotate 100">
<param name=TxFilter9 value="$3|rotate 120">
<param name=TxFilter10 value="$1|rotate 140">
<param name=TxFilter11 value="$2|rotate 160">
<param name=TxFilter12 value="$3|rotate 180">
<param name=TxFilter13 value="$1|rotate 200">
<param name=TxFilter14 value="$2|rotate 220">
<param name=TxFilter15 value="$3|rotate 240">
<param name=TxFilter16 value="$1|rotate 260">
<param name=TxFilter17 value="$2|rotate 280">
<param name=TxFilter18 value="$3|rotate 300">
<param name=TxFilter19 value="$1|rotate 320">
<param name=TxFilter20 value="$2|rotate 340">
<param name=TxFilter21 value="$3">
</applet>
```

Because we set **ImgInitialImage** to 4, the first three images are not included in the animation sequence. However, the images are created according to **TxFilter1**, **TxFilter2**, and **TxFilter3**, which specify the **multicolor** filter. By creating these three image we save time; for images 3 through 21 we have only to rotate existing images, rather than creating new ones. This speeds up the image manipulation phase of the animation.

Controlling Animation Speed

The speed of each applet in this chapter can be controlled by the user. There are two delay speeds which can be controlled: **DelayBetweenImages** and **DelayBetweenRuns**. By changing the delay times the animation can be sped up or slowed down. The **DelayBetweenRuns** setting affects only those applets which run continuously. Animation applets which run once and stop (such as **AnimateOnButton**) do not use the **DelayBetweenRuns** parameter.

The applets in this chapter respond to the following keyboard input:

f	Animation 10% faster (**DelayBetweenImages** descreased)
s	Animation 10% slower (**DelayBetweenImages** increased)
F	Animation sequences repeat 10% more rapidly (**DelayBetweenRuns** descreased)
S	Animation sequences repeat 10% more slowly (**DelayBetweenRuns** increased)

Common Settings

The following parameters are common to all the applets in this chapter.

Name	Description	Default
TxNumImages	The number of text images in the text animation sequence	0
ImgNumImages	The number of images in the image animation sequence	0
ImgFilter*N*	The filter with which to manipulate the *N*th image in the image animation sequence	(none)
TxFilter*N*	The filter with which to manipulate the *N*th image in the text animation sequence	(none)
TxDelayBetweenImages	The delay (in milliseconds) between images in the text animation sequence	100
TxDelayBetweenRuns	The delay (in milliseconds) between text animation sequences	2000
ImgDelayBetweenImages	The delay (in milliseconds) between images in the image animation sequence	100
ImgDelayBetweenRuns	The delay (in milliseconds) between image animation sequences	2000
TxInitialImage	The sequence number of the first image to display in the text animation sequence	1
ImgInitialImage	The sequence number of the first image to use in the image animation sequence	1
ImgDisplayFirst	If true, display Image1 while the rest of the images in the image animation sequence are being loaded and filtered	false
TxXOffset*N*	The horizontal distance (in pixels) from the top of the applet to the upper left corner of the *N*th image in the text animation sequence	0
TxYOffset*N*	The vertical distance (in pixels) from the top of the applet to the upper left corner of the *N*th image in the text animation sequence	0
ImgXOffset*N*	The horizontal distance (in pixels) from the top of the applet to the upper left corner of the *N*th image in the image animation sequence	0
ImgYOffset*N*	The vertical distance (in pixels) from the top of the applet to the upper left corner of the *N*th image in the image animation sequence	0
AppNumMaps	The number of image maps (required for use of image maps)	0
Map*N*_X1	The left X coordinate for map *N*	0
Map*N*_Y1	The top Y coordinate for map *N*	0
Map*N*_X2	The right X coordinate for map *N*	0

Name	Description	Default
Map*N*_Y2	The bottom Y coordinate for map *N*	0
Map*N*_URL	The URL for map *N*	(none)
TestMode	If true, the pointer position is displayed in the status line	false
AppBGImage	The background image	(none)
AppBGImageXOffset	The horizontal offset at which to position the background image	0
AppBGImageYOffset	The vertical offset at which to position the background image	0
AppTile	If true, tile the background image	false
TxURL	The URL to load when the pointer is within the text and any mouse button is pressed	(none)
ImgURL	The URL to load when the pointer is within the image and any mouse button is pressed	(none)
TxAudio	The audio file to play when the pointer enters the text	(none)
ImgAudio	The audio file to play when the pointer enters the image	(none)
TxAudio*N*	The audio file to play when the *N*th text in the animation sequence is displayed	(none)
ImgAudio*N*	The audio file to play when the *N*th image in the animation sequence is displayed	(none)
Image*N*	The *N*th image to display	(none)
ImgXOffset	The horizontal distance (in pixels) from the left side of the applet to the image	0
ImgYOffset	The vertical distance (in pixels) from the top of the applet to the image	0
ImgHorizCenter	If true, the image is horizontally centered	false
ImgVertCenter	If true, the image is vertically centered	false
ImgBorderWidth	The width of the image border (must be greater than 0 in order for a border to be drawn)	0
ImgBorderColor	The color of the image border	Set by browser
ImgBorderMargin	The distance (in pixels) from the image border to the image on all sides	0
ImgFrameThickness	The thickness of the image frame (must be greater than 0 in order for a frame to be drawn)	0
ImgFrameType	The type of image frame: **ShadowIn**, **ShadowOut**, **ShadowEtchedIn**, or **ShadowEtchedOut**	**ShadowIn**

Name	Description	Default
ImgFrameMargin	The distance (in pixels) from the image frame to the image	0
Text	The string of characters to display	(none)
TxColor	The text color	Set by browser
TxBGColor	The text background color	transparent
TxHorizCenter	If true, the text is horizontally centered	false
TxVertCenter	If true, the text is vertically centered	false
TxFont	The font of the text: **TimesRoman, Helvetica, Courier, Dialog, DialogInput,** or **ZapfDingbats**	**Dialog**
TxStyle	The style of the font: **Plain, Bold, Italic,** or **BoldItalic**	**Plain**
TxPointSize	The size of the font in points	10
TxUnderLine	If true, the text is underlined	false
TxBorderWidth	The width of the text border (must be greater than 0 in order for a border to be drawn)	0
TxBorderColor	The color of the text border	black
TxBorderMargin	The distance (in pixels) from the text border to the text on all sides	0
TxFrameThickness	The thickness of the text frame (must be greater than 0 in order for a frame to be drawn)	0
TxFrameType	The type of text frame: **ShadowIn, ShadowOut, ShadowEtchedIn,** or **ShadowEtchedOut**	**ShadowIn**
TxFrameMargin	The distance (in pixels) from the text frame to the text	0
AppBGColor	The background color of the applet	Set by browser
AppBorderWidth	The width of the applet border (must be greater than 0 in order for a border to be drawn)	0
AppBorderColor	The color of the applet border	black
AppFrameThickness	The thickness of the applet frame (must be greater than 0 in order for a frame to be drawn)	0
AppFrameType	The type of applet frame: **ShadowIn, ShadowOut, ShadowEtchedIn,** or **ShadowEtchedOut**	**ShadowIn**

AnimateContinuous
Continuous forward animation

Description

The **AnimateContinuous** applet animates the images in the specified sequence. When the end of the sequence is reached, animation pauses for the specified number of milliseconds and then repeats itself.

Using **AnimateContinuous** in HTML Code

The following HTML code uses the **AnimateContinuous** applet to create the animation shown at the top of this page:

```
<applet code=AnimateContinuous.class width=200 height=200>
<param name=AppBGImage value=pattern.gif>
<Param name=AppTile value=true>

<param name=Text value="Attention!">
<param name=TxFont value=Helvetica>
<param name=TxHorizCenter value=true>
<param name=TxVertCenter value=true>
<param name=TxStyle value=Bold>
<param name=TxPointSize value=36>
<param name=TxDelayBetweenRuns value=2000>
<param name=TxDelayBetweenImages value=250>
<param name=TxNumImages value=8>
<param name=TxInitialImage value=4>
<param name=TxFilter1 value="multicolor white blue red">
<param name=TxFilter2 value="multicolor blue red white">
<param name=TxFilter3 value="multicolor red white blue">
<param name=TxFilter4 value="$1">
<param name=TxFilter5 value="$2|rotate 20">
<param name=TxFilter6 value="$3|rotate 40">
<param name=TxFilter7 value="$1|rotate 60">
<param name=TxFilter8 value="$2|rotate 80">
</applet>
```

Here's another example of continuous animation using **AnimateContinuous** and a prepared series of images. It includes an audio file that is played when the hammer hits the anvil.

```
<applet code=AnimateContinuous.class width=800 height=200>
<param name=AppBGImage value=../images/pattern.gif>
<param name=AppTile value=true>
<param name=ImgdisplayFirst value=true>

<param name=ImgNumImages value=16>
```

```
<param name=Image1 value=../images/mw1.gif>
<param name=Image2 value=../images/mw2.gif>
<param name=Image3 value=../images/mw3.gif>
<param name=Image4 value=../images/mw4.gif>
<param name=Image5 value=../images/mw5.gif>
<param name=Image6 value=../images/mw6.gif>
<param name=Image7 value=../images/mw7.gif>
<param name=Image8 value=../images/mw8.gif>
<param name=Image9 value=../images/mw9.gif>
<param name=Image10 value=../images/mw10.gif>
<param name=Image11 value=../images/mw11.gif>
<param name=Image12 value=../images/mw12.gif>
<param name=Image13 value=../images/mw13.gif>
<param name=Image14 value=../images/mw14.gif>
<param name=Image15 value=../images/mw15.gif>
<param name=Image16 value=$1>
<param name=ImgDelayBetweenRuns value=250>
<param name=ImgDelayBetweenImages value=250>
<param name=ImgRunOnce value=true>
<param name=ImgYOffset1 value=1>
<param name=ImgYOffset2 value=0>
<param name=ImgXOffset9 value=3>
<param name=ImgXOffset10 value=0>
<param name=ImgYOffset14 value=-1>
<param name=ImgYOffset15 value=0>
<param name=ImgYOffset16 value=1>
<param name=ImgAudio13 value="audio/hammer.au">
</applet>
```

Settings

All settings for **AnimateContinuous** are included in the settings described on page 150.

See Also

Related applets: **AnimateTwoWay** on page 156

URL for **AnimateContinuous**

```
http://www.vivids.com/java/animate/AnimateContinuous.html
```

AnimateTwoWay

Continuous forward and backward animation

Description

The **AnimateTwoWay** applet animates the images in the specified sequence. When the end of the sequence is reached, the animation pauses the specified number of milliseconds, then reverses itself by displaying the images in reverse order. Backward and forward animation repeats continuously.

Forward

Backward

Using AnimateTwoWay in HTML Code

The following HTML code uses the **AnimateTwoWay** applet to create the animation shown at the top of this page:

```
<applet code=AnimateTwoWay.class width=200 height=200>
<param name=AppBGImage value=../images/pattern.gif>
<Param name=AppTile value=true>

<param name=Text value="Attention!">
<param name=TxFont value=Helvetica>
<param name=TxHorizCenter value=true>
<param name=TxVertCenter value=true>
<param name=TxStyle value=Bold>
<param name=TxPointSize value=36>
<param name=TxDelayBetweenRuns value=250>
<param name=TxDelayBetweenImages value=250>
<param name=TxNumImages value=8>
<param name=TxInitialImage value=4>
<param name=TxFilter1 value="multicolor white blue red">
<param name=TxFilter2 value="multicolor blue red white">
<param name=TxFilter3 value="multicolor red white blue">
<param name=TxFilter4 value="$1">
<param name=TxFilter5 value="$2|rotate 20">
<param name=TxFilter6 value="$3|rotate 40">
<param name=TxFilter7 value="$1|rotate 60">
<param name=TxFilter8 value="$2|rotate 80">
</applet>
```

Here's another example of continuous two-way animation using **AnimateTwoWay**. This animation shrinks an image using the **scale** filter.

```
<applet code=AnimateTwoWay.class width=120 height=531>
<param name=Image1 value=../images/face.gif>
<param name=ImgHorizCenter value=true>
<param name=ImgVertCenter value=true>
<param name=ImgDelayBetweenRuns value=2000>
<param name=ImgDelayBetweenImages value=250>
<param name=ImgNumImages value=12>
<param name=ImgFilter2 value="scale 95 90">
<param name=ImgFilter3 value="scale 90 80">
<param name=ImgFilter4 value="scale 85 70">
<param name=ImgFilter5 value="scale 80 60">
<param name=ImgFilter6 value="scale 75 50">
<param name=ImgFilter7 value="scale 70 40">
<param name=ImgFilter8 value="scale 65 30">
<param name=ImgFilter9 value="scale 60 20">
<param name=ImgFilter10 value="scale 55 10">
<param name=ImgFilter11 value="scale 50 2">
<param name=ImgFilter12 value="scale 0 0">
</applet>
```

Settings

All settings for **AnimateTwoWay** are included in the settings described on page 150.

See Also

Related applets: **AnimateContinuous** on page 153

URL for **AnimateTwoWay**:

```
http://www.vivids.com/java/animate/AnimateTwoWay.html
```

AnimateOnButton

Forward animation activated by mouse button

Description

The **AnimateOnButton** applet animates the images in the specified sequence when any mouse button is pressed in the image area or text area. The animation runs one time. When a mouse button is pressed again the animation repeats itself.

Forward on mouse press

Forward on mouse press

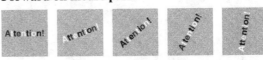

Using AnimateOnButton in HTML Code

The following HTML code uses the **AnimateOnButton** applet to create the animation shown at the top of this page.

```
<applet code=AnimateOnButton.class width=200 height=200>
<param name=AppBGImage value=../images/pattern.gif>
<Param name=AppTile value=true>

<param name=Text value="Attention!">
<param name=TxFont value=Helvetica>
<param name=TxHorizCenter value=true>
<param name=TxVertCenter value=true>
<param name=TxStyle value=Bold>
<param name=TxPointSize value=36>
<param name=TxDelayBetweenRuns value=250>
<param name=TxDelayBetweenImages value=250>
<param name=TxNumImages value=8>
<param name=TxInitialImage value=4>
<param name=TxRunOnce value=true>
<param name=TxFilter1 value="multicolor white blue red">
<param name=TxFilter2 value="multicolor blue red white">
<param name=TxFilter3 value="multicolor red white blue">
<param name=TxFilter4 value="$1">
<param name=TxFilter5 value="$2|rotate 20">
<param name=TxFilter6 value="$3|rotate 40">
<param name=TxFilter7 value="$1|rotate 60">
<param name=TxFilter8 value="$2|rotate 80">
</applet>
```

Here's another example using **AnimateOnButton** with a prepared series of images. This animation displays a car moving across a button. It is activated by button press.

```
<applet code=AnimateOnButton.class width=106 height=106>
<param name=AppBGImage value=../images/pattern.gif>
<Param name=AppTile value=true>

<param name=ImgHorizCenter value=true>
<param name=ImgVertCenter value=true>
<param name=ImgDelayBetweenImages value=200>
<param name=ImgDisplayFirst value=true>
<param name=ImgNumImages value=7>
<param name=ImgInitialImage value=1>
<param name=Image1 value=../images/car1.gif>
<param name=Image2 value=../images/car2.gif>
<param name=Image3 value=../images/car3.gif>
<param name=Image4 value=../images/car4.gif>
<param name=Image5 value=../images/car5.gif>
<param name=Image6 value=../images/car6.gif>
<param name=Image7 value=../images/car7.gif>
<param name=Image8 value=$1>
</applet>
```

Settings

The common settings described on page 150 apply to the **AnimateOnButton** applet. Two additional parameters specify whether the text and image animation sequence should run once at launch time, independent of any mouse activity.

Name	Description	Default
TxRunOnce	If true, the text animation sequence runs once at launch time	false
ImgRunOnce	If true, the image animation sequence runs once at launch time	false

See Also

Related applets: **AnimateOnButtonTwoWay** on page 162

URL for **AnimateOnButton**:

`http://www.vivids.com/java/animate/AnimateOnButton.html`

AnimateOnButtonTwoWay

Forward and backward animation activated by mouse button

Description

The **AnimateOnButtonTwoWay** applet animates the images in the specified sequence when any mouse button is pressed in the image or text area. The animation runs one time. When a mouse button is pressed again the animation reverses itself.

Forward on mouse press

Backward on mouse press

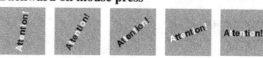

Using AnimateOnButtonTwoWay in HTML Code

The following HTML code uses the **AnimateOnButtonTwoWay** applet to create the animation shown at the top of this page:

```
<applet code=AnimateOnButtonTwoWay.class width=200 height=200>
<param name=AppBGImage value=../images/pattern.gif>
<Param name=AppTile value=true>

<param name=Text value="Attention!">
<param name=TxFont value=Helvetica>
<param name=TxHorizCenter value=true>
<param name=TxVertCenter value=true>
<param name=TxStyle value=Bold>
<param name=TxPointSize value=36>
<param name=TxDelayBetweenRuns value=250>
<param name=TxDelayBetweenImages value=250>
<param name=TxNumImages value=8>
<param name=TxInitialImage value=4>
<param name=TxRunOnce value=true>
<param name=TxFilter1 value="multicolor white blue red">
<param name=TxFilter2 value="multicolor blue red white">
<param name=TxFilter3 value="multicolor red white blue">
<param name=TxFilter4 value="$1">
<param name=TxFilter5 value="$2|rotate 20">
<param name=TxFilter6 value="$3|rotate 40">
<param name=TxFilter7 value="$1|rotate 60">
<param name=TxFilter8 value="$2|rotate 80">
</applet>
```

Here's another example using **AnimateOnButtonTwoWay**. This animation displays a sign that has been processed with the **waveimage** filter.

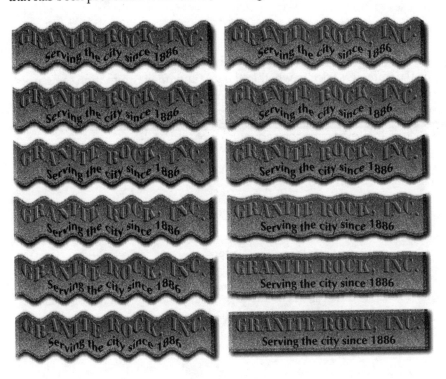

```
<applet code=AnimateOnButtonTwoWay.class width=300 height=150>
<param name=Image1 value=../images/granite2.gif>
<param name=AppBGColor value=#ffffff>
<param name=ImgDelayBetweenImages value=250>
<param name=ImgHorizCenter value=true>
<param name=ImgVertCenter value=true>
<param name=ImgNumImages value=13>
<param name=ImgInitialImage value=2>
<param name=ImgFilter1 value="scale 60 60">
<param name=ImgFilter2 value="$1|waveimage 8 10 0">
<param name=ImgFilter3 value="$1|waveimage 8 10 10">
<param name=ImgFilter4 value="$1|waveimage 8 10 20">
<param name=ImgFilter5 value="$1|waveimage 8 10 30">
<param name=ImgFilter6 value="$1|waveimage 8 10 40">
<param name=ImgFilter7 value="$1|waveimage 8 10 50">
<param name=ImgFilter8 value="$1|waveimage 8 10 60">
<param name=ImgFilter9 value="$1|waveimage 8 10 70">
<param name=ImgFilter10 value="$1|waveimage 6 10 80">
<param name=ImgFilter11 value="$1|waveimage 4 10 90">
```

```
<param name=ImgFilter12 value="$1|waveimage 2 10 100">
<param name=ImgFilter13 value="$1">
</applet>
```

Settings

The common settings described on page 150 apply to the **AnimateOnButtonTwoWay**
applet. Two additional parameters specify whether the text and image animation sequences
should run once at launch time, independent of any mouse activity.

Name	Description	Default
TxRunOnce	If true, the text animation sequence runs once at launch time	false
ImgRunOnce	If true, the image animation sequence runs once at launch time	false

See Also

Related applets: **AnimateOnButton** on page 159

URL for **AnimateOnButtonTwoWay**

   http://www.vivids.com/java/animate/AnimateOnButtonTwoWay.html

Pages for source code: **AnimateOnButtonTwoWay.java** on page 282

AnimateOnEntry

**Continuous forward animation
activated by pointer entry**

Description

The **AnimateOnEntry** applet animates the
images in the specified sequence when the
pointer enters the text or image area. The
animation runs continuously while the

Forward when pointer enters

pointer remains within the boundaries of the text or image. When the pointer leaves the
area, the animation stops.

You can specify that when the pointer leaves the text or image area, the image reverts to its
original state. Otherwise, the image remains as it was when the pointer left the area.

Using AnimateOnEntry in HTML Code

The following HTML code uses the **AnimateOnEntry** applet to create the animation shown
at the top of this page:

```
<applet code=AnimateOnEntry.class width=200 height=200>
<param name=AppBGImage value=../images/pattern.gif>
<Param name=AppTile value=true>

<param name=Text value="Attention!">
<param name=TxFont value=Helvetica>
<param name=TxHorizCenter value=true>
<param name=TxVertCenter value=true>
<param name=TxStyle value=Bold>
<param name=TxPointSize value=36>
<param name=TxDelayBetweenRuns value=250>
<param name=TxDelayBetweenImages value=250>
<param name=TxNumImages value=21>
<param name=TxInitialImage value=4>
<param name=TxReturnStart value=true>
<param name=TxRunOnce value=true>
<param name=TxFilter1 value="multicolor white blue red">
<param name=TxFilter2 value="multicolor blue red white">
<param name=TxFilter3 value="multicolor red white blue">
<param name=TxFilter4 value="$1">
<param name=TxFilter5 value="$2|rotate 20">
<param name=TxFilter6 value="$3|rotate 40">
<param name=TxFilter7 value="$1|rotate 60">
```

```
<param name=TxFilter8 value="$2|rotate 80">
<param name=TxFilter9 value="$3|rotate 100">
<param name=TxFilter10 value="$1|rotate 120">
<param name=TxFilter11 value="$2|rotate 140">
<param name=TxFilter12 value="$3|rotate 160">
<param name=TxFilter13 value="$1|rotate 180">
<param name=TxFilter14 value="$2|rotate 200">
<param name=TxFilter15 value="$3|rotate 220">
<param name=TxFilter16 value="$1|rotate 240">
<param name=TxFilter17 value="$2|rotate 260">
<param name=TxFilter18 value="$3|rotate 280">
<param name=TxFilter19 value="$3|rotate 300">
<param name=TxFilter20 value="$3|rotate 320">
<param name=TxFilter21 value="$3|rotate 340">
</applet>
```

The following example uses the **AnimateOnEntry** applet with a prepared series of images to "ring the telephone" when the pointer enters the image region. The "ringing" continues until the pointer leaves the region.

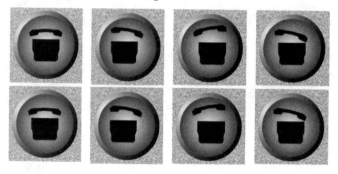

```
<applet code=AnimateOnEntry.class width=120 height=120>
<param name=AppBGImage value=../images/pattern.gif>
<param name=AppTile value=true>

<param name=Image1 value=../images/phone1.gif>
<param name=Image2 value=../images/phone2.gif>
<param name=Image3 value=../images/phone3.gif>
<param name=Image4 value=../images/phone4.gif>
<param name=ImgHorizCenter value=true>
<param name=ImgVertCenter value=true>
<param name=ImgDelayBetweenImages value=100>
<param name=ImgDelayBetweenRuns value=100>
<param name=ImgNumImages value=4>
<param name=ImgReturnStart value=true>
<param name=ImgAudio value=audio/phone.au>
</applet>
```

Settings

The common settings described on page 150 apply to the **AnimateOnEntry** applet. Two additional parameters specify whether the text and image animation sequence should revert to the initial image when the pointer leaves the region.

Name	Description	Default
TxReturnStart	If true, the text animation sequence reverts to the initial image when the pointer leaves the text region	false
ImgReturnStart	If true, the image animation sequence reverts to the initial image when the pointer leaves the image region	false

See Also

Related applets: **AnimateOnEntryTwoWay** on page 168

URL for **AnimateOnEntry**:

http://www.vivids.com/java/animate/AnimateOnEntry.html

AnimateOnEntryTwoWay

**Forward animation activated
by pointer entry**

**Backward animation
activated by pointer exit**

Forward when pointer enters

Description

The **AnimateOnEntryTwoWay** applet
animates the images in the specified
sequence when the pointer enters the text
or image area. The animation runs once.
When the pointer leaves the area, the animation reverses itself.

Backward when pointer leaves

Using AnimateOnEntryTwoWay in HTML Code

The following HTML code uses the **AnimateOnEntryTwoWay** applet to create the animation shown at the top of this page.

```
<applet code=AnimateOnEntryTwoWay.class width=200 height=200>
<param name=AppBGImage value=pattern.gif>
<Param name=AppTile value=true>

<param name=Text value="Attention!">
<param name=TxFont value=Helvetica>
<param name=TxHorizCenter value=true>
<param name=TxVertCenter value=true>
<param name=TxStyle value=Bold>
<param name=TxPointSize value=36>
<param name=TxDelayBetweenRuns value=250>
<param name=TxDelayBetweenImages value=250>
<param name=TxNumImages value=14>
<param name=TxInitialImage value=4>
<param name=TxFilter1 value="multicolor white blue red">
<param name=TxFilter2 value="multicolor blue red white">
<param name=TxFilter3 value="multicolor red white blue">
<param name=TxFilter4 value="$1">
<param name=TxFilter5 value="$2|rotate 20">
<param name=TxFilter6 value="$3|rotate 40">
<param name=TxFilter7 value="$1|rotate 60">
<param name=TxFilter8 value="$2|rotate 80">
<param name=TxFilter9 value="$2|rotate 100">
```

```
<param name=TxFilter10 value="$2|rotate 120">
<param name=TxFilter11 value="$2|rotate 140">
<param name=TxFilter12 value="$2|rotate 160">
<param name=TxFilter13 value="$2|rotate 180">
<param name=TxFilter14 value="$2|rotate 200">
</applet>
```

Here's an example that uses both text and an image. When the pointer moves within the image, the **transparent** filter makes the image become gradually transparent. At the same time, the text gradually becomes less transparent. The effect is of the image disappearing while the text appears.

```
<applet code=AnimateOnEntryTwoWay.class width=240 height=200>
<param name=AppBGImage value=../images/pattern.gif>
<Param name=AppTile value=true>

<param name=Text value="Welcome!">
<param name=TxFont value=Helvetica>
<param name=TxHorizCenter value=true>
<param name=TxVertCenter value=true>
<param name=TxStyle value=Bold>
<param name=TxPointSize value=42>
<param name=TxDelayBetweenImages value=250>
<param name=TxNumImages value=7>
<param name=TxInitialImage value=2>
<param name=TxFilter1 value="text">
<param name=TxFilter2 value="$1|transparent 100">
<param name=TxFilter3 value="$1|transparent 80">
<param name=TxFilter4 value="$1|transparent 60">
<param name=TxFilter5 value="$1|transparent 40">
<param name=TxFilter6 value="$1|transparent 20">
```

```
<param name=TxFilter7 value="$1|transparent 0">

<param name=Image1 value=../images/vivid.gif>
<param name=ImgHorizCenter value=true>
<param name=ImgVertCenter value=true>
<param name=ImgDelayBetweenImages value=250>
<param name=ImgNumImages value=6>
<param name=ImgFilter2 value="transparent 20">
<param name=ImgFilter3 value="transparent 40">
<param name=ImgFilter4 value="transparent 60">
<param name=ImgFilter5 value="transparent 80">
<param name=ImgFilter6 value="transparent 100">
</applet>
```

Settings

All settings for **AnimateOnEntryTwoWay** are included in the settings described on page 150.

See Also

Related applets: **AnimateOnEntry** on page 165

URL for **AnimateOnEntryTwoWay**:

> http://www.vivids.com/java/animate/AnimateOnEntryTwoWay.html

AnimateMultiple

Multiple simultaneous animations

Description

The **AnimateMultiple** applet animates multiple strings and images simultaneously.

AnimateMultiple is the most complex applet in the book. You should use it only if you cannot accomplish your task with one of the other applets in this chapter.

If you want to create multiple animations, you always have the option of using several animation applets on the same Web page. The one limitation of this method, however, is that the animation applets cannot touch or overlap each other. If you want several animation sequences to touch each other, overlap each other, or run on top of each other you need to use **AnimateMultiple**. In all other cases you will probably find it easier to use the other animation applets discussed earlier in this chapter.

Using AnimateMultiple in HTML Code

The following HTML code uses the **AnimateMultiple** applet to create the three text animations and two image animations shown in the illustration..

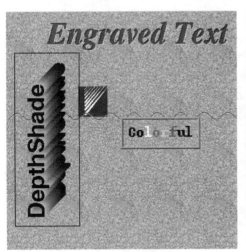

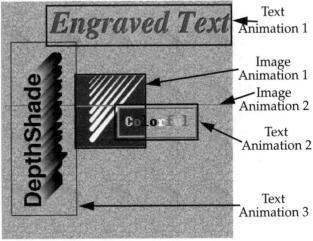

```
<applet code=AnimateMultiple.class width=320 height=240>
<param name=AppTile value=true>
<param name=AppBgImage value=../images/pattern.gif>
<param name=AppFrameThickness value=4>
<param name=AppFrameType value=ShadowEtchedIn>
```

```
<param name=TxCount value=3>

<param name=Text1 value="Engraved Text">
<param name=Tx1DelayBetweenImages value=100>
<param name=Tx1DelayBetweenRuns value=1000>
<param name=Tx1PointSize value=48>
<param name=Tx1Font value=TimesRoman>
<param name=Tx1Style value=BoldItalic>
<param name=Tx1XOffset1 value=20>
<param name=Tx1YOffset1 value=10>
<param name=Tx1NumImages value=16>
<param name=Tx1Filter1 value="engrave 1 10">
<param name=Tx1Filter2 value="engrave 1 20">
<param name=Tx1Filter3 value="engrave 1 30">
<param name=Tx1Filter4 value="engrave 1 40">
<param name=Tx1Filter5 value="engrave 1 50">
<param name=Tx1Filter6 value="engrave 1 60">
<param name=Tx1Filter7 value="engrave 1 70">
<param name=Tx1Filter8 value="engrave 1 80">
<param name=Tx1Filter9 value="engrave 1 70">
<param name=Tx1Filter10 value="engrave 1 60">
<param name=Tx1Filter11 value="engrave 1 50">
<param name=Tx1Filter12 value="engrave 1 40">
<param name=Tx1Filter13 value="engrave 1 30">
<param name=Tx1Filter14 value="engrave 1 20">
<param name=Tx1Filter15 value="engrave 1 10">
<param name=Tx1Filter16 value="engrave 1 0">
<param name=Tx1URL value=http://www.sun.com>
<param name=Tx1XOffset1 value=10>
<param name=Tx1XOffset2 value=20>
<param name=Tx1XOffset3 value=30>
<param name=Tx1XOffset4 value=40>
<param name=Tx1XOffset5 value=50>
<param name=Tx1XOffset6 value=60>
<param name=Tx1XOffset7 value=70>
<param name=Tx1XOffset8 value=80>

<param name=Text2 value="Colorful">
<param name=Tx2DelayBetweenImages value=100>
<param name=Tx2DelayBetweenRuns value=100>
<param name=Tx2PointSize value=24>
<param name=Tx2Font value=Courier>
<param name=Tx2Style value=Bold>
<param name=Tx2XOffset1 value=200>
<param name=Tx2YOffset1 value=180>
<param name=Tx2FrameThickness value=4>
<param name=Tx2FrameMargin value=12>
<param name=Tx2FrameType value=ShadowEtchedOut>
```

```
<param name=Tx2NumImages value=4>
<param name=Tx2Filter1 value="multicolor yellow green blue black white
salmon">
<param name=Tx2Filter2 value="multicolor green blue black white salmon
yellow">
<param name=Tx2Filter3 value="multicolor blue black white salmon yellow
green">
<param name=Tx2Filter4 value="multicolor black white salmon yellow green
blue">
<param name=Tx2Audio value=audio/sun.au>
<param name=Tx2URL value=http://www.vivids.com>

<param name=Text3 value="DepthShade">
<param name=Tx3DelayBetweenImages value=400>
<param name=Tx3DelayBetweenRuns value=1000>
<param name=Tx3AnimationType value=TwoWay>
<param name=Tx3PointSize value=36>
<param name=Tx3Font value=Helvetica>
<param name=Tx3Style value=Bold>
<param name=Tx3XOffset1 value=30>
<param name=Tx3YOffset1 value=80>
<param name=Tx3BorderWidth value=1>
<param name=Tx3BorderMargin value=13>
<param name=Tx3NumImages value=6>
<param name=Tx3Filter1 value="depthshade 10 10 yellow|rotate 90">
<param name=Tx3Filter2 value="depthshade 15 15 yellow|rotate 90">
<param name=Tx3Filter3 value="depthshade 20 20 yellow|rotate 90">
<param name=Tx3Filter4 value="depthshade 25 25 yellow|rotate 90">
<param name=Tx3Filter5 value="depthshade 30 30 yellow|rotate 90">
<param name=Tx3Filter6 value="depthshade 35 35 yellow|rotate 90">

<param name=ImgCount value=2>

<param name=Img1Image1 value=../images/vivid.gif>
<param name=Img1DelayBetweenImages value=100>
<param name=Img1DelayBetweenRuns value=100>
<param name=Img1XOffset1 value=120>
<param name=Img1YOffset1 value=120>
<param name=Img1NumImages value=19>
<param name=Img1Filter1 value="scale 10 10">
<param name=Img1Filter2 value="scale 20 20">
<param name=Img1Filter3 value="scale 30 30">
<param name=Img1Filter4 value="scale 40 40">
<param name=Img1Filter5 value="scale 50 50">
<param name=Img1Filter6 value="scale 60 60">
<param name=Img1Filter7 value="scale 70 70">
<param name=Img1Filter8 value="scale 80 80">
<param name=Img1Filter9 value="scale 90 90">
```

```
<param name=Img1Image10 value=$1>
<param name=Img1Filter11 value=$9>
<param name=Img1Filter12 value=$8>
<param name=Img1Filter13 value=$7>
<param name=Img1Filter14 value=$6>
<param name=Img1Filter15 value=$5>
<param name=Img1Filter16 value=$4>
<param name=Img1Filter17 value=$3>
<param name=Img1Filter18 value=$2>
<param name=Img1Filter19 value=$1>
<param name=Img1Audio value=audio/welcome.au>

<param name=Img2Image1 value=../images/hr.gif>
<param name=Img2DelayBetweenImages value=100>
<param name=Img2DelayBetweenRuns value=3000>
<param name=Img2XOffset1 value=0>
<param name=Img2YOffset1 value=160>
<param name=Img2NumImages value=10>
<param name=Img2Filter1 value="transcolor #c0c0c0">
<param name=Img2Filter2 value="$1|waveimage 2 6 10">
<param name=Img2Filter3 value="$1|waveimage 4 6 20">
<param name=Img2Filter4 value="$1|waveimage 6 6 30">
<param name=Img2Filter5 value="$1|waveimage 8 6 40">
<param name=Img2Filter6 value="$5">
<param name=Img2Filter7 value="$4">
<param name=Img2Filter8 value="$3">
<param name=Img2Filter9 value="$2">
<param name=Img2Filter10 value="$1">
<param name=Img2YOffset2 value=158>
<param name=Img2YOffset3 value=156>
<param name=Img2YOffset4 value=154>
<param name=Img2YOffset5 value=152>
<param name=Img2YOffset6 value=152>
<param name=Img2YOffset7 value=154>
<param name=Img2YOffset8 value=156>
<param name=Img2YOffset9 value=158>
<param name=Img2YOffset10 value=160>

</applet>
```

Settings

All settings for **AnimateMultiple** are included in the settings described on page 150. However, the parameters that begin with **Tx** must instead begin with **Tx*N***, and parameters that begin with **Img** must instead begin with **Img*N***. The ***N*** specifies the text or image animation involved.

The parameters that specify filters include two numbers: one that specifies the animation number, and the other the filter number. **Tx*N*Filter*M*** specifies the *N*th text animation and the *M*th filter for that animation sequence. **Img2Filter1**, for example, specifies the filter for the first image in image animation sequence 2.

Name	Description	Default
TxCount	The number of text animation sequences	0
ImgCount	The number of image animation sequences	0
Img*N*Image*M*	The *M*th image of the *N*th image animation sequence	
Tx*N*AnimationType	The animation type of the Nth text animation: **Continuous, TwoWay, OnButton, OnButtonTwoWay, OnEntry, OnEntryTwoWay**	**Continuous**
Img*N*AnimationType	The animation type of the Nth image animation: **Continuous, TwoWay, OnButton, OnButtonTwoWay, OnEntry, OnEntryTwoWay**	**Continuous**
Tx*N*XCenter	The horizontal position at which to center the *N*th text animation sequence	(do not center)
Tx*N*YCenter	The vertical position at which to center the *N*th text animation sequence	(do not center)
Img*N*XCenter	The horizontal position at which to center the *N*th image animation sequence	(do not center)
Img*N*YCenter	The vertical position at which to center the *N*th image animation sequence	(do not center)
Tx*N*ReturnStart	If true, the *N*th text animation sequence reverts to the initial image when the pointer leaves the text region	false
Img*N*ReturnStart	If true, the *N*th image animation sequence reverts to the initial image when the pointer leaves the image region	false
Tx*N*Filter*M*	The filter with which to manipulate the *M*th text in the *N*th text animation sequence	(none)
Img*N*Filter*M*	The filter with which to manipulate the *M*th image in the *N*th image animation sequence	(none)

See Also

URL for AnimateMultiple:

> http://www.vivids.com/java/animate/AnimateMultiple.html

CHAPTER
6

Assorted Applets

The applets in this chapter are presented together because they don't fit into any particular category. They are, however, some of the most useful and interesting applets in the book. The **Coalesce** applet is my personal favorite.

These applets fit into two categories: string animation and slide shows.

The string animation applets are useful for displaying text in an eye-catching manner. They are not as flexible as the ones introduced in the previous chapters—you can't, for example, play an audio file or load a URL, or combine them as with filters—but they are not as complicated and have less overhead, so they will load and display faster than many of the other applets.

The slide show applets are designed to display a series of images with optional audio. Each slide show applet moves between images in a different way. Enjoy!

Common Settings for String Animation Applets

The first seven applets in this chapter animate strings. The following table shows parameters that are common to these applets.

Name	Description	Default
AppBGColor	The applet background color	Set by browser
AppBGImage	The applet background image	(none)
AppTile	If true, tile the background image	false
DelayBetweenChars	The delay (in milliseconds) between character movements	20
DelayBetweenRuns	The delay (in milliseconds) between strings	3000
XOffset	The horizontal distance (in pixels) from the left side of the applet to the text	0
YOffset	The vertical distance (in pixels) from the top of the applet to the baseline of the text	The height of the text
TextColor	The text color	Set by browser
HorizCenter	If true, the text is horizontal centered	false
VertCenter	If true, the text is vertical centered	false
Font	The font of the text: **TimesRoman, Helvetica, Courier, Dialog, DialogInput,** or **ZapfDingbats**	**Dialog**
Style	The style of the font: **Plain, Bold, Italic,** or **BoldItalic**	**Plain**
PointSize	The size of the font in points	10

Tracker

Highlights each character in a string from left to right

Displays multiple strings in succession

![The Quick Brown Fox highlighted sequence, then Jumps Over highlighted sequence]

Description

The **Tracker** applet highlights each character in a string from left to right. You can select the color of the text and the color of the highlighting.

After a specified delay, the next string in the sequence, if any, is displayed in the same manner. There is no limit to the number of strings that can be displayed. After all of the strings have been displayed, the process starts again with the first string.

Interaction

The **Tracker** applet responds to the following keyboard input:

f	Highlighting speed 10% faster
s	Highlighting speed 10% slower
F	Delay between strings 10% shorter
S	Delay between strings 10% longer

Using Tracker in HTML Code

The following HTML code uses the **Tracker** applet to display the string *The Quick Brown Fox Jumps Over the Lazy Dog* as shown at the top of the page.

```
<applet code=Tracker.class width=250 height=35>
<param name=TextCount value=3>
<param name=text1 value="The Quick Brown Fox">
<param name=text2 value="Jumps Over">
<param name=text3 value="the Lazy Dog">
<param name=DelayBetweenChars value=50>
<param name=DelayBetweenRuns value=2000>
<param name=HorizCenter value=true>
<param name=VertCenter value=true>
<param name=style value=bold>
<param name=pointsize value=20>
</applet>
```

Settings

The common settings described on page 178 all apply to the **Tracker** applet. Three additional parameters specify the number of strings to display, the strings themselves, and the highlight color.

Name	Description	Default
TextCount	The number of strings to display (required)	0
Text*N*	The *N*th string of characters	(none)
HighlightColor	The highlight color	white

See Also

Related applets: **TrackFade** on page 181

URL for **Tracker**: `http://www.vivids.com/java/assorted/Tracker.html`

TrackFade

Highlights each character in a fading string from left to right

Displays multiple strings in succession

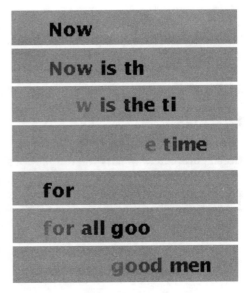

Description

The **TrackFade** applet displays each character in a string and then begins to fade that character as others are displayed. When the specified number of characters are displayed together, the leftmost character disappears entirely as each new character is added on the right. Characters in between are partially faded, depending on how far to the left they are. You can select the color of the text and the color of the highlighting.

After a specified delay, the next string in the sequence, if any, is displayed in the same manner. There is no limit to the number of strings that can be displayed. After all of the strings have been displayed, the process starts again with the first string.

Interaction

The **TrackFade** applet responds to the following keyboard input:

f	Highlighting speed 10% faster
s	Highlighting speed 10% slower
F	Delay between strings 10% shorter
S	Delay between strings 10% longer

Using TrackFade in HTML Code

The following HTML code uses the **TrackFade** to display the string *Now is the time for all good men to come to the aid of their country* as shown at the top of the page.

```
<applet code=TrackFade.class width=250 height=35>
<param name=TextCount value=4>
<param name=text1 value="Now is the time">
<param name=text2 value="for all good men">
<param name=text3 value="to come to the aid">
<param name=text4 value="of their country!">
<param name=FadeSize value=12>
<param name=DelayBetweenChars value=50>
```

```
<param name=DelayBetweenRuns value=1000>
<param name=HorizCenter value=true>
<param name=VertCenter value=true>
<param name=Style value=bold>
<param name=Pointsize value=20>
</applet>
```

Settings

The common settings described on page 178 all apply to the **TrackFade** applet. Four additional parameters specify the number of strings to display, the strings themselves, the color to which to fade, and the number of characters to display at once.

Name	Description	Default
TextCount	The number of strings to display (required)	0
Text*N*	The *N*th string of characters	(none)
FadeToColor	The color to which the string fades	The background color
FadeSize	The number of characters to display simultaneously	10

The bigger the value of **FadeSize**, the more characters can be read together at any given time. Each displayed character will be a different color—some shade between **TextColor** and **FadeToColor**.

By default, **FadeToColor** is set to the background color of the applet. If you set **FadeToColor** to some other color, each character eventually appears drawn entirely in that color, rather than disappearing by fading to the background color.

See Also

Related applets: **Tracker** on page 179

URL for **TrackFade**: http://www.vivids.com/java/assorted/TrackFade.html

Coalesce

Displays characters from a string at random positions

The string coalesces when the pointer enters the applet

Returns the characters to random positions when the pointer leaves the applet

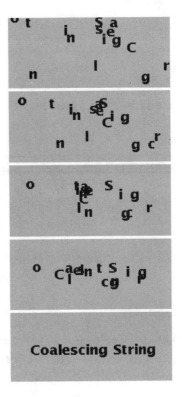

Coalescing String

Description

The **Coalesce** applet displays the characters in a string at random positions within the applet. When the pointer enters the applet, the characters begin to coalesce, until the specified string is displayed. When the pointer leaves the applet, the characters move to new random positions.

If the pointer enters or leaves the applet while the characters are moving, the direction of movement reverses. In other words, if the characters are coalescing and the pointer leaves the applet, the characters change direction—moving toward their random positions. If the characters are moving toward their random positions and the pointer enters the applet, the characters begin to coalesce.

Interaction

The **Coalesce** applet responds to the following keyboard input:

f   Character movement 10% faster

s   Character movement 10% slower

Using Coalesce in HTML Code

The following HTML code uses the **Coalesce** to display the string *Coalescing String* as shown at the top of the page.

```
<applet code=Coalesce.class width=250 height=100>
<param name=text value="Coalescing String">
<param name=AppBGImage value=../images/pattern.gif>
<param name=AppTile value=true>
<param name=Steps value=30>
<param name=DelayBetweenChars value=50>
<param name=HorizCenter value=true>
<param name=VertCenter value=true>
```

```
<param name=style value=bold>
<param name=pointsize value=20>
</applet>
```

Settings

The common settings described on page 178 all apply to the **Coalesce** applet. Two additional parameters specify the string to display and the number of steps in the coalescing sequence.

Name	Description	Default
Text	The string of characters to display	(none)
Steps	The number of steps in the coalescing sequence	50

The value of **Steps**, combined with the value of the **DelayBetweenChars** parameter, determines the speed with which the string coalesces.

See Also

URL for **Coalesce**:   `http://www.vivids.com/java/assorted/Coalesce.html`

Pages for source code: **Coalesce.java** on page 292

MoveLeft

Each character in a string moves left to takes its position

Displays multiple strings in succession

Description

The **MoveLeft** applet displays each character as it moves left into its position in the string.

After a specified delay, the next string in the sequence, if any, is displayed in the same manner. There is no limit to the number of strings that can be displayed. After all of the strings have been displayed, the process starts again with the first string.

Interaction

The **MoveLeft** applet responds to the following keyboard input:

f   Character movement 10% faster

s   Character movement 10% slower

F   Delay between strings 10% shorter

S   Delay between strings 10% longer

Using MoveLeft in HTML Code

The following HTML code uses the **MoveLeft** to display the string *Mary had a little lamb* as shown at the top of the page.

```
<applet code=MoveLeft.class width=250 height=35>
<param name=TextCount value=2>
<param name=text1 value="Mary had">
<param name=text2 value="a little lamb">
<param name=DelayBetweenChars value=50>
<param name=DelayBetweenRuns value=1000>
<param name=HorizCenter value=true>
<param name=VertCenter value=true>
<param name=Style value=bold>
<param name=Pointsize value=20>
</applet>
```

Settings

The common settings described on page 178 all apply to the **MoveLeft** applet. Two additional parameters specify the number of strings to display, and the strings themselves.

Name	Description	Default
TextCount	The number of strings to display (required)	0
Text*N*	The *N*th string of characters	(none)

See Also

Related applets: **MoveUp** on page 187
UpAndOver on page 189

URL for **MoveLeft**: `http://www.vivids.com/java/assorted/MoveLeft.html`

MoveUp

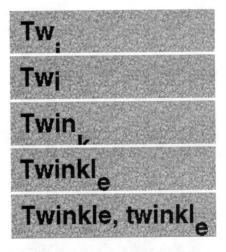

Each character in a string moves up to takes its position in the string

Displays multiple strings in succession

Description

The **MoveUp** applet displays each character as it moves up into its position in the string.

After a specified delay, the next string in the sequence, if any, is displayed in the same manner. There is no limit to the number of strings that can be displayed. After all of the strings have been displayed, the process starts again with the first string.

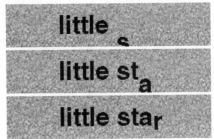

Interaction

The **MoveUp** applet responds to the following keyboard input:

f   Character movement 10% faster

s   Character movement 10% slower

F   Delay between strings 10% shorter

S   Delay between strings 10% longer

Using MoveUp in HTML Code

The following HTML code uses the **MoveUp** to display the string *Twinkle, twinkle little star* as shown at the top of the page.

```
<applet code=MoveUp.class width=250 height=50>
<param name=TextCount value=2>
<param name=text1 value="Twinkle, twinkle">
<param name=text2 value="little star">
<param name=AppBGImage value=../images/pattern.gif>
<param name=AppTile value=true>
<param name=DelayBetweenChars value=50>
<param name=DelayBetweenRuns value=2000>
<param name=HorizCenter value=true>
<param name=VertCenter value=true>
<param name=Font value=Helvetica>
```

```
<param name=Style value=bold>
<param name=Pointsize value=30>
</applet>
```

Settings

The common settings described on page 178 all apply to the **MoveUp** applet. Two additional parameters specify the number of strings to display, and the strings themselves.

Name	Description	Default
TextCount	The number of strings to display (required)	0
TextN	The Nth string of characters	(none)

See Also

Related applets: **MoveLeft** on page 185
UpAndOver on page 189

URL for **MoveUp**: `http://www.vivids.com/java/assorted/MoveUp.html`

UpAndOver

Each character in a string moves up to takes its position

The string moves left out of view

Displays multiple strings in succession

Description

The **UpAndOver** applet displays each character as it moves up into its position in the string.

After a specified delay, the string moves out of view to the left and the next string in the sequence, if any, is displayed in the same manner. There is no limit to the number of strings that can be displayed. After all of the strings have been displayed, the process starts again with the first string.

Interaction

The **UpAndOver** applet responds to the following keyboard input:

f	Character movement 10% faster
s	Character movement 10% slower
F	Delay between strings 10% shorter
S	Delay between strings 10% longer

Using UpAndOver in HTML Code

The following HTML code uses the **UpAndOver** to display the string *Twinkle, twinkle little star* as shown at the top of the page.

```
<applet code=UpAndOver.class width=250 height=50>
<param name=TextCount value=2>
<param name=text1 value="Twinkle, twinkle">
<param name=text2 value="little star">
<param name=AppBGImage value=../images/pattern.gif>
<param name=AppTile value=true>
<param name=DelayBetweenChars value=50>
<param name=DelayBetweenRuns value=5000>
<param name=HorizCenter value=true>
<param name=VertCenter value=true>
```

```
<param name=Font value=Helvetica>
<param name=Style value=bold>
<param name=Pointsize value=30>
</applet>
```

Settings

The common settings described on page 178 all apply to the **UpAndOver** applet. Three additional parameters specify the number of strings to display, the strings themselves, and the distance to move the string each time during exit.

Name	Description	Default
TextCount	The number of strings to display (required)	0
Text*N*	The text for the *N*th string of characters	(none)
MoveLeftDist	The distance (in pixels) to move the string left each time during exit from the applet	10

The speed of the text as it moves out of view is controlled by two parameters: **DelayBetweenChars** and **MoveLeftDist**. Smaller values of **MoveLeftDist** will make the movement smoother but slower because it will be moving a few number of pixels each time. Smaller values of **DelayBetweenChars** will speed the movement, but values that are too small will result in applets that do no run on slower machines.

See Also

Related applets:

    MoveLeft on page 185
    MoveUp on page 187

URL for **UpAndOver**:

    http://www.vivids.com/java/assorted/UpAndOver.html

Ticker

Displays a scrolling string of characters

Displays multiple strings in succession

Description

The **Ticker** applet scrolls a string of characters from right to left across the applet. The effect is similar to that of a scrolling electronic display.

After a specified delay, the next string in the sequence, if any, is displayed in the same manner. There is no limit to the number of strings that can be displayed. After all of the strings have been displayed, the process starts again with the first string.

Interaction

The **Ticker** applet responds to the following mouse input:

Button Press	The text stops scrolling. Press again and it restarts
Shift Button Press	The text scrolls in the reverse direction

The **Ticker** applet also responds to the following keyboard input:

f	Character movement 10% faster
s	Character movement 10% slower
F	Delay between strings 10% shorter
S	Delay between strings 10% longer
m	Increase the move distance by one pixel
l	Decrease the move distance by one pixel

Using Ticker in HTML Code

The following HTML code uses the **Ticker** to display *Welcome to the Instant Java Home Page* as shown at the top of the page.

```
<applet code=Ticker.class width=250 height=50>
<param name=TextCount value=2>
<param name=text1 value="Welcome to the Instant Java Home Page">
<param name=text2 value="Brought to you by Vivid Solutions">
```

```
<param name=AppBGImage value=../images/pattern.gif>
<param name=AppTile value=true>
<param name=DelayBetweenChars value=30>
<param name=DelayBetweenRuns value=30>
<param name=MoveDist value=5>
<param name=VertCenter value=true>
<param name=Font value=Helvetica>
<param name=Style value=BoldItalic>
<param name=Pointsize value=36>
</applet>
```

Settings

The common settings described on page 178 all apply to the **Ticker** applet. Four additional parameters specify the number of strings to display, the strings themselves, the distance to move the string each time, and the initial direction of movement.

Name	Description	Default
TextCount	The number of strings to display (required)	0
Text*N*	The *N*th string of characters	(none)
MoveDist	The distance (in pixels) to move the string each time	20
Reverse	If true, the initial direction of the moving text is from left to right	false

The speed of the moving text is controlled by two parameters: **DelayBetweenChars** and **MoveDist**. Smaller values of **MoveDist** will make the movement smoother but slower because it will be moving a few number of pixels each time. Smaller values of **DelayBetweenChars** will speed the movement, but values that are too small will result in applets that do not run on slower machines.

The **HorizCenter** parameter is not used in this applet.

See Also

URL for **Ticker**: http://www.vivids.com/java/assorted/Ticker.html

Pages for source code: **Ticker.java** on page 295

Slide Show Applets

The following six applets are slide show applets. Each displays a series of images in sequence. What makes each applet unique is the way in which it moves from one image to the next.

The slide show applets all share some common features. Each can operate automatically (the image changes without user interaction), or they can be manually operated by the user. Parameters allow you to specify automatic or manual play.

The following table includes parameters that are common to all six slide show applets.

Name	Description	Default
NumImages	The number of images to display (required)	0
Image*N*	The *N*th image	(none)
Sound*N*	The sound file played when the *N*th image is displayed	(none)
Controls	If true, the slide show includes Next and Previous buttons and an Audio checkbox	false
AutoPlay	If true, the images are displayed in sequence without user interaction (overrides **Controls**)	false
DelayBetweenImages	The delay (in seconds) between images (**AutoPlay** only)	5
AppBGColor	The applet background color	Set by browser

The slide show applets were originally designed to display images of the same size. However, you may use images of different sizes. The dimensions of the largest image determine the size of the image area. Smaller images are displayed within a rectangular region the width and height of the largest image.

If you set the **Controls** parameter to true (and do not set **AutoPlay** to true) then the slide show applets include *Next* and *Previous* buttons and the *Audio* checkbox, as shown below:

If you specify neither **AutoPlay** nor **Controls**, the images are displayed manually without controls. To change images you must use the mouse. With the pointer over the applet, press any mouse button to advance to the next image. Hold down the Shift key and press any mouse button to move to the previous image. To toggle the audio between on and off, press **a**.

SlideShow

Displays a series of images in sequence with optional audio and controls

Description

The **SlideShow** applet displays a series of images in sequence.

It can optionally include controls for displaying the next or previous image in the sequence. If the **AutoPlay** parameter is true, the images in the sequence automatically change every **DelayBetweenImages** seconds.

Interaction

The **SlideShow** applet responds to the following mouse input:

Button Press	Advance to next slide (if **AutoPlay** is false)
Shift Button Press	View slides in reverse order

The **SlideShow** applet also responds to the following keyboard input:

F	Interval between images 10% shorter (if **AutoPlay** is true)
S	Interval between images 10% longer (if **AutoPlay** is true)
a	Toggle audio

Using SlideShow in HTML Code

The following HTML code uses **SlideShow** to display three images in sequence as shown at the top of the page. Each image has an associated audio file, **AutoPlay** is true, and the delay between images is 7 seconds.

```
<applet code=SlideShow.class width=432 height=72>
<param name=NumImages value=3>
<param name=Image1 value=../images/duotone.gif>
<param name=Image2 value=../images/machine.gif>
<param name=Image3 value=../images/powertr.gif>
<param name=Sound1 value=audio/duotone.au>
<param name=Sound2 value=audio/machine.au>
<param name=Sound3 value=audio/powertr.au>
<param name=AutoPlay value=true>
<param name=DelayBetweenImages value=7>
</applet>
```

Settings

The common settings described on page page 193 all apply to the **SlideShow** applet.

See Also

URL for **SlideShow**:   `http://www.vivids.com/java/assorted/SlideShow.html`

Related applets: **SlideShowPush** on page 196
                             SlideShowSlide on page 198
                             SlideShowSplit on page 200
                             SlideShowSwap on page 202
                             SlideShowFade on page 204

SlideShowPush

Displays a series of images in sequence with optional audio and controls

Transition between images is by pushing

Description

The **SlideShowPush** applet displays a series of images in sequence. The transition from one image to the next is by pushing; the new image pushes the old image out of view to the right.

SlideShowPush can optionally include controls for displaying the next or previous image in the sequence. If the **AutoPlay** parameter is true, the images in the sequence automatically change every **DelayBetweenImages** seconds.

Interaction

The **SlideShowPush** applet responds to the following mouse input:

Button Press	Advance to next slide (if **AutoPlay** is false)
Shift Button Press	View slides in reverse order

The **SlideShowPush** applet also responds to the following keyboard input:

f	Interval between image movements 10% shorter
s	Interval between image movements 10% longer
F	Interval between images 10% shorter (if **AutoPlay** is true)
S	Interval between images 10% longer (if **AutoPlay** is true)
m	Increase image movement by one pixel per movement
l	Decrease image movement by one pixel per movement
a	Toggle audio

Using SlideShowPush in HTML Code

The following HTML code uses **SlideShowPush** to display three images in sequence as shown at the top of the page. Each image has an associated audio file, **Controls** is true—which adds the *Next*, *Previous*, and *Audio* buttons—and the delay between images is 2 seconds.

```
<applet code=SlideShowPush.class width=432 height=72>
<param name=NumImages value=3>
```

```
<param name=Image1 value=../images/duotone.gif>
<param name=Image2 value=../images/machine.gif>
<param name=Image3 value=../images/powertr.gif>
<param name=Sound1 value=audio/duotone.au>
<param name=Sound2 value=audio/machine.au>
<param name=Sound3 value=audio/powertr.au>
<param name=Controls value=true>
<param name=DelayBetweenMoves value=25>
<param name=DelayBetweenImages value=2>
</applet>
```

Settings

The common settings described on page page 193 all apply to the **SlideShowPush** applet. Two additional parameters specify the transition speed and movement.

Name	Description	Default
DelayBetweenMoves	The delay (in milliseconds) between image movements	20
MoveSize	The distance (in pixels) of each image movement	5

See Also

URL for **SlideShowPush**:   `http://www.vivids.com/java/assorted/SlideShowPush.html`

Related applets:

SlideShow on page 194
SlideShowSlide on page 198
SlideShowSplit on page 200
SlideShowSwap on page 202
SlideShowFade on page 204

SlideShowSlide

Displays a series of images in sequence with optional audio and controls

Transition between images is by sliding the older image out of view

Description

The **SlideShowSlide** applet displays a series of images in sequence. The transition from one image to the next is by sliding the older image out of view to the right.

SlideShowSlide can optionally include controls for displaying the next or previous image in the sequence. If the **AutoPlay** parameter is true, the images in the sequence automatically change every **DelayBetweenImages** seconds. The speed of the transition is controlled by the **DelayBetweenMoves** and **MoveSize** parameters.

Interaction

The **SlideShowSlide** applet responds to the following mouse input:

Button Press	Advance to next slide (if **AutoPlay** is false)
Shift Button Press	View slides in reverse order

The **SlideShowSlide** applet also responds to the following keyboard input:

f	Interval between image movements 10% shorter
s	Interval between image movements 10% longer
F	Interval between images 10% shorter (if **AutoPlay** is true)
S	Interval between images 10% longer (if **AutoPlay** is true)
m	Increase image movement by one pixel per movement
l	Decrease image movement by one pixel per movement
a	Toggle audio

Using SlideShowSlide in HTML Code

The following HTML code uses **SlideShowSlide** to display three images in sequence, as shown at the top of the page. The first image has an associated audio file, **AutoPlay** is true, and the delay between images is 3 seconds.

```
<applet code=SlideShowSlide.class width=432 height=150>
<param name=NumImages value=3>
<param name=Image1 value=../images/duotone.gif>
```

```
<param name=Image2 value=../images/machine.gif>
<param name=Image3 value=../images/powertr.gif>
<param name=Sound1 value=audio/duotone.au>
<param name=AutoPlay value=true>
<param name=DelayBetweenMoves value=20>
<param name=DelayBetweenImages value=3>
</applet>
```

Settings

The common settings described on page page 193 all apply to the **SlideShowSlide** applet. Two additional parameters specify the transition speed and movement.

Name	Description	Default
DelayBetweenMoves	The delay (in milliseconds) between image movements	20
MoveSize	The distance (in pixels) of each image movement	5

See Also

URL for **SlideShowSlide**:   http://www.vivids.com/java/assorted/SlideShowSlide.html

Related applets:
SlideShow on page 194
SlideShowPush on page 196
SlideShowSplit on page 200
SlideShowSwap on page 202
SlideShowFade on page 204

SlideShowSplit

Displays a series of images in sequence with optional audio and controls

Transition between images is by splitting the current image down the middle

Description

The **SlideShowSplit** applet displays a series of images in sequence. The transition from one image to the next is by splitting the current image in half and sliding each half out of view, one to the right and one to the left.

SlideShowSplit can optionally include controls for displaying the next or previous image in the sequence. If the **AutoPlay** parameter is true, the images in the sequence automatically change every **DelayBetweenImages** seconds. The speed of the transition is controlled by the **DelayBetweenMoves** and **MoveSize** parameters.

Interaction

The **SlideShowSplit** applet responds to the following mouse input:

Button Press	Advance to next slide (if **AutoPlay** is false)
Shift Button Press	View slides in reverse order

The **SlideShowSplit** applet also responds to the following keyboard input:

f	Interval between image movements 10% shorter
s	Interval between image movements 10% longer
F	Interval between images 10% shorter (if **AutoPlay** is true)
S	Interval between images 10% longer (if **AutoPlay** is true)
m	Increase image movement by one pixel per movement
l	Decrease image movement by one pixel per movement
a	Toggle audio

Using SlideShowSplit in HTML Code

The following HTML code uses **SlideShowSplit** to display three images in sequence as shown at the top of the page. Each image has an associated audio file, **Controls** is true—which adds the *Next*, *Previous*, and *Audio* buttons—and the delay between images is 5 seconds.

```
<applet code=SlideShowSplit.class width=432 height=72>
<param name=NumImages value=3>
<param name=AppBGColor value=red>
<param name=Controls value=true>
<param name=Image1 value=../images/duotone.gif>
<param name=Image2 value=../images/powertr.gif>
<param name=Image3 value=../images/machine.gif>
<param name=Sound1 value=audio/duotone.au>
<param name=Sound2 value=audio/powertr.au>
<param name=Sound3 value=audio/machine.au>
<param name=DelayBetweenMoves value=5>
<param name=DelayBetweenImages value=2>
<param name=MoveSize value=2>
</applet>
```

Settings

The common settings described on page page 193 all apply to the **SlideShowSplit** applet. Two additional parameters specify the transition speed and movement.

Name	Description	Default
DelayBetweenMoves	The delay (in milliseconds) between image movements	20
MoveSize	The distance (in pixels) of each image movement	5

See Also

URL for **SlideShowSplit**:

> http://www.vivids.com/java/assorted/SlideShowSplit.html

Related applets:

SlideShow on page 194
SlideShowPush on page 196
SlideShowSlide on page 198
SlideShowSwap on page 202
SlideShowFade on page 204

SlideShowSwap

Displays a series of images in sequence with optional audio and controls

Transition between images is by swapping

Description

The **SlideShowSwap** applet displays a series of images in sequence. The transition from one image to the next is by swapping. First one image moves to the right and the other to the left until the half-way point is reached. Then the images swap positions: the one that was behind comes to the front, the one that was in front goes to the back, and the direction each is travelling reverses. The effect is similar to automated shuffling of a stack of pictures.

SlideShowSwap can optionally include controls for displaying the next or previous image in the sequence. If the **AutoPlay** parameter is true, the images in the sequence automatically change every **DelayBetweenImages** seconds. The speed of the transition is controlled by the **DelayBetweenMoves** and **MoveSize** parameters.

Interaction

The **SlideShowSwap** applet responds to the following mouse input:

Button Press	Advance to next slide (if **AutoPlay** is false)
Shift Button Press	View slides in reverse order

The page 202applet also responds to the following keyboard input:

f	Interval between image movements 10% shorter
s	Interval between image movements 10% longer
F	Interval between images 10% shorter (if **AutoPlay** is true)
S	Interval between images 10% longer (if **AutoPlay** is true)
m	Increase image movement by one pixel per movement
l	Decrease image movement by one pixel per movement
a	Toggle audio

Using SlideShowSwap in HTML Code

The following HTML code uses **SlideShowSwap** to display three images in sequence, as shown at the top of the page. Each image has an associated audio file, **AutoPlay** is true, and the delay between images defaults to 5 seconds.

```
<applet code=SlideShowSwap.class width=432 height=72>
<param name=NumImages value=3>
<param name=Image1 value=../images/duotone.gif>
<param name=Image2 value=../images/powertr.gif>
<param name=Image3 value=../images/machine.gif>
<param name=Sound1 value=audio/duotone.au>
<param name=Sound2 value=audio/powertr.au>
<param name=Sound3 value=audio/machine.au>
<param name=AutoPlay value=true>
</applet>
```

Settings

The common settings described on page page 193 all apply to the **SlideShowSwap** applet. Two additional parameters specify the transition speed and movement.

Name	Description	Default
DelayBetweenMoves	The delay (in milliseconds) between image movements	20
MoveSize	The distance (in pixels) of each image movement	5

See Also

URL for **SlideShowSwap**:

http://www.vivids.com/java/assorted/SlideShowSwap.html

Related applets:

SlideShow on page 194
SlideShowPush on page 196
SlideShowSlide on page 198
SlideShowSplit on page 200
SlideShowFade on page 204

SlideShowFade

Displays a series of images in sequence with optional audio and controls

Transition between images is by fading to the background color

Description

The **SlideShowFade** applet displays a series of images in sequence. The transition from one image to the next is by fading. First the older image fades to the background color, then the next image fades in from the background color.

SlideShowFade can optionally include controls for displaying the next or previous image in the sequence. If the **AutoPlay** parameter is true, the images in the sequence automatically change every **DelayBetweenImages** seconds. The speed of the transition is controlled by the **DelayBetweenMoves** and **MoveSize** parameters.

Interaction

The **SlideShowFade** applet responds to the following mouse input:

Button Press	Advance to next slide (if **AutoPlay** is false)
Shift Button Press	View slides in reverse order

The **SlideShowSplit** applet also responds to the following keyboard input:

f	Interval between image movements 10% shorter
s	Interval between image movements 10% longer
F	Interval between images 10% shorter (if **AutoPlay** is true)
S	Interval between images 10% longer (if **AutoPlay** is true)
a	Toggle audiot

Using SlideShowFade in HTML Code

The following HTML code uses **SlideShowFade** to display three images in sequence, as shown at the top of the page. Each image has an associated audio file, **AutoPlay** is true, the delay between images is 7 seconds, and the delay between transitional faded images is 150 milliseconds.

```
<applet code=SlideShowFade.class width=432 height=72>
<param name=NumImages value=3>
```

```
<param name=FadeSize value=8>
<param name=DelayBetweenFades value=150>
<param name=DelayBetweenImages value=7>
<param name=Controls value=true>
<param name=Image1 value=../images/duotone.gif>
<param name=Image2 value=../images/powertr.gif>
<param name=Image3 value=../images/machine.gif>
<param name=AutoPlay value=true>
<param name=Sound1 value=audio/duotone.au>
<param name=Sound2 value=audio/powertr.au>
<param name=Sound3 value=audio/machine.au>
</applet>
```

Settings

The common settings described on page page 193 all apply to the **SlideShowFade** applet. Two additional parameters specify the transition speed and number of transitional images in the fade effect.

Name	Description	Default
DelayBetweenFades	The delay (in milliseconds) between transitional images	20
FadeSize	The number of transitional images to use to create fade effect	10

See Also

URL for **SlideShowFade**:

http://www.vivids.com/java/assorted/SlideShowFade.html

Related applets: **SlideShow** on page 194
                        SlideShowPush on page 196
                        SlideShowSlide on page 198
                        SlideShowSplit on page 200
                        SlideShowSwap on page 202

Pages for source code: **SlideShowFade.java** on page 298

APPENDIX A

Selected
Source Code
Listings

AdjColor.java

```
import java.awt.Color;

public class AdjColor {
    static int CalcFade(int from, int to, int perc, int scale) {

        return((from > to) ?
            to + ((from - to) * (scale-perc) / scale) :
            from + ((to - from) * perc / scale));
    }

    static Color darkenit(int r, int g, int b, double factor) {
        return new Color(Math.max((int)(r * (1 - factor)), 0),
                         Math.max((int)(g * (1 - factor)), 0),
                         Math.max((int)(b * (1 - factor)), 0));
    }

    //
    // The brightenit method in awt/Color.java doesn't really do
    // it right.  If your color is black (#000000) their brighter
    // method does not make it brighter.  You put in black
    // and you get back black.  I think this algorithm makes more
    // sense.
    static Color brightenit(int r, int g, int b, double factor) {
        int r2, g2, b2;
        r2 = r + (int)((255 - r) * factor);
```

```java
            g2 = g + (int)((255 - g) * factor);
            b2 = b + (int)((255 - b) * factor);
            return new Color(r2, g2, b2);
    }

    static Color darkenit(Color c, double factor) {
        int r, g, b;
        r = c.getRed();
        g = c.getGreen();
        b = c.getBlue();
        return darkenit(r, g, b, factor);
    }

    static Color brightenit(Color c, double factor) {
        int r, g, b;
        r = c.getRed();
        g = c.getGreen();
        b = c.getBlue();
        return brightenit(r, g, b, factor);
    }

    static Color Fade(Color from, Color to, double factor) {
        int from_r, from_g, from_b;
        int to_r, to_g, to_b;
        int r, g, b;

        from_r = from.getRed();
        from_g = from.getGreen();
        from_b = from.getBlue();
        to_r = to.getRed();
        to_g = to.getGreen();
        to_b = to.getBlue();
        if(from_r > to_r)
            r = to_r + (int)((from_r - to_r)*factor);
        else
            r = to_r - (int)((to_r - from_r)*factor);
        if(from_g > to_g)
            g = to_g + (int)((from_g - to_g)*factor);
        else
            g = to_g - (int)((to_g - from_g)*factor);
        if(from_b > to_b)
            b = to_b + (int)((from_b - to_b)*factor);
        else
            b = to_b - (int)((to_b - from_b)*factor);

        return new Color(r, g, b);
    }
}
```

Filter.java

```java
import java.applet.*;
import java.awt.*;
import java.awt.image.*;
import java.net.*;
import java.util.*;

public class Filter {
    int new_w = -1;
    int new_h = -1;

    public int[] invoke(Applet applet, String tx, String f_str,
                        int[] p1, int w, int h,
                        boolean maketransparent, Color bgcolor,
                        boolean underline) {
        return invoke(applet, tx, f_str, p1, w, h, maketransparent,
                      bgcolor, underline, applet.getFont());
    }

    public int[] invoke(Applet applet, String tx, String f_str,
                        int[] p1, int w, int h,
                        boolean maketransparent, Color bgcolor,
                        boolean underline, Font font) {

        StringTokenizer st, st2;
        int             num_elements;
        int             num_params[];
        String          filter_strings[];
        String          param_strings[][];
        int             i, j;
        Class           cl;
        ImgFilt         filterclass;

        new_w = w;
        new_h = h;
        if(f_str != null) {
            st = new StringTokenizer(f_str, "|");
            num_elements = st.countTokens();
            filter_strings = new String[num_elements];
            param_strings  = new String[num_elements][];
            num_params     = new int[num_elements];

            for(i=0;i<num_elements;i++) {
                String tmp_str, tmp_str2;
                tmp_str = st.nextToken();
                tmp_str2 = new String(tmp_str);
                st2 = new StringTokenizer(tmp_str2, " ");
                num_params[i] = st2.countTokens();
                if(num_params[i] == 1) {
                    filter_strings[i] = tmp_str;
```

```
                        param_strings[i] = null;
                  } else {
                        param_strings[i] = new String[num_params[i]-1];
                        filter_strings[i] = st2.nextToken();
                        for(j=0;j<num_params[i]-1;j++) {
                              param_strings[i][j] = st2.nextToken();
                        }
                  }
            }
            for(i=0;i<num_elements;i++) {
                  try {
                        cl = Class.forName("f" + filter_strings[i]);
                        filterclass = (ImgFilt)cl.newInstance();
                        for(j=0;j<num_params[i]-1;j++)
                              filterclass.setparameter(param_strings[i][j], j);
                        filterclass.setBackground(bgcolor);
                        filterclass.setForeground(applet.getForeground());
                        filterclass.setFont(font);
                        filterclass.setApplet(applet);
                        filterclass.setText(tx);
                        filterclass.setUnderline(underline);
                        // When we call setTransparent(true) this
                        // means that the background color will be
                        // used as the transparent color
                        filterclass.setTransparent(maketransparent);
                        p1 = filterclass.filter(p1, new_w, new_h);
                        new_w = filterclass.getWidth();
                        new_h = filterclass.getHeight();
                  } catch (ClassNotFoundException e) {
                        System.err.println("Can't find class " + filter_strings[i]);
                  } catch (InstantiationException e) {
                        System.err.println("Couldn't instantiate class " +
                                                        filter_strings[i]);
                  } catch (IllegalAccessException e) {
                        System.err.println("Couldn't access class " +
                                                        filter_strings[i]);
                  }
            }
      }
      return p1;
}

public int getWidth() {
      return new_w;
}

public int getHeight() {
      return new_h;
}
}
```

GetParm.java

```java
import java.applet.Applet;
import java.awt.Color;
import java.net.URL;
import java.awt.Font;
import java.net.MalformedURLException;

public class GetParm {

    public static int toInt(Applet applet, String par, int defaultval) {
        String s = applet.getParameter(par);
        if(s == null)
            return defaultval;
        else
            return(Integer.parseInt(s));
    }

    public static String toString(Applet applet, String par, String defaultval) {
        String s = applet.getParameter(par);
        if(s == null)
            return defaultval;
        else
            return(s);
    }

    public static boolean toBoolean(
                        Applet applet,
                        String par,
                        boolean defaultval) {
        String s = applet.getParameter(par);
        if(s == null)
            return defaultval;
        else
            return(s.equalsIgnoreCase("true"));
    }

    public static Color toColor(
                        Applet applet,
                        String par,
                        Color defaultval) {
        Color color;

        String s = applet.getParameter(par);
        if(s == null)
            return defaultval;
        else {
            try {
                if(s.charAt(0) == '#') {
                    char chars[];
                    // Get rid of leading #
```

```
                         chars =  new char [s.length()];
                         s.getChars(0, s.length(), chars, 0);
                         color = new Color(Integer.parseInt(
                                 new String(chars, 1, s.length()-1),16));
                         return(new Color(Integer.parseInt(
                                 new String(chars, 1, s.length()-1), 16)));
                     } else {
                         color = new Color(Integer.parseInt(s, 16));
                         return(color);
                     }
                 } catch (NumberFormatException e) {
                     String retcolor;
                     retcolor = ColrLook.getColor(s);
                     if(retcolor != null)
                         return(new Color(Integer.parseInt(retcolor, 16)));
                     else
                         System.out.println("Bad color specification: " +
                                                             e.getMessage());

                     return null;
                 }
             }
         }
     }

     public static URL toURL(
                         Applet applet,
                         String par) {
         URL url = null;
         String s = applet.getParameter(par);
         if(s == null)
             return null;
         else {
             try {
                 url = new URL(s);
             } catch(MalformedURLException e) {
                 url = null;
             }
             if(url == null) {
                 // The URL may be specified as relative to
                 // the HTML document base in which the URL resides
                 // We should be able to handle that
                 try {
                     url = new URL(applet.getDocumentBase(), s);
                 } catch(MalformedURLException e) {
                     url = null;
                 }
             }
             if(url == null) {
                 // The URL may be specified as relative to
                 // the Code base (though that seems rather
                 // unlikely)
                 //
                 try {
```

```java
                    url = new URL(applet.getCodeBase(), s);
                } catch(MalformedURLException e) {
                    url = null;
                }
            }
            if(url == null)
                System.out.println("Unable to load URL: " + s);
        }
        return url;
    }

    public static Font toFont(
                            Applet applet,
                            String par1,
                            String par2,
                            String par3) {

        String fontname;
        String fontstyle;
        int style = -1;
        int psize;
        Font font;
        Font currentfont;
        String psize_str;

        currentfont = applet.getFont();
        fontname = applet.getParameter(par1);
        if(fontname == null)
            fontname = currentfont.getName();
        fontstyle = applet.getParameter(par2);
        if(fontstyle == null)
            style = currentfont.getStyle();

        // Get the Font
        if(fontname.equalsIgnoreCase("TimesRoman")   ||
           fontname.equalsIgnoreCase("Helvetica")    ||
           fontname.equalsIgnoreCase("Courier")      ||
           fontname.equalsIgnoreCase("Dialog")       ||
           fontname.equalsIgnoreCase("DialogInput") ||
           fontname.equalsIgnoreCase("ZapfDingbats")) {
                // Do Nothing, we got a valid font
        } else {
            fontname = currentfont.getName();
        }

        if(style == -1) {
            // Get the Font Style
            if(fontstyle.equalsIgnoreCase("bold"))
                style = Font.BOLD;
            else if(fontstyle.equalsIgnoreCase("italic"))
                style = Font.ITALIC;
            else if(fontstyle.equalsIgnoreCase("bolditalic"))
                style = Font.ITALIC|Font.BOLD;
```

```
            else
                style = Font.PLAIN;
        }
        psize_str = applet.getParameter(par3);
        if(psize_str == null)
            psize = currentfont.getSize();
        else {
            try {
                psize = Integer.parseInt(psize_str);
            } catch (NumberFormatException e) {
                psize = currentfont.getSize();
                System.out.println("NumberformatException: " + psize_str);
            }
        }


        // Set up the font stuff
        font = new Font(fontname, style, psize);
        return font;
    }
}
```

ImgFilt.java

```java
import java.awt.*;
import java.applet.*;

public abstract class ImgFilt {
    protected int new_width;
    protected int new_height;
    protected int newpixels[];
    protected Color trans_color;
    protected int trans_color_value;
    protected boolean transparent = false;
    protected Color bg = Color.white;
    protected Color fg = Color.black;
    protected Font font;
    protected String tx;
    protected Applet applet;
    protected boolean underline;

    public ImgFilt() {
        new_width  = -1;
        new_height = -1;
    }

    public abstract int[] filter(int[] p1, int w, int h);

    public int getWidth() {
        return new_width;
    }

    public int getHeight() {
        return new_height;
    }

    public void setparameter(String s, int i) {
        // Do nothing
    }

    public void setparameter(String s) {
        // Do nothing
    }

    public void setTransparentColor(Color color) {
        transparent = true;
        trans_color = color;
        trans_color_value = (0xFF << 24) |
                            (color.getRed()   << 16) |
                            (color.getGreen() <<  8) |
                            (color.getBlue());
    }
```

```java
public void setTransparentColor(boolean t, Color color) {
    transparent = t;
    trans_color = color;
    trans_color_value = (0xFF << 24) |
                        (color.getRed()   << 16) |
                        (color.getGreen() <<  8) |
                        (color.getBlue());
}

public void setTransparent(boolean t) {
    transparent = t;
}

public void setBackground(Color bg) {
    this.bg = bg;
}

public void setForeground(Color fg) {
    this.fg = fg;
}

public void setFont(Font font) {
    this.font = font;
}

public void setApplet(Applet a) {
    applet = a;
}

public void setText(String t) {
    tx = t;
}

public void setUnderline(boolean b) {
    underline = b;
}

public Color String2Color(String s) {
    String retcolor;

    if(s == null)
        return null;
    try {
        if(s.charAt(0) == '#') {
            char chars[];
            // Get rid of leading #
            chars = new char [s.length()];
            s.getChars(0, s.length(), chars, 0);
            return(new Color(Integer.parseInt(
                    new String(chars, 1, s.length()-1), 16)));
        } else {
            return(new Color(Integer.parseInt(s, 16)));
        }
```

```
        } catch (NumberFormatException e) {
            retcolor = ColrLook.getColor(s);
            if(retcolor != null)
                return(new Color(Integer.parseInt(retcolor, 16)));
            else
                System.out.println("Bad color specification: " + e.getMessage());

            return null;
        }
    }


    //
    // The drawUnderline method draws an underline
    // The underline is actually a filled rectangle
    // whose size is based on the width of a pipe
    // character from the same font.  It works!
    //
    protected void drawUnderline(Graphics g,
                            FontMetrics fm,
                            int x,
                            int y,
                            int w,
                            Color c) {
        if(underline) {
            int pipewidth = fm.charWidth('|');
            g.setColor(c);
            g.fillRect(x, y, w, Math.max(1, pipewidth/4));
        }
    }
}
```

ImgGetr.java

```java
import java.awt.*;
import java.awt.image.*;
import java.applet.Applet;
import java.net.*;
import java.io.*;

/**
 * ImgGetr is a utility class to get images.  It is
 * similar and simpler than MediaTracker.  The one
 * advantage of ImgGetr is that if an error occurs
 * getting the image (such as the url or file specified
 * does not exist) an image is created which can be used
 * to display an error message indicating to the user that
 * the image was not "gotten".
 *
 * @author      John Pew
 */
public class ImgGetr {
    Image        image;          // The image
    String       image_file;     // The name of the image file
    int          image_width;    // Width of the image
    int          image_height;   // Height of the image
    URL          complete_url;
    InputStream  in;
    String       errormsg;
    boolean      image_load;
    Applet       applet;

    /**
     * Construct an ImageGetter object.
     *
     * @param a The applet that has created this object
     */
    public ImgGetr(Applet a) {
        applet = a;
    }

    /**
     * Process the image. Check the usr and file and make sure that
     * we can actually load this thing. If not, then call the
     * createErrorMessageImage method to return an image with
     * the error message displayed in it.
     *
     * @param url The URL to load
     * @param file The file to load
     * @param loadnow If true, wait for the file to load before returning
     */
    public Image process(URL url, String file, boolean loadnow) {
        image_file = file;
        image_load = loadnow;
        int i;
```

```
        // See if the user specified an Image parameter
        // If not, then notify
        if(image_file == null) {
            String errormsg[] = { "Missing \"Image\" parameter!!" };
            return createErrorMessageImage(errormsg);
        }

        // If the user did specify an Image parameter
        if(image_file != null) {

            // First, check the URL and makes sure it's valid
            // We can't just do a getImage() on the specified
            // URL because getImage() returns immediately
            // and if the user has specified an invalid URL
            // (file) we don't get notified.
            try {
                complete_url = new URL(url, image_file);
            } catch(MalformedURLException e) {
                // It's unlikely that this execption will ever be
                // thrown because the calling class is
                // probably using getCodeBase()
                String errormsg[] = {
                        "Invalid \"Image\" value!!",
                        "MalformedURLException" };
                return createErrorMessageImage(errormsg);
            }
            if(complete_url != null) {
                image = applet.getImage(complete_url);
                if(image == null) {
                    String errormsg[] = { "getImage failed"};
                    System.out.println(errormsg[0]);
                    return createErrorMessageImage(errormsg);
                }
                if(loadnow)
                    loadImageAndWait(image, applet);
            }
        }
        return image;
    }

/**
 * Checks to see if the specified image is actually
 * prepared (loaded) and ready to display
 * Return true if loaded, otherwise false
 *
 * @param image the image to check
 * @param applet the applet
 */
public boolean isImagePrepared(Image image, Applet applet) {
    boolean ImagePrepared;
    ImagePrepared = applet.prepareImage(image, applet);
    return ImagePrepared;
}
```

```
/**
 * Begins the preparation (loading) of the image
 * This function returns immediately
 * The image is loaded in a thread
 *
 * @param image the image to prepare
 * @param applet the applet
 */
public void prepareImage(Image image, Applet applet) {
    boolean ImagePrepared;
    ImagePrepared = applet.prepareImage(image, applet);
}


/**
 * Prepares (loads) the image and does not return
 * until the loading is complete
 *
 * @param image the image to load
 * @param applet the applet
 */
public synchronized void loadImageAndWait(Image image, Applet applet) {
    int checkImageFlags;
    boolean ImagePrepared;

    ImagePrepared = applet.prepareImage(image, applet);
    if(ImagePrepared == false) {
        while(((checkImageFlags =
                applet.checkImage(image, applet)) &
                    ImageObserver.ALLBITS) == 0) {
            try {
                wait(100);
            } catch (InterruptedException e){}
        }
    }
}


/**
 * Create an error message as an image so that
 * the applet can display the error message where
 * the image would have otherwise been displayed
 *
 * @param e An array of error messages
 */
public Image createErrorMessageImage(String e[]) {
    Image errorImage;
    Graphics errorGC;
    Font font;
    Font errorfont;
    FontMetrics fontmetrics;
    int height;
    int position = 25;
    int i;
```

```
        errorImage = applet.createImage(applet.size().width,
                                              applet.size().height);

        errorGC = errorImage.getGraphics();
        errorGC.setColor(applet.getBackground());
        errorGC.fillRect(0, 0, applet.size().width, applet.size().height);
        errorGC.setColor(applet.getForeground());
        font = applet.getFont();
        errorfont = new Font("Dialog", Font.BOLD, 12);
        applet.setFont(errorfont);
        fontmetrics = applet.getFontMetrics(errorfont);
        height = fontmetrics.getHeight();

        errorGC.setFont(new Font(errorfont.getName(),
                           Font.BOLD, errorfont.getSize()+4));
        errorGC.drawString("ERROR:", 10, position);
        errorGC.setFont(errorfont);
        for(i = 0;i<e.length;i++) {
            if(e[i] != null) {
                position += height;
                errorGC.drawString(e[i], 25, position);
            }
        }
        applet.setFont(font);
        return errorImage;
    }

    public synchronized int getWidth(Image image, ImageObserver observer) {
        int width;
        while((width = image.getWidth(observer)) == -1) {
            try {wait(100);} catch (InterruptedException e){}
        }
        return width;
    }

    public synchronized int getHeight(Image image, ImageObserver observer) {
        int height;
        while((height = image.getHeight(observer)) == -1) {
            try {wait(100);} catch (InterruptedException e){}
        }
        return height;
    }

    public int[] getPixels(Image image, ImageObserver observer) {
        int pixels[];
        int w, h;
        PixGrab tmp_pg;
        boolean retval;

        w = getWidth(image, observer);
        h = getHeight(image, observer);
        loadImageAndWait(image, applet);
        pixels = new int[w * h];
        tmp_pg = new PixGrab(image, 0, 0, w, h, pixels, 0, w);
```

```
        try {
            retval = tmp_pg.grabPixels(0);
        } catch (InterruptedException e) {
            System.err.println("Interrupted waiting for pixels");
        }
        return pixels;
    }

    public int[] getPixels(Image image, Applet applet) {
        int pixels[];
        int w, h;
        PixGrab tmp_pg;
        boolean retval;

        w = getWidth(image, applet);
        h = getHeight(image, applet);
        loadImageAndWait(image, applet);
        pixels = new int[w * h];
        tmp_pg = new PixGrab(image, 0, 0, w, h, pixels, 0, w);
        try {
            retval = tmp_pg.grabPixels(0);
        } catch (InterruptedException e) {
            System.err.println("Interrupted waiting for pixels");
        }
        return pixels;
    }


    /*
     * This is an alternative way of grabbing the pixels.
     * It may be necessary to use this version if the PixelGrabber
     * continues to cause fatal errors
     */

    /*
    public static int[] getPixels(Image image,
                                  Applet applet) {
        int w, h;
        int pixels[];
        Image tmpimage, tmpimage2;
        Graphics tmpGC;

        w = getWidth(image, applet);
        h = getHeight(image, applet);
        loadImageAndWait(image, applet);
        CatchFlt catchFilter = new CatchFlt();
        catchFilter.setsize(applet, w, h);
        tmpimage = applet.createImage(new FilteredImageSource(image.getSource(),
                                                catchFilter));
        tmpimage2 = applet.createImage(w, h);
        tmpGC = tmpimage2.getGraphics();
        tmpGC.drawImage(tmpimage, 0, 0, applet);
        loadImageAndWait(tmpimage2, applet);
```

```
                pixels = catchFilter.getPixels();
                return pixels;
        }
        */
}


/*
class CatchFlt extends RGBImageFilter {
        int index;
        int w, h;
        int pixels[];
        Applet applet;
        int mul;
        Color fg, bg;

        public CatchFlt() {
                // The filter's operation does not depend on the
                // pixel's location, so IndexColorModels can be
                // filtered directly.
                canFilterIndexColorModel = false;
        }
        public CatchFlt(Applet applet, int wid, int hei) {
                this.applet = applet;
                // The two sizes may not exactly be equal proportional, so
                // choose the bigger
                w = wid;
                h = hei;
                pixels = new int[h*w];
                canFilterIndexColorModel = false;
        }

        public void setsize(Applet applet, int wid, int hei) {
                this.applet = applet;
                // The two sizes may not exactly be equal proportional, so
                // choose the bigger
                w = wid;
                h = hei;
                pixels = new int[h*w];
                return;
        }

        public int filterRGB(int x, int y, int rgb) {

                pixels[(y*w)+x] = rgb;

                return rgb;
        }

        public int[] getPixels() {
                return pixels;
        }
}
*/
```

fsoftshadow.java

```java
import java.awt.*;
import java.awt.image.*;

public class fsoftshadow extends ImgFilt {
    int shadow_xoffset = 2;
    int shadow_yoffset = 2;
    Color shadow_color = new Color(150, 150, 150);
    int soft_thickness = 2;
    Color light_shadow[];

    public void setparameter(String str, int i) {
        switch(i) {
        case 0:
            shadow_xoffset = Integer.parseInt(str);
            break;
        case 1:
            shadow_yoffset = Integer.parseInt(str);
            break;
        case 2:
            shadow_color = String2Color(str);
            break;
        case 3:
            soft_thickness = Integer.parseInt(str);
            break;
        }
    }

    public int[] filter(int[] p1, int w, int h) {
        int i;
        int x, y;
        Image image;
        Graphics g;
        int ascent, descent;
        FontMetrics fontmetrics;
        int pixels[];
        boolean retval;
        ftransp tp;
        ImgGetr ig;

        // Ignore p1, w, and h

        fontmetrics = applet.getFontMetrics(font);
        ascent = fontmetrics.getAscent();
        descent = fontmetrics.getDescent();
        new_width = fontmetrics.stringWidth(tx) + Math.abs(shadow_xoffset);
        new_height = fontmetrics.getHeight() + Math.abs(shadow_yoffset);

        image = applet.createImage(new_width, new_height);
        g = image.getGraphics();
```

```
        g.setFont(font);
        g.setColor(bg);
        g.fillRect(0, 0, new_width, new_height);

        x = (shadow_xoffset < 0) ? 0 : Math.abs(shadow_xoffset);
        y = (shadow_yoffset < 0) ? 0 : Math.abs(shadow_yoffset);

        // Draw text in lighter shadow color offset by xoffset+1, yoffset+1
        light_shadow = new Color[soft_thickness];
        for(i=0;i<soft_thickness;i++)
            light_shadow[i] = AdjColor.Fade(shadow_color,
                              bg, 0.8*(i+1)/soft_thickness);


        // Draw text in shadow color offset by xoffset, yoffset
        // The size of soft_thickness determines how much work
        // we put into creating the "soft shadow". Too big a number
        // creates a silly looking shadow
        for(i=0;i<soft_thickness;i++) {
            int soft_offset = soft_thickness-i;
            g.setColor(light_shadow[i]);
            for(int j=-soft_offset;j<soft_offset;j++)
                for(int k=-soft_offset;k<soft_offset;k++) {
                    g.drawString(tx, x+j, y+ascent+k);
                    drawUnderline(g, fontmetrics, x+j,
                        y+ascent+k+Math.max(1, (descent/4)),
                        new_width, light_shadow[i]);
                }
        }

        // If the shadow is negative then we must offset the position
        // of the non-shadow text to allow room for the shadow
        x = (shadow_xoffset < 0) ? Math.abs(shadow_xoffset) : 0;
        y = (shadow_yoffset < 0) ? Math.abs(shadow_yoffset) : 0;

        // Now draw the main foreground text
        g.setColor(fg);
        g.drawString(tx, x, y+ascent);
        drawUnderline(g, fontmetrics, x,
                      y+ascent+Math.max(1, (descent/4)),
                      new_width, fg);

        // Grab the pixels
        ig = new ImgGetr(applet);
        pixels = ig.getPixels(image, applet);
        if(transparent) {
            tp = new ftransp();
            tp.setTransparentColor(bg);
            pixels = tp.filter(pixels, new_width, new_height);
        }
        return pixels;
    }
}
```

femboss.java

```java
import java.awt.*;
import java.awt.image.*;

public class femboss extends ImgFilt {
    int depth = 1;
    double intensity = .50;

    public void setparameter(String str, int i) {
        switch(i) {
        case 0:
            depth = Integer.parseInt(str);
            break;
        case 1:
            intensity = (double)(Integer.parseInt(str)/100.0);
            break;
        }
    }

    public int[] filter(int[] p1, int w, int h) {
        int i;
        int x, y;
        int divisor;
        double xoff, yoff, ddivisor;
        int ascent, descent;
        FontMetrics fontmetrics;
        Image image;
        Graphics g;
        int pixels[];
        boolean retval;
        ftransp tp;
        Color   dark;
        Color   bright;
        ImgGetr ig;

        fontmetrics = applet.getFontMetrics(font);
        ascent = fontmetrics.getAscent();
        descent = fontmetrics.getDescent();
        new_width = fontmetrics.stringWidth(tx);
        new_height = fontmetrics.getHeight();

        // Clear out whatever might already be there
        image = applet.createImage(new_width, new_height);
        g = image.getGraphics();
        g.setFont(font);
        g.setColor(bg);
        g.fillRect(0, 0, new_width, new_height);

        // To Create the embossed look, draw the string in a darker
        // and brighter shade than the background, offset by depth
```

```
        dark = AdjColor.darkenit(bg, intensity);
        bright = AdjColor.brightenit(bg, intensity);

        // Upper Left edge
        g.setColor(bright);
        g.drawString(tx, 0, ascent-depth);
        drawUnderline(g, fontmetrics, 0,
                        ascent-depth+Math.max(1, (descent/4))+depth,
                        new_width, dark);

        // Lower Right edge
        g.setColor(dark);
        g.drawString(tx, depth*2, ascent+depth);
        drawUnderline(g, fontmetrics, depth*2,
                        ascent+depth+Math.max(1, (descent/4))-depth,
                        new_width, bright);

        // The main body of the characters
        g.setColor(bg);
        g.drawString(tx, depth, ascent);
        drawUnderline(g, fontmetrics, depth,
                        ascent+Math.max(1, (descent/4)),
                        new_width, bg);

        // Now grab the pixels for use with filters
        ig = new ImgGetr(applet);
        pixels = ig.getPixels(image, applet);
        if(transparent) {
            tp = new ftransp();
            tp.setTransparentColor(bg);
            pixels = tp.filter(pixels, new_width, new_height);
        }
        return pixels;
    }
}
```

fnegative.java

```java
public class fnegative extends ImgFilt {
    int subfrom = 255;

    public void setparameter(String str, int i) {
        switch(i) {
        case 0:
            subfrom = Integer.parseInt(str);
            break;
        }
    }

    public int[] filter(int[] p1, int w, int h) {
        int x, y, i;
        int index, new_index;
        int alpha, red, green, blue;
        int nalpha, nred, ngreen, nblue;

        if(p1.length != (w*h)) {
            System.out.println("negative filter: wrong size array");
            System.out.println("p1.length = " + p1.length + " (w,h) = "
                                + w + "," + h);
            return null;
        }

        newpixels = new int[h * w];

        new_index = 0;
        for(y=0;y<h;y++) {
            for(x=0;x<w;x++) {
                index = (y*w) + x;
                alpha = (p1[index] & 0xff000000) >>> 24;
                red   = (p1[index] & 0x00ff0000) >> 16;
                green = (p1[index] & 0x0000ff00) >> 8;
                blue  = (p1[index] & 0x000000ff);

                nred   = Math.abs(subfrom - red);
                ngreen = Math.abs(subfrom - green);
                nblue  = Math.abs(subfrom - blue);
                newpixels[new_index++] =
                    (alpha << 24) | (nred << 16) | (ngreen << 8) | nblue;
            }
        }
        new_width  = w;
        new_height = h;
        return newpixels;
    }
}
```

fscale.java

```java
public class fscale extends ImgFilt {
    int perc_width = 100;
    int perc_height = 100;

    public void setparameter(String str, int i) {
        switch(i) {
        case 0:
            perc_width = Integer.parseInt(str);
            break;
        case 1:
            perc_height = Integer.parseInt(str);
            break;
        }
    }

    public int[] filter(int[] p1, int w, int h) {
        int x, y;
        int old_index, new_index;
        int old_size,  new_size;

        if(p1.length != (w*h)) {
            System.out.println("scale filter: got array of wrong size");
            return null;
        }

        new_width = (int)(w * perc_width/ 100);
        new_height = (int)(h * perc_height/ 100);
        old_size = w * h;
        new_size = new_width * new_height;

        newpixels = new int[new_width * new_height];
        new_index = 0;
        for(y=0;y<new_height;y++) {
            for(x=0;x<new_width;x++) {
                old_index =  ((y*100/perc_height)*w) + (x*100/perc_width);
                try {
                    newpixels[new_index++] = p1[old_index];
                } catch (ArrayIndexOutOfBoundsException e) {
                    System.out.println("y = " + y + " x = " + x);
                }
            }
        }
        return newpixels;
    }
}
```

BasicText.java

```java
import java.awt.*;
import java.applet.Applet;
import java.net.*;
import java.io.*;

//
// BasicText is the base class applet upon which most of the
// applets in the Fundamentals chapter are based.
// Basic handles lots of generic things like drawing
// borders, frames, and underline.  Many of the basic
// parameters are gotten here.
//
public class BasicText extends Applet {
    // Parameters that apply to the entire applet
    protected int          app_borderwidth;      // Applet border width
    protected Color        app_bordercolor;      // Applet border color
    protected String       app_fr_type;          // Applet frame type
    protected int          app_fr_thick;         // Applet frame thickness
    protected Color        app_bg_color;         // Applet background color

    // Parameters specific to Text
    protected String       tx;                   // Text
    protected int          tx_xoffset;           // Text X offset
    protected int          tx_yoffset;           // Text Y offset
    protected Color        tx_color;             // Text color
    protected boolean      tx_horizcenter;       // Text horizontally centered
    protected boolean      tx_vertcenter;        // Text vertically centered
    protected Font         tx_font;              // Text font
    protected FontMetrics  tx_fontmetrics;       // Text font metrics
    protected boolean      tx_underline;         // Text underline
    protected int          tx_width;             // Text width
    protected int          tx_height;            // Text height
    protected int          tx_ascent;            // Text ascent
    protected int          tx_descent;           // Text descent
    protected int          tx_borderwidth;       // Text border width
    protected Color        tx_bordercolor;       // Text border color
    protected int          tx_bordermargin;      // Text border margin
    protected String       tx_fr_type;           // Text frame type
    protected int          tx_fr_thick;          // Text frame thickness
    protected int          tx_fr_margin;         // Text frame margin
    protected int          tx_x_coord;           // Text X Coordinate
    protected int          tx_y_coord;           // Text Y Coordinate

    public void init() {
        // Applet parameters
        app_borderwidth = GetParm.toInt(this,    "AppBorderWidth", 0);
        app_bordercolor = GetParm.toColor(this,  "AppBorderColor", Color.black);
        app_fr_type     = GetParm.toString(this, "AppFrameType", "ShadowIn");
        app_fr_thick    = GetParm.toInt(this,    "AppFrameThickness", 0);
```

fscale.java

```java
public class fscale extends ImgFilt {
    int perc_width = 100;
    int perc_height = 100;

    public void setparameter(String str, int i) {
        switch(i) {
        case 0:
            perc_width = Integer.parseInt(str);
            break;
        case 1:
            perc_height = Integer.parseInt(str);
            break;
        }
    }

    public int[] filter(int[] p1, int w, int h) {
        int x, y;
        int old_index, new_index;
        int old_size,  new_size;

        if(p1.length != (w*h)) {
            System.out.println("scale filter: got array of wrong size");
            return null;
        }

        new_width = (int)(w * perc_width/ 100);
        new_height = (int)(h * perc_height/ 100);
        old_size = w * h;
        new_size = new_width * new_height;

        newpixels = new int[new_width * new_height];
        new_index = 0;
        for(y=0;y<new_height;y++) {
            for(x=0;x<new_width;x++) {
                old_index =  ((y*100/perc_height)*w) + (x*100/perc_width);
                try {
                    newpixels[new_index++] = p1[old_index];
                } catch (ArrayIndexOutOfBoundsException e) {
                    System.out.println("y = " + y + " x = " + x);
                }
            }
        }
        return newpixels;
    }
}
```

BasicText.java

```java
import java.awt.*;
import java.applet.Applet;
import java.net.*;
import java.io.*;

//
// BasicText is the base class applet upon which most of the
// applets in the Fundamentals chapter are based.
// Basic handles lots of generic things like drawing
// borders, frames, and underline.  Many of the basic
// parameters are gotten here.
//
public class BasicText extends Applet {
    // Parameters that apply to the entire applet
    protected int       app_borderwidth;      // Applet border width
    protected Color     app_bordercolor;      // Applet border color
    protected String    app_fr_type;          // Applet frame type
    protected int       app_fr_thick;         // Applet frame thickness
    protected Color     app_bg_color;         // Applet background color

    // Parameters specific to Text
    protected String    tx;                   // Text
    protected int       tx_xoffset;           // Text X offset
    protected int       tx_yoffset;           // Text Y offset
    protected Color     tx_color;             // Text color
    protected boolean   tx_horizcenter;       // Text horizontally centered
    protected boolean   tx_vertcenter;        // Text vertically centered
    protected Font      tx_font;              // Text font
    protected FontMetrics tx_fontmetrics;     // Text font metrics
    protected boolean   tx_underline;         // Text underline
    protected int       tx_width;             // Text width
    protected int       tx_height;            // Text height
    protected int       tx_ascent;            // Text ascent
    protected int       tx_descent;           // Text descent
    protected int       tx_borderwidth;       // Text border width
    protected Color     tx_bordercolor;       // Text border color
    protected int       tx_bordermargin;      // Text border margin
    protected String    tx_fr_type;           // Text frame type
    protected int       tx_fr_thick;          // Text frame thickness
    protected int       tx_fr_margin;         // Text frame margin
    protected int       tx_x_coord;           // Text X Coordinate
    protected int       tx_y_coord;           // Text Y Coordinate

    public void init() {
        // Applet parameters
        app_borderwidth = GetParm.toInt(this,    "AppBorderWidth", 0);
        app_bordercolor = GetParm.toColor(this,  "AppBorderColor", Color.black);
        app_fr_type     = GetParm.toString(this, "AppFrameType", "ShadowIn");
        app_fr_thick    = GetParm.toInt(this,    "AppFrameThickness", 0);
```

```
        app_bg_color    = GetParm.toColor(this,   "AppBGColor", null);

        // Text parameters
        tx              = GetParm.toString(this, "Text", "");
        tx_xoffset      = GetParm.toInt(this,    "TxXOffset", 0);
        tx_yoffset      = GetParm.toInt(this,    "TxYOffset", -1);
        tx_color        = GetParm.toColor(this,  "TxColor", null);
        tx_horizcenter  = GetParm.toBoolean(this, "TxHorizCenter", false);
        tx_vertcenter   = GetParm.toBoolean(this, "TxVertCenter", false);
        tx_font         = GetParm.toFont(this,   "TxFont",
                                                 "TxStyle",
                                                 "TxPointSize");
        tx_underline    = GetParm.toBoolean(this, "TxUnderLine", false);
        tx_borderwidth  = GetParm.toInt(this,    "TxBorderWidth", 0);
        tx_bordercolor  = GetParm.toColor(this,  "TxBorderColor", Color.black);
        tx_bordermargin = GetParm.toInt(this,    "TxBorderMargin", 0);
        tx_fr_thick     = GetParm.toInt(this,    "TxFrameThickness", 0);
        tx_fr_type      = GetParm.toString(this, "TxFrameType", "ShadowIn");
        tx_fr_margin    = GetParm.toInt(this,    "TxFrameMargin", 0);

        setFont(tx_font);
        tx_fontmetrics = getFontMetrics(tx_font);

        tx_width  = tx_fontmetrics.stringWidth(tx);
        tx_height = tx_fontmetrics.getHeight();
        tx_ascent = tx_fontmetrics.getMaxAscent();
        tx_descent = tx_fontmetrics.getDescent();

        // Set the background and foreground colors, if specified
        if(app_bg_color != null)
            setBackground(app_bg_color);
        else
            app_bg_color = getBackground();
        if(tx_color != null)
            setForeground(tx_color);
        else
            tx_color = getForeground();
    }


//
// Overwrite the default update method
// This may not be necessary for this case
// but it certainly doesn't hurt
//
public void update(Graphics g) {
    paint(g);
}


//
// Our paint method handles several tasks:
//     Calculates the x and y coordinates base on params
//     Draws the applet frame
//     Draws the applet border
```

```
//      Draws the text frame
//      Draws the text border
//      Draws the underline
//      Draws the text
//
public void paint(Graphics g) {
    // We never know when the size might change so if horizcenter
    // is true then recalculate the x_coord every time
    tx_x_coord = calcULXcoord(tx_horizcenter, size().width, tx_width,
                              tx_xoffset);
    tx_y_coord = calcLLYcoord(tx_vertcenter, size().height, tx_height,
                              tx_descent, tx_yoffset);

    // Draw frame for applet
    drawFrame(g, 0, 0, size().width, size().height,
                       app_fr_type, app_fr_thick, 0);
    // Draw border for applet
    drawBorder(g, 0, 0, size().width, size().height,
                       app_borderwidth, 0, app_bordercolor);
    // Draw frame for text
    drawFrame(g, tx_x_coord, tx_y_coord-tx_ascent,
                       tx_width, tx_height,
                       tx_fr_type, tx_fr_thick, tx_fr_margin);
    // Draw border for text
    drawBorder(g, tx_x_coord, tx_y_coord-tx_ascent,
                       tx_width, tx_height,
                       tx_borderwidth, tx_bordermargin, tx_bordercolor);
    drawUnderline(g, tx_x_coord, tx_y_coord+Math.max(1, (tx_descent/4)),
                       tx_width, tx_color);
    g.setColor(tx_color);
    g.drawString(tx, tx_x_coord, tx_y_coord);
}


//
// Calculate the upper left corner position when centering
// an item that's drawn in relation to its upper left corner
// such as images
//
protected int calcULCenter(int panelsize, int objectsize) {
    return ((panelsize / 2) - (objectsize / 2));
}


//
// Calculate the lower left corner position when centering
// an item that's drawn in relation to its lower left corner
// such as text
//
protected int calcLLCenter(int panelsize, int objectsize) {
    return ((panelsize / 2) + (objectsize / 2));
}


//
// A general purpose text drawing method
```

```
// This method is used by the Img class
//
protected void drawText(Graphics g, String txt, int x, int y,
                                      Color c, Font f) {
    if(txt != null) {
        g.setColor(c);
        g.setFont(f);
        g.drawString(txt, x, y);
    }

}


//
// The drawBorder method draws a border at the
// specified x and y position
//
protected void drawBorder(Graphics g,
                    int x,
                    int y,
                    int w,
                    int h,
                    int borderwidth,
                    int margin,
                    Color c) {
    if(borderwidth > 0) {
        g.setColor(c);
        for(int i=0;i<borderwidth;i++) {
            g.drawRect(x-margin+i,
                    y-margin+i,
                    w+(margin*2)-(i*2)-1,
                    h+(margin*2)-(i*2)-1);
        }
    }
}

void drawTopLine(Graphics g,
            int x, int y, int w, int h, int i, int margin) {
    g.drawLine(x-margin+i, y-margin+i, x+w+margin-i-1, y-margin+i);
}

void drawBottomLine(Graphics g,
            int x, int y, int w, int h, int i, int margin) {
    g.drawLine(x-margin+i, y+h+margin-i-1, x+w+margin-i-1, y+h+margin-i-1);
}

void drawLeftLine(Graphics g,
            int x, int y, int w, int h, int i, int margin) {
    g.drawLine(x-margin+i, y-margin+i, x-margin+i, y+h+margin-i-1);
}

void drawRightLine(Graphics g,
            int x, int y, int w, int h, int i, int margin) {
    g.drawLine(x+w+margin-i-1, y-margin+i, x+w+margin-i-1, y+h+margin-i-1);
```

```
    }


    //
    // The drawFrame draws a frame at the specified x and y position
    // A frame can be one of the following four types: ShadowIn,
    // ShadowOut, ShadowEtchedIn, ShadowEtchedOut
    //
    protected void drawFrame(Graphics g,        // Graphics to draw to
                             int x,             // X upper left position
                             int y,             // Y upper left position
                             int w,             // width
                             int h,             // height
                             String type,       // Type of frame
                             int thickness,     // thickness of frame
                             int margin) {      // Margin around object
        int i;
        if(thickness == 0)
            return;
        Color darker = AdjColor.darkenit(app_bg_color, .50);
        Color slightlydarker = AdjColor.darkenit(app_bg_color, .10);
        Color brighter = AdjColor.brightenit(app_bg_color, .50);

        if(thickness > 0) {
            if(type.equalsIgnoreCase("shadowout")) {
                for(i=0;i<thickness;i++) {
                    g.setColor(brighter);
                    // TOP
                    drawTopLine(g, x, y, w, h, i, margin);
                    // LEFT
                    drawLeftLine(g, x, y, w, h, i, margin);

                    g.setColor(darker);
                    // BOTTOM
                    drawBottomLine(g, x, y, w, h, i, margin);
                    // RIGHT
                    drawRightLine(g, x, y, w, h, i, margin);
                }
            } else if(type.equalsIgnoreCase("shadowetchedin")) {
                for(i=0;i<thickness;i++) {
                    if(i == 0)
                        g.setColor(darker);
                    else if (i == thickness-1)
                        g.setColor(brighter);
                    else
                        g.setColor(slightlydarker);
                    // TOP
                    drawTopLine(g, x, y, w, h, i, margin);
                    // LEFT
                    drawLeftLine(g, x, y, w, h, i, margin);

                    if(i == 0)
                        g.setColor(brighter);
```

```
            else if (i == thickness-1)
                g.setColor(darker);
            else
                g.setColor(slightlydarker);
            // BOTTOM
            drawBottomLine(g, x, y, w, h, i, margin);
            // RIGHT
            drawRightLine(g, x, y, w, h, i, margin);
        }

    } else if(type.equalsIgnoreCase("shadowetchedout")) {
        for(i=0;i<thickness;i++) {
            if(i == 0)
                g.setColor(brighter);
            else if (i == thickness-1)
                g.setColor(darker);
            else
                g.setColor(app_bg_color);
            // TOP
            drawTopLine(g, x, y, w, h, i, margin);
            // LEFT
            drawLeftLine(g, x, y, w, h, i, margin);

            if(i == 0)
                g.setColor(darker);
            else if (i == thickness-1)
                g.setColor(brighter);
            else
                g.setColor(app_bg_color);
            // BOTTOM
            drawBottomLine(g, x, y, w, h, i, margin);
            // RIGHT
            drawRightLine(g, x, y, w, h, i, margin);
        }

    } else {    // Default to "shadowin"
        for(i=0;i<thickness;i++) {
            g.setColor(darker);
            // TOP
            drawTopLine(g, x, y, w, h, i, margin);
            // LEFT
            drawLeftLine(g, x, y, w, h, i, margin);

            g.setColor(brighter);
            // BOTTOM
            drawBottomLine(g, x, y, w, h, i, margin);
            // RIGHT
            drawRightLine(g, x, y, w, h, i, margin);
        }
    }
  }
}
```

```
//
// The drawUnderline method draws an underline
// The underline is actually a filled rectangle
// whose size is based on the width of a pipe
// character from the same font.  It works!
//
protected void drawUnderline(Graphics g,
                             int x,
                             int y,
                             int w,
                             Color c) {
    if(tx_underline == true) {
        int pipewidth = tx_fontmetrics.charWidth('|');;
        g.setColor(c);
        g.fillRect(x, y, w, Math.max(1, pipewidth/4));
    } .
}


//
// Calculate the upper left X coordinate based
// on parameters such as horizcenter and xoffset
//
protected int calcULXcoord(boolean hcent, int appletwidth,
                           int objectwidth, int xoffset) {
    int x;

    // Horizontal (x coordinate) Position
    if(hcent)
        x = calcULCenter(appletwidth, objectwidth);
    else if (xoffset == -1)
        x = 0;
    else
        x = xoffset;

    return x;
}


//
// Calculate the upper left Y coordinate based
// on parameters such as vertcenter and yoffset
//
protected int calcULYcoord(boolean hcent, int appletheight,
                           int objectheight, int yoffset) {
    int y;

    // Vertical (y coordinate) Position
    if(hcent)
        y = calcULCenter(appletheight, objectheight);
    else if (yoffset == -1)
        y = 0;
    else
        y = yoffset;
```

```
        return y;
    }

    //
    // Calculate the lower left Y coordinate based
    // on parameters such as vertcenter and yoffset
    //
    protected int calcLLYcoord(boolean hcent, int appletheight,
                    int objectheight, int objectdescent, int yoffset) {
        int y;

        // Vertical (y coordinate) Position
        if(hcent)
            y = calcLLCenter(appletheight, objectheight) - objectdescent;
        else if (yoffset == -1)
            y = objectheight - objectdescent;
        else
            y = yoffset;

        return y;
    }
}
```

AudioText.java

```java
import java.awt.*;
import java.applet.*;
import java.net.*;
import java.io.*;


//
// AudioText displays a string and also plays
// an audio file when the pointer enters the text.
// If the pointer moves out of the text before the
// audio has finished playing then the audio is terminated.
//
public class AudioText extends BasicText {
    protected AudioClip   tx_clip;           // The Audio Clip
    protected String      tx_audio_file;     // The name of the audio file
    protected boolean     tx_playing;        // Is the clip currently playing

    public void init() {
        super.init();
        tx_audio_file = GetParm.toString(this, "TxAudio", null);

        // If the user specified an non-existent or invalid
        // file, then print error message and exit
        if(tx_audio_file != null) {
            tx_clip = getAudioClip(getDocumentBase(), tx_audio_file);
            if(tx_clip == null) {
                System.out.println(
                    "Error getting " + tx_audio_file + ". " +
                    "Make sure the file exists and is an audio file");
            }
        }
    }


    //
    // Check the x and y coordinates to see if we're actually
    // inside the boundaries of the text
    //
    public boolean mouseMove(Event evt, int x, int y) {
        if(x > tx_x_coord && x < tx_x_coord + tx_width &&
           y < tx_y_coord+tx_descent && y > tx_y_coord - tx_ascent) {
            if(!tx_playing) {
                tx_playing = true;
                if(tx_clip != null)
                    tx_clip.play();
            } // else it's already playing, leave it alone
        } else {
            // Since we don't get any kind of notification when the audio
            // clip has terminated (due to playing to completion) we set
            // playing to false everytime we move out of the boundaries
            // of the string
```

```
            tx_playing = false;
            if(tx_clip != null) {
                tx_clip.stop();
            }
        }
        return true;
    }


    //
    // Just to be sure, when we exit the applet, stop the clip
    // It should already be stopped
    //
    public boolean mouseExit(Event evt, int x, int y) {
        tx_playing = false;
        if(tx_clip != null)
            tx_clip.stop();
        return true;
    }
}
```

OffScr.java

```java
import java.awt.*;
import java.awt.image.*;
import java.applet.*;
import java.net.*;
import java.io.*;

//
// BasicTxt is the base class applet upon which most of the
// applets in the Fundamentals chapter are based.
// Basic handles lots of generic things like drawing
// borders, frames, and underline.  Many of the basic
// parameters are gotten here.
//
public class OffScr extends Applet {
    // Parameters that apply to the entire applet
    protected int        app_borderwidth;       // Applet border width
    protected Color      app_bordercolor;       // Applet border color
    protected String     app_fr_type;           // Applet frame type
    protected int        app_fr_thick;          // Applet frame thickness
    protected Color      app_bg_color;          // Applet background color

    // Parameters specific to Text
    protected String      tx;                   // Text
    protected int         tx_xoffset;           // Text X offset
    protected int         tx_yoffset;           // Text Y offset
    protected Color       tx_color;             // Text color
    protected Color       tx_bg_color;          // Text background color
    protected boolean     tx_horizcenter;       // Text horizontally centered
    protected boolean     tx_vertcenter;        // Text vertically centered
    protected Font        tx_font;              // Text font
    protected FontMetrics tx_fontmetrics;       // Text font metrics
    protected boolean     tx_underline;         // Text underline
    protected int         tx_width;             // Text width
    protected int         tx_height;            // Text height
    protected int         tx_ascent;            // Text ascent
    protected int         tx_descent;           // Text descent
    protected int         tx_borderwidth;       // Text border width
    protected Color       tx_bordercolor;       // Text border color
    protected int         tx_bordermargin;      // Text border margin
    protected String      tx_fr_type;           // Text frame type
    protected int         tx_fr_thick;          // Text frame thickness
    protected int         tx_fr_margin;         // Text frame margin
    protected int         tx_x_coord;           // Text X Coordinate
    protected int         tx_y_coord;           // Text Y Coordinate

    // Parameters specific to the Image
    protected String      img_file;             // Image file name
    protected ImgGetr     img_gettr;            // The Image Getter class
    protected boolean     img_wait_load;        // Load flag
```

```
protected int           img_width;          // Image width
protected int           img_height;         // Image height
protected int           img_xoffset;        // Image X offset
protected int           img_yoffset;        // Image Y offset
protected int           img_y_coord;        // Image X coordinate
protected int           img_x_coord;        // Image Y coordinate
protected boolean       img_horizcenter;    // Image horizontally centered
protected boolean       img_vertcenter;     // Image vertically centered
protected int           img_borderwidth;    // Image border width
protected Color         img_bordercolor;    // Image border color
protected int           img_bordermargin;   // Image border margin
protected String        img_fr_type;        // Image frame type
protected int           img_fr_thick;       // Image frame thickness
protected int           img_fr_margin;      // Image frame margin
Font                    loading_font;

// Parameters specific to Audio
protected AudioClip     tx_clip;            // The Text Audio Clip
protected String        tx_audio_file;      // The Text audio file
protected boolean       tx_playing;         // Text clip currently playing
protected AudioClip     img_clip;           // The Image Audio Clip
protected String        img_audio_file;     // The Image audio file
protected boolean       img_playing;        // Image clip currently playing

// Parameters specific to URLs
protected URL           tx_url;             // The Text URL
protected URL           img_url;            // The Image URL

protected boolean       tile;               // Tiled?
protected Image         bgimage;            // The background image
protected String        bgimage_file;       // Name of the background image
protected ImgGetr       ig;                 // The Image Getter class
protected int           bgimage_width;      // Background image width
protected int           bgimage_height;     // Background image height
protected int           bgimageXoffset;     // BG image X ofset
protected int           bgimageYoffset;     // BG image Y ofset
protected Image         tiled_bgimage;      // Tile BG?
protected int           app_width;          // App width
protected int           app_height;         // App height
protected Graphics      bg_g;               // Background Graphics

// Parameters specific to Image Maps
protected int           num_maps;           // Number of Maps
protected int           map_x1[];           // X1 coord for map
protected int           map_y1[];           // Y1 coord for map
protected int           map_x2[];           // X2 coord for map
protected int           map_y2[];           // Y2 coord for map
protected URL           map_url[];          // URLs for maps
protected boolean       testmode;           // Test mode

// Parameters specific to OffScreen images
protected  Image        tx_osi;             // Text Off-Screen Image
protected  Graphics     tx_g;               // Graphics of tx_osi
```

```
protected    int            tx_pixels[];      // The text image
protected    String         tx_filter_str;    // Text filters in string format
protected    Image          img_osi;          // Image Off-Screen Image
protected    Graphics       img_g;            // Graphics of img_osi
protected    int            img_pixels[];     // The text image
protected    String         img_filter_str;   // Img filters in string format
boolean                     retval;           // Retval from grabPixels;


public void init() {
    int i;

    // ======== Applet ===========
    app_borderwidth = GetParm.toInt(this,      "AppBorderWidth", 0);
    app_bordercolor = GetParm.toColor(this,    "AppBorderColor", Color.black);
    app_fr_type     = GetParm.toString(this,   "AppFrameType", "ShadowIn");
    app_fr_thick    = GetParm.toInt(this,      "AppFrameThickness", 0);
    app_bg_color    = GetParm.toColor(this,    "AppBGColor", null);

    // ======== Text ===========
    tx              = GetParm.toString(this, "Text", null);
    tx_xoffset      = GetParm.toInt(this,      "TxXOffset", 0);
    tx_yoffset      = GetParm.toInt(this,      "TxYOffset", -1);
    tx_color        = GetParm.toColor(this,    "TxColor", null);
    tx_bg_color     = GetParm.toColor(this,    "TxBGColor", null);
    tx_horizcenter  = GetParm.toBoolean(this,  "TxHorizCenter", false);
    tx_vertcenter   = GetParm.toBoolean(this,  "TxVertCenter",  false);
    tx_font         = GetParm.toFont(this,     "TxFont",
                                               "TxStyle",
                                               "TxPointSize");
    tx_underline    = GetParm.toBoolean(this,  "TxUnderLine", false);
    tx_borderwidth  = GetParm.toInt(this,      "TxBorderWidth", 0);
    tx_bordercolor  = GetParm.toColor(this,    "TxBorderColor", Color.black);
    tx_bordermargin = GetParm.toInt(this,      "TxBorderMargin", 0);
    tx_fr_thick     = GetParm.toInt(this,      "TxFrameThickness", 0);
    tx_fr_type      = GetParm.toString(this,   "TxFrameType", "ShadowIn");
    tx_fr_margin    = GetParm.toInt(this,      "TxFrameMargin", 0);

    setFont(tx_font);
    tx_fontmetrics = getFontMetrics(tx_font);

    // Set the background and foreground colors, if specified
    // We must set these colors here before using them
    // in the next block of code
    if(app_bg_color != null)
        setBackground(app_bg_color);
    else
        app_bg_color = getBackground();
    if(tx_color != null)
        setForeground(tx_color);
    else
        tx_color = getForeground();
```

```
if(tx != null) {
    // This is somewhat wasteful to create this
    // because it may not be needed if the user
    // has specified TxFilter.  However, if
    // not then we must generate the pixels
    ftext ps = new ftext();
    ps.setText(tx);
    ps.setApplet(this);
    ps.setFont(tx_font);
    ps.setBackground(app_bg_color);
    ps.setForeground(tx_color);
    tx_pixels = ps.filter(null, 0, 0);
    tx_width = ps.getWidth();
    tx_height = ps.getHeight();

    tx_width   = tx_fontmetrics.stringWidth(tx);
    tx_height  = tx_fontmetrics.getHeight();
    tx_ascent  = tx_fontmetrics.getMaxAscent();
    tx_descent = tx_fontmetrics.getDescent();
}

// ======== Image ===========
img_file      = GetParm.toString(this,  "Image", null);
img_wait_load = GetParm.toBoolean(this, "ImgLoadWait", false);
img_xoffset   = GetParm.toInt(this,     "ImgXOffset", 0);
img_yoffset   = GetParm.toInt(this,     "ImgYOffset", -1);
img_horizcenter = GetParm.toBoolean(this, "ImgHorizCenter", false);
img_vertcenter = GetParm.toBoolean(this, "ImgVertCenter",  false);
img_borderwidth = GetParm.toInt(this,   "ImgBorderWidth", 0);
img_bordercolor = GetParm.toColor(this,  "ImgBorderColor",
                                         Color.black);
img_bordermargin= GetParm.toInt(this,   "ImgBorderMargin", 0);
img_fr_thick  = GetParm.toInt(this,     "ImgFrameThickness", 0);
img_fr_type   = GetParm.toString(this,  "ImgFrameType", "ShadowIn");
img_fr_margin = GetParm.toInt(this,     "ImgFrameMargin", 0);


if(img_file != null) {
    img_gettr     = new ImgGetr(this);
    if(img_wait_load)
        repaint();
    img_osi = img_gettr.process(getDocumentBase(), img_file, false);
    img_gettr.prepareImage(img_osi, this);
    img_width = img_gettr.getWidth(img_osi, this);
    img_height = img_gettr.getHeight(img_osi, this);
    img_gettr.loadImageAndWait(img_osi, this);

    img_pixels = img_gettr.getPixels(img_osi, this);
}

// ======== Audio ===========
tx_audio_file = GetParm.toString(this, "TxAudio", null);
img_audio_file = GetParm.toString(this, "ImgAudio", null);
```

```java
// If the user specified an non-existent or invalid
// file, then print error message and exit
if(tx_audio_file != null) {
    tx_clip = getAudioClip(getDocumentBase(), tx_audio_file);
    if(tx_clip == null) {
        System.out.println(
            "Error getting " + tx_audio_file + ". " +
            "Make sure the file exists and is an audio file");
    }
}
// If the user specified an non-existent or invalid
// file, then print error message and exit
if(img_audio_file != null) {
    img_clip = getAudioClip(getDocumentBase(), img_audio_file);
    if(img_clip == null) {
        System.out.println(
            "Error getting " + img_audio_file + ". " +
            "Make sure the file exists and is an audio file");
    }
}


// ======== URL ===========
tx_url     = GetParm.toURL(this, "TxURL");
img_url    = GetParm.toURL(this, "ImgURL");

// ======== BG Image ===========
tile          = GetParm.toBoolean(this, "AppTile",     false);
bgimage_file  = GetParm.toString(this,  "AppBGImage",  null);
bgimageXoffset = GetParm.toInt(this,    "AppBGImageXOffset", 0);
bgimageYoffset = GetParm.toInt(this,    "AppBGImageYOffset", 0);

if(bgimage_file != null) {
    ig = new ImgGetr(this);
    bgimage = ig.process(getDocumentBase(), bgimage_file, false);
    ig.prepareImage(bgimage, this);
    bgimage_width = ig.getWidth(bgimage, this);
    bgimage_height = ig.getHeight(bgimage, this);
}


// ========== Image Maps ===========
testmode = GetParm.toBoolean(this, "TestMode",  false);
num_maps = GetParm.toInt(this,     "AppNumMaps", 0);

if(num_maps > 0) {
    map_x1  = new int[num_maps];
    map_y1  = new int[num_maps];
    map_x2  = new int[num_maps];
    map_y2  = new int[num_maps];
    map_url = new URL[num_maps];
}

for(i=0;i<num_maps;i++) {
```

```
            map_x1[i]  = GetParm.toInt(this, "Map"+(i+1)+"_X1",  0);
            map_y1[i]  = GetParm.toInt(this, "Map"+(i+1)+"_Y1",  0);
            map_x2[i]  = GetParm.toInt(this, "Map"+(i+1)+"_X2",  0);
            map_y2[i]  = GetParm.toInt(this, "Map"+(i+1)+"_Y2",  0);
            map_url[i] = GetParm.toURL(this, "URL"+(i+1));
        }

        // ======== Filters ===========
        tx_filter_str  = GetParm.toString(this, "TxFilter",  null);
        img_filter_str = GetParm.toString(this, "ImgFilter", null);
    }


    //
    // Overwrite the default update method
    // This may not be necessary for this case
    // but it certainly doesn't hurt
    //
    public void update(Graphics g) {
        paint(g);
    }


    //
    // Our paint method handles several tasks:
    //     Calculates the x and y coordinates base on params
    //     Draws the applet frame
    //     Draws the applet border
    //     Draws the text frame
    //     Draws the text border
    //     Draws the underline
    //     Draws the text
    //
    public void paint(Graphics g) {
        tilebackground(g);
        if(img_osi != null) {

            img_x_coord = calcULXcoord(img_horizcenter, size().width,
                                        img_width, img_xoffset);
            img_y_coord = calcULYcoord(img_vertcenter, size().height,
                                        img_height, img_yoffset);

            g.drawImage(img_osi, img_x_coord, img_y_coord, this);
            drawFrame(g, img_x_coord, img_y_coord, img_width,
                            img_height, img_fr_type,
                            img_fr_thick, img_fr_margin);
            drawBorder(g, img_x_coord, img_y_coord, img_width,
                            img_height, img_borderwidth,
                            img_bordermargin, img_bordercolor);
        }
        // We never know when the size might change so if horizcenter
        // is true then recalculate the x_coord every time
        if(tx_osi != null) {
            tx_x_coord = calcULXcoord(tx_horizcenter, size().width,
                            tx_width, tx_xoffset);
```

```
        tx_y_coord = calcULYcoord(tx_vertcenter, size().height,
                        tx_height, tx_yoffset);

        // Draw frame for applet
        drawFrame(g, 0, 0, size().width, size().height,
                        app_fr_type, app_fr_thick, 0);
        // Draw border for applet
        drawBorder(g, 0, 0, size().width, size().height,
                        app_borderwidth, 0, app_bordercolor);

        // Draw the text
        g.drawImage(tx_osi, tx_x_coord, tx_y_coord, this);

        // Draw frame for text
        drawFrame(g, tx_x_coord, tx_y_coord,
                        tx_width, tx_height,
                        tx_fr_type, tx_fr_thick, tx_fr_margin);


        // Draw border for text
        drawBorder(g, tx_x_coord, tx_y_coord,
                        tx_width, tx_height,
                        tx_borderwidth, tx_bordermargin,
                        tx_bordercolor);
    }
}


//
// If the user clicks the mouse then load the URL
// We check the text position first, so if there is
// overlapping text and image then the text URL will
// be loaded, not the imgae URL
//
public boolean mouseDown(Event evt, int x, int y) {
    int i;

    // Handle the image maps first
    for(i=0;i<num_maps;i++) {
        if(x > map_x1[i] && x < map_x2[i] &&
           y > map_y1[i] && y < map_y2[i]) {
            if(map_url[i] != null) {
                if(testmode) {
                    getAppletContext().showStatus("Loading URL: " +
                            map_url[i].toString());
                    System.out.println("Loading URL: " +
                            map_url[i].toString());
                } else
                    getAppletContext().showDocument(map_url[i]);
                return true;
            }
        }
    }
```

```java
        // Handle the text next (Text takes precedence over images)
        if(x > tx_x_coord && x < tx_x_coord + tx_width &&
           y > tx_y_coord && y < tx_y_coord + tx_height) {
            if(tx_url != null) {
                getAppletContext().showDocument(tx_url);
                System.out.println("loading " + tx_url.toString());
                return true;
            }
        }

        // Handle the image last
        if(x > img_x_coord && x < img_x_coord + img_width &&
           y > img_y_coord && y < img_y_coord + img_height) {
            if(img_url != null) {
                getAppletContext().showDocument(img_url);
                System.out.println("loading " + img_url.toString());
                return true;
            }
        }
        return true;
    }


    //
    // Check the x and y coordinates to see if we're actually
    // inside the boundaries of the text or image or both
    //
    public boolean mouseMove(Event evt, int x, int y) {
        boolean tx_status_shown = false;
        boolean img_status_shown = false;
        int i;

        if(testmode) {
            getAppletContext().showStatus("X: " + x + " Y: " + y);
            return true;
        }

        //
        // If a image map url was found (hence tx_status_shown == true)
        // then return and don't bother to call the other mouseMove
        // stuff would simply display the url for the text or image.
        //
        if(tx_status_shown == true) {
            return true;
        }

        // ========== AUDIO =============
        // Process the image first
        if(x > img_x_coord && x < img_x_coord + img_width &&
           y > img_y_coord && y < img_y_coord + img_height) {
            if(!img_playing) {
                img_playing = true;
                if(img_clip != null)
                    img_clip.play();
```

```
            } // else it's already playing, leave it alone
        } else {
            // Since we don't get any kind of notification when the audio
            // clip has terminated (due to playing to completion) we set
            // playing to false everytime we move out of the boundaries
            // of the string
            img_playing = false;
            if(img_clip != null) {
                img_clip.stop();
            }
        }


        // Process the text last
        if(x > tx_x_coord && x < tx_x_coord + tx_width &&
           y > tx_y_coord && y < tx_y_coord + tx_height) {
            if(!tx_playing) {
                tx_playing = true;
                if(tx_clip != null)
                    tx_clip.play();
            } // else it's already playing, leave it alone
        } else {
            // Since we don't get any kind of notification when the audio
            // clip has terminated (due to playing to completion) we set
            // playing to false everytime we move out of the boundaries
            // of the string
            tx_playing = false;
            if(tx_clip != null) {
                tx_clip.stop();
            }
        }


        // ========== IMAGE MAPS ==============
        for(i=0;i<num_maps;i++) {
            if(x > map_x1[i] && x < map_x2[i] &&
               y > map_y1[i] && y < map_y2[i]) {
                if(map_url[i] != null) {
                    getAppletContext().showStatus(map_url[i].toString());
                    tx_status_shown = true;
                }
            }
        }


        // ========== URLs ==============
        // Handle the text first
        if(x > tx_x_coord && x < tx_x_coord + tx_width &&
           y > tx_y_coord && y < tx_y_coord + tx_height) {
            if(tx_url != null) {
                getAppletContext().showStatus(tx_url.toString());
                tx_status_shown = true;
            }
        }


        // Handle the image last
```

```
        // If a Text URL is being displayed then don't
        // display the image URL
        if(x > img_x_coord && x < img_x_coord + img_width &&
           y > img_y_coord && y < img_y_coord + img_height) {
            if(img_url != null && tx_status_shown == false) {
                getAppletContext().showStatus(img_url.toString());
                img_status_shown = true;
            }
        }
        // If we are not over either text or image that has
        // a corresponding URL then clear the status line
        if(tx_status_shown == false && img_status_shown == false)
            getAppletContext().showStatus(null);
        return true;
    }

    //
    // Just to be sure, when we exit the applet, stop the clips
    // It should already be stopped
    //
    public boolean mouseExit(Event evt, int x, int y) {
        // Just to be sure
        tx_playing = false;
        if(tx_clip != null)
            tx_clip.stop();
        img_playing = false;
        if(img_clip != null)
            img_clip.stop();
        getAppletContext().showStatus(null);
        return true;
    }

    //
    // Calculate the upper left corner position when centering
    // an item that's drawn in relation to its upper left corner
    // such as images
    //
    protected int calcULCenter(int panelsize, int objectsize) {
        return ((panelsize / 2) - (objectsize / 2));
    }

    //
    // Calculate the lower left corner position when centering
    // an item that's drawn in relation to its lower left corner
    // such as text
    //
    protected int calcLLCenter(int panelsize, int objectsize) {
        return ((panelsize / 2) + (objectsize / 2));
    }

    //
    // A general purpose text drawing method
    // This method is used by the Img class
    //
```

```java
protected void drawText(Graphics g, String txt, int x, int y,
                                        Color c, Font f) {
    if(txt != null) {
        g.setColor(c);
        g.setFont(f);
        g.drawString(txt, x, y);
    }

}


//
// The drawBorder method draws a border at the
// specified x and y position
//
protected void drawBorder(Graphics g,
                          int x,
                          int y,
                          int w,
                          int h,
                          int borderwidth,
                          int margin,
                          Color c) {
    if(borderwidth > 0) {
        g.setColor(c);
        for(int i=0;i<borderwidth;i++) {
            g.drawRect(x-margin+i,
                       y-margin+i,
                       w+(margin*2)-(i*2)-1,
                       h+(margin*2)-(i*2)-1);
        }
    }
}

void drawTopLine(Graphics g,
            int x, int y, int w, int h, int i, int margin) {
    g.drawLine(x-margin+i, y-margin+i, x+w+margin-i-1, y-margin+i);
}

void drawBottomLine(Graphics g,
            int x, int y, int w, int h, int i, int margin) {
    g.drawLine(x-margin+i, y+h+margin-i-1, x+w+margin-i-1, y+h+margin-i-1);
}

void drawLeftLine(Graphics g,
            int x, int y, int w, int h, int i, int margin) {
    g.drawLine(x-margin+i, y-margin+i, x-margin+i, y+h+margin-i-1);
}

void drawRightLine(Graphics g,
            int x, int y, int w, int h, int i, int margin) {
    g.drawLine(x+w+margin-i-1, y-margin+i, x+w+margin-i-1, y+h+margin-i-1);
}
```

```
//
// The drawFrame draws a frame at the specified x and y position
// A frame can be one of the following four types: ShadowIn,
// ShadowOut, ShadowEtchedIn, ShadowEtchedOut
//
protected void drawFrame(Graphics g,      // Graphics to draw to
                         int x,           // X upper left position
                         int y,           // Y upper left position
                         int w,           // width
                         int h,           // height
                         String type,     // Type of frame
                         int thickness,   // thickness of frame
                         int margin) {    // Margin around object
    int i;
    if(thickness == 0)
        return;
    Color darker = AdjColor.darkenit(app_bg_color, .50);
    Color slightlydarker = AdjColor.darkenit(app_bg_color, .10);
    Color brighter = AdjColor.brightenit(app_bg_color, .50);

    if(thickness > 0) {
        if(type.equalsIgnoreCase("shadowout")) {
            for(i=0;i<thickness;i++) {
                g.setColor(brighter);
                // TOP
                drawTopLine(g, x, y, w, h, i, margin);
                // LEFT
                drawLeftLine(g, x, y, w, h, i, margin);

                g.setColor(darker);
                // BOTTOM
                drawBottomLine(g, x, y, w, h, i, margin);
                // RIGHT
                drawRightLine(g, x, y, w, h, i, margin);
            }
        } else if(type.equalsIgnoreCase("shadowetchedin")) {
            for(i=0;i<thickness;i++) {
                if(i == 0)
                    g.setColor(darker);
                else if (i == thickness-1)
                    g.setColor(brighter);
                else
                    g.setColor(slightlydarker);
                // TOP
                drawTopLine(g, x, y, w, h, i, margin);
                // LEFT
                drawLeftLine(g, x, y, w, h, i, margin);

                if(i == 0)
                    g.setColor(brighter);
                else if (i == thickness-1)
                    g.setColor(darker);
                else
```

```
                    g.setColor(slightlydarker);
                // BOTTOM
                drawBottomLine(g, x, y, w, h, i, margin);
                // RIGHT
                drawRightLine(g, x, y, w, h, i, margin);
            }

        } else if(type.equalsIgnoreCase("shadowetchedout")) {
            for(i=0;i<thickness;i++) {
                if(i == 0)
                    g.setColor(brighter);
                else if (i == thickness-1)
                    g.setColor(darker);
                else
                    g.setColor(app_bg_color);
                // TOP
                drawTopLine(g, x, y, w, h, i, margin);
                // LEFT
                drawLeftLine(g, x, y, w, h, i, margin);

                if(i == 0)
                    g.setColor(darker);
                else if (i == thickness-1)
                    g.setColor(brighter);
                else
                    g.setColor(app_bg_color);
                // BOTTOM
                drawBottomLine(g, x, y, w, h, i, margin);
                // RIGHT
                drawRightLine(g, x, y, w, h, i, margin);
            }

        } else {     // Default to "shadowin"
            for(i=0;i<thickness;i++) {
                g.setColor(darker);
                // TOP
                drawTopLine(g, x, y, w, h, i, margin);
                // LEFT
                drawLeftLine(g, x, y, w, h, i, margin);

                g.setColor(brighter);
                // BOTTOM
                drawBottomLine(g, x, y, w, h, i, margin);
                // RIGHT
                drawRightLine(g, x, y, w, h, i, margin);
            }
        }
    }
}


//
// The drawUnderline method draws an underline
// The underline is actually a filled rectangle
```

```
// whose size is based on the width of a pipe
// character from the same font.  It works!
//
protected void drawUnderline(Graphics g,
                             int x,
                             int y,
                             int w,
                             Color c) {
    if(tx_underline == true) {
        int pipewidth = tx_fontmetrics.charWidth('|');;
        g.setColor(c);
        g.fillRect(x, y, w, Math.max(1, pipewidth/4));
    }
}


//
// Calculate the upper left X coordinate based
// on parameters such as horizcenter and xoffset
//
protected int calcULXcoord(boolean hcent, int appletwidth,
                           int objectwidth, int xoffset) {
    int x;

    // Horizontal (x coordinate) Position
    if(hcent)
        x = calcULCenter(appletwidth, objectwidth);
    else if (xoffset == -1)
        x = 0;
    else
        x = xoffset;

    return x;
}


//
// Calculate the upper left Y coordinate based
// on parameters such as vertcenter and yoffset
//
protected int calcULYcoord(boolean hcent, int appletheight,
                           int objectheight, int yoffset) {
    int y;

    // Vertical (y coordinate) Position
    if(hcent)
        y = calcULCenter(appletheight, objectheight);
    else if (yoffset == -1)
        y = 0;
    else
        y = yoffset;

    return y;
}
```

```
//
// Calculate the lower left Y coordinate based
// on parameters such as vertcenter and yoffset
//
protected int calcLLYcoord(boolean hcent, int appletheight,
               int objectheight, int objectdescent, int yoffset) {
    int y;

    // Vertical (y coordinate) Position
    if(hcent)
        y = calcLLCenter(appletheight, objectheight) - objectdescent;
    else if (yoffset == -1)
        y = objectheight - objectdescent;
    else
        y = yoffset;

    return y;
}


//
// Tile the background with the specified image
//
protected void tilebackground(Graphics g) {
    int i, j;

    if(bgimage == null)
        return;
    if(ig.isImagePrepared(bgimage, this) == false)
        ig.loadImageAndWait(bgimage, this);
    //
    // If the applet has changed size or this is the first time
    // tilebackground has been called then create the bg image
    //
    if(app_width != size().width || app_height != size().height) {
        app_width  = size().width;
        app_height = size().height;

        tiled_bgimage = createImage(size().width, size().height);
        bg_g = tiled_bgimage.getGraphics();
        bg_g.setColor(app_bg_color);
        bg_g.fillRect(0, 0, size().width, size().height);
        if(tile & (bgimageXoffset != 0 || bgimageYoffset != 0)) {
            for(i=-bgimage_height;i<app_height;i+=bgimage_height) {
                for(j=-bgimage_width;j<app_width;j+=bgimage_width) {
                    bg_g.drawImage(bgimage, j+bgimageYoffset,
                                   i+bgimageXoffset, this);
                }
            }

        } else if(tile) {
            for(i=-bgimage_height;i<app_height;i+=bgimage_height) {
                for(j=-bgimage_width;j<app_width;j+=bgimage_width) {
                    bg_g.drawImage(bgimage, j+2, i+2, this);
```

```
                }
            }
        } else {
            bg_g.drawImage(bgimage, bgimageXoffset,
                                    bgimageYoffset, this);
        }
    }

    if(tiled_bgimage != null) {
        g.drawImage(tiled_bgimage, 0, 0, this);
    }
}

public void doStandardFilters() {
    Filter f;

    //========= INVOKE IMAGE FILTERS ==============
    f = new Filter();
    if(img_osi != null && img_filter_str != null) {
        img_pixels = f.invoke(this, null, img_filter_str, img_pixels,
                        img_width, img_height, false, app_bg_color,
                        false);
        img_width  = f.getWidth();
        img_height = f.getHeight();
    }

    //========= CREATE IMAGE FROM PIXELS ==============
    if(img_osi != null) {
        img_osi = createImage(new MemoryImageSource(img_width,
                        img_height, ColorModel.getRGBdefault(),
                        img_pixels, 0, img_width));
    }

    //========= INVOKE FILTERS ==============
    if(tx != null && tx_filter_str != null) {
        if(tx_bg_color == null) {
            tx_pixels = f.invoke(this, tx, tx_filter_str, tx_pixels,
                        tx_width, tx_height, true, app_bg_color,
                        tx_underline);
        } else {
            tx_pixels = f.invoke(this, tx, tx_filter_str, tx_pixels,
                        tx_width, tx_height, false, tx_bg_color,
                        tx_underline);
        }
        tx_width  = f.getWidth();
        tx_height = f.getHeight();
    }

    //========= CREATE IMAGE FROM PIXELS ==============
    if(tx != null) {
        tx_osi = createImage(new MemoryImageSource(tx_width,
                        tx_height, ColorModel.getRGBdefault(),
                        tx_pixels, 0, tx_width));
```

```
            }
        }


    public synchronized boolean imageUpdate(Image img,
                                            int infoflags,
                                            int x, int y,
                                            int width,
                                            int height){
        if((infoflags & ERROR) != 0) {
            if(img.equals(this.img_osi))
                System.out.println("Error getting image = " + img_file);
            else if(img.equals(bgimage))
                System.out.println("Error getting image = " + bgimage_file);
            img.flush();
            img = null;
            return false;
        }
        if((infoflags & ABORT) != 0) {
            if(img.equals(this.img_osi))
                System.out.println("Abort image = " + img_file);
            else if(img.equals(bgimage))
                System.out.println("Abort image = " + bgimage_file);
            img.flush();
            img = null;
            return false;
        }
        if((infoflags & ALLBITS) != 0) {
            return true;
        }
        return super.imageUpdate(img, infoflags, x, y, width, height);
    }
}
```

SoftShadow.java

```java
import java.awt.*;
import java.awt.image.*;

public class SoftShadow extends OffScr {
    protected String    shadow_color;
    protected String    shadow_xoffset;
    protected String    shadow_yoffset;
    protected String    soft_thickness;
    protected Color     light_shadow[];

    public void init() {
        int x, y;

        super.init();

        shadow_color   = GetParm.toString(this,"ShadowColor", "#646464");
        shadow_xoffset = GetParm.toString(this, "ShadowXOffset", "2");
        shadow_yoffset = GetParm.toString(this, "ShadowYOffset", "2");
        soft_thickness = GetParm.toString(this, "SoftThickness", "2");

        //========= SHADOW THE TEXT ==============
        fsoftshadow sh;
        sh = new fsoftshadow();
        sh.setText(tx);
        sh.setApplet(this);
        sh.setFont(tx_font);
        sh.setForeground(tx_color);
        sh.setBackground(tx_bg_color!=null ? tx_bg_color : app_bg_color);
        sh.setTransparent(tx_bg_color!=null ? false : true);
        sh.setUnderline(tx_underline);
        sh.setparameter(shadow_xoffset, 0);
        sh.setparameter(shadow_yoffset, 1);
        sh.setparameter(shadow_color, 2);
        sh.setparameter(soft_thickness, 3);
        tx_pixels = sh.filter(null, 0, 0);       // These params get ignored
        tx_width = sh.getWidth();
        tx_height = sh.getHeight();

        doStandardFilters();
    }
}
```

Emboss.java

```java
import java.awt.*;
import java.awt.image.*;

public class Emboss extends OffScr {
    protected String      depth;
    protected String      contrast;

    public void init() {

        super.init();
        depth            = GetParm.toString(this, "Depth", "1");
        contrast         = GetParm.toString(this, "Contrast", "50");

        //========= EMBOSS THE TEXT ==============
        femboss em;
        em = new femboss();
        em.setText(tx);
        em.setApplet(this);
        em.setFont(tx_font);
        em.setBackground(tx_bg_color!=null ? tx_bg_color : app_bg_color);
        em.setTransparent(tx_bg_color!=null ? false : true);
        em.setForeground(tx_color);
        em.setUnderline(tx_underline);
        em.setparameter(depth, 0);
        em.setparameter(contrast, 1);
        tx_pixels = em.filter(null, 0, 0);        // These params get ignored
        tx_width = em.getWidth();
        tx_height = em.getHeight();

        doStandardFilters();
    }
}
```

Negative.java

```java
import java.awt.image.*;
import java.awt.Color;
import java.awt.*;

public class Negative extends OffScr {

    public void init() {
        fnegative n;
        String subfrom;

        super.init();
        subfrom  = GetParm.toString(this, "SubFrom", "255");

        //========= MAKE THE IMAGE NEGATIVE ==============
        n = new fnegative();
        n.setparameter(subfrom, 0);
        img_pixels = n.filter(img_pixels, img_width, img_height);
        img_width = n.getWidth();
        img_height = n.getHeight();

        doStandardFilters();
    }
}
```

Scale.java

```java
import java.awt.image.*;
import java.awt.Color;
import java.awt.*;

public class Scale extends OffScr {

    public void init() {
        fscale sc;
        String perc_x;
        String perc_y;
        String perc;

        super.init();

        perc_x  = GetParm.toString(this, "ScaleX", "100");
        perc_y  = GetParm.toString(this, "ScaleY", "100");
        perc    = GetParm.toString(this, "Scale",   null);
        if(perc != null) {
            perc_x = perc;
            perc_y = perc;
        }

        //========= SCALE THE IMAGE =============
        sc = new fscale();
        sc.setparameter(perc_x, 0);
        sc.setparameter(perc_y, 1);
        img_pixels = sc.filter(img_pixels, img_width, img_height);
        img_width  = sc.getWidth();
        img_height = sc.getHeight();

        doStandardFilters();
    }
}
```

Animate.java

```java
import java.awt.*;
import java.awt.image.*;
import java.applet.*;
import java.awt.MediaTracker;
import java.util.*;

public abstract class Animate extends OffScr implements Runnable {
    protected Thread    tx_animator;
    protected Thread    img_animator;

    protected int       tx_index;
    protected int       tx_num_images;
    protected int       tx_xoffset[];           // Text X offset
    protected int       tx_yoffset[];           // Text Y offset
    protected int       tx_width[];             // Text width
    protected int       tx_height[];            // Text height
    protected int       tx_x_coord[];           // Text X Coordinate
    protected int       tx_y_coord[];           // Text Y Coordinate
    protected Image     tx_osi[];
    protected int       tx_delay_images;
    protected int       tx_delay_runs;
    protected String    tx_filter_str[];
    protected int       tx_lower_bound;
    protected int       tx_filtered_pixels[][];
    protected AudioClip tx_pi_clip[];           // The per text Audio Clip
    protected String    tx_pi_audio_file[];     // The per text audio file

    protected Image     img[];                  // The image
    protected String    img_file[];
    protected int       img_index;
    protected ImgGetr   img_gettr;              // The Image Getter class
    protected int       img_pixels[][];            // The text image
    protected int       img_num_images;
    protected int       img_xoffset[];          // Image X offset
    protected int       img_yoffset[];          // Image Y offset
    protected int       img_width[];            // Image width
    protected int       img_height[];           // Image height
    protected int       img_width_orig[];       // Image width
    protected int       img_height_orig[];      // Image height
    protected int       img_x_coord[];          // Image X Coordinate
    protected int       img_y_coord[];          // Image Y Coordinate
    protected Image     img_osi[];
    protected int       img_delay_images;
    protected int       img_delay_runs;
    protected String    img_filter_str[];
    protected int       img_lastimage_index;
    protected int       img_lower_bound;
    protected boolean   img_loaded[];
    protected boolean   img_copyfrom[];
```

```
protected int        img_reuseval[];
protected boolean    img_nofilespec[];
protected boolean    img_display_first;
protected int        img_filtered_pixels[][];
protected AudioClip  img_pi_clip[];            // The per image Audio Clip
protected String     img_pi_audio_file[];      // The per image audio file

protected Image      offScreen;
protected Graphics   offGC;

protected int        tmp_pixels[];
int applet_width = -1;
int applet_height = -1;
protected Filter f;
protected boolean debugflag;
protected boolean all_images_loaded;

public void init() {
    int i;

    super.init();
    tx_index = -1;
    img_index = -1;
    all_images_loaded = false;
    debugflag        = GetParm.toBoolean(this, "Debug", false);
    tx_num_images    = GetParm.toInt(this, "TxNumImages", 0);
    tx_delay_images  = GetParm.toInt(this, "TxDelayBetweenImages", 100);
    tx_delay_runs    = GetParm.toInt(this, "TxDelayBetweenRuns", 2000);
    tx_lower_bound   = GetParm.toInt(this, "TxInitialImage", 0);

    img_num_images   = GetParm.toInt(this, "ImgNumImages", 0);
    img_delay_images = GetParm.toInt(this, "ImgDelayBetweenImages", 100);
    img_delay_runs   = GetParm.toInt(this, "ImgDelayBetweenRuns", 2000);
    img_lower_bound  = GetParm.toInt(this, "ImgInitialImage", 0);
    img_display_first= GetParm.toBoolean(this, "ImgDisplayFirst", false);

    // Since user number start at 1 not 0
    if(tx_lower_bound > 0)
        tx_lower_bound--;
    if(img_lower_bound > 0)
        img_lower_bound--;


    if(tx_num_images > 0) {
        tx_width      = new int[tx_num_images];
        tx_height     = new int[tx_num_images];
        tx_xoffset    = new int[tx_num_images];
        tx_yoffset    = new int[tx_num_images];
        tx_x_coord    = new int[tx_num_images];
        tx_y_coord    = new int[tx_num_images];
        tx_filter_str = new String[tx_num_images];
        tx_osi        = new Image[tx_num_images];
        tx_filtered_pixels = new int[tx_num_images][];
```

```
            tx_pi_clip      = new AudioClip[tx_num_images];
            tx_pi_audio_file = new String[tx_num_images];
    }

    if(img_num_images > 0) {
            img_file        = new String[img_num_images];
            img_width       = new int[img_num_images];
            img_height      = new int[img_num_images];
            img_width_orig  = new int[img_num_images];
            img_height_orig = new int[img_num_images];
            img_xoffset     = new int[img_num_images];
            img_yoffset     = new int[img_num_images];
            img_x_coord     = new int[img_num_images];
            img_y_coord     = new int[img_num_images];
            img_filter_str  = new String[img_num_images];
            img_osi         = new Image[img_num_images];
            img             = new Image[img_num_images];
            img_pixels      = new int[img_num_images][];
            img_loaded      = new boolean[img_num_images];
            img_copyfrom    = new boolean[img_num_images];
            img_nofilespec  = new boolean[img_num_images];
            img_reuseval    = new int[img_num_images];
            img_filtered_pixels = new int[img_num_images][];
            img_pi_clip     = new AudioClip[img_num_images];
            img_pi_audio_file = new String[img_num_images];
    }

    f = new Filter();


    if(tx_num_images > 0 && tx != null) {
            ftext ps = new ftext();
            ps.setBackground(tx_bg_color!=null ? tx_bg_color : app_bg_color);
            ps.setTransparent(tx_bg_color!=null ? false : true);
            ps.setForeground(tx_color);
            ps.setFont(tx_font);
            ps.setApplet(this);
            ps.setText(tx);
            ps.setUnderline(tx_underline);
            tx_pixels = ps.filter(null, 0, 0);
            tx_width[0] = ps.getWidth();
            tx_height[0] = ps.getHeight();
            tx_ascent = tx_fontmetrics.getMaxAscent();
            tx_descent = tx_fontmetrics.getDescent();
    }


    for(i=0;i<tx_num_images;i++) {
        tx_filter_str[i] = GetParm.toString(this,
                                "TxFilter"+(i+1), "noop");
        tx_xoffset[i]    = GetParm.toInt(this,
                                "TxXOffset" + (i+1), 0x7FFFFFFF);
        tx_yoffset[i]    = GetParm.toInt(this,
```

```
                                    "TxYOffset" + (i+1), 0x7FFFFFFF);

        if(i == 0) {
            if(tx_xoffset[0] == 0x7FFFFFFF)
                tx_xoffset[0] = 0;
            if(tx_yoffset[0] == 0x7FFFFFFF)
                tx_yoffset[0] = 0;
        } else {
            if(tx_xoffset[i] == 0x7FFFFFFF)
                tx_xoffset[i] = tx_xoffset[i-1];
            if(tx_yoffset[i] == 0x7FFFFFFF)
                tx_yoffset[i] = tx_yoffset[i-1];
        }
        tx_pi_audio_file[i]   = GetParm.toString(this,
                                "TxAudio"+(i+1), null);
        if(tx_pi_audio_file[i] != null)
            tx_pi_clip[i] = getAudioClip(getDocumentBase(),
                                tx_pi_audio_file[i]);
    }

    img_lastimage_index = -1;
    for(i=0;i<img_num_images;i++) {

        // Get X and X offsets for Images
        img_xoffset[i] = GetParm.toInt(this,"ImgXOffset"+(i+1),0x7FFFFFFF);
        img_yoffset[i] = GetParm.toInt(this,"ImgYOffset"+(i+1),0x7FFFFFFF);

        if(i == 0) {
            if(img_xoffset[0] == 0x7FFFFFFF)
                img_xoffset[0] = 0;
            if(img_yoffset[0] == 0x7FFFFFFF)
                img_yoffset[0] = 0;
        } else {
            if(img_xoffset[i] == 0x7FFFFFFF)
                img_xoffset[i] = img_xoffset[i-1];
            if(img_yoffset[i] == 0x7FFFFFFF)
                img_yoffset[i] = img_yoffset[i-1];
        }

        // See if the user specified an image file
        img_file[i] = GetParm.toString(this,  "Image"+(i+1), null);

        // Get the Image filter
        img_filter_str[i] = GetParm.toString(this,
                            "ImgFilter"+(i+1),
                            "noop");
        img_pi_audio_file[i]   = GetParm.toString(this,
                                "ImgAudio"+(i+1), null);
        if(img_pi_audio_file[i] != null) {
            img_pi_clip[i] = getAudioClip(getDocumentBase(),
                                img_pi_audio_file[i]);
        }
    }
```

```
        debug("exiting init");
}

public void doTxFilters() {
    int i;
    Filter f;

    f = new Filter();
    for(i=0;i<tx_num_images;i++) {
        // This may get called because the thread was stopped but
        // is now being restarted.  No need to go through all of this
        // again
        if(tx_osi[i] != null)
            continue;
        getAppletContext().showStatus("Getting Text "
                                + (i+1) + " of " + tx_num_images + ": "
                                + tx_filter_str[i]);
        tx_filtered_pixels[i] = doStandardTxFilters(tx_pixels,
                        tx_width[i], tx_height[i],
                        f, tx_filter_str[i], i);
        tx_width[i] = f.getWidth();
        tx_height[i] = f.getHeight();
        tx_osi[i] = createImage(new MemoryImageSource(tx_width[i],
                            tx_height[i],
                            ColorModel.getRGBdefault(),
                            tx_filtered_pixels[i], 0, tx_width[i]));
        Thread.yield();
    }
    getAppletContext().showStatus("");
}

public synchronized void loadImages() {
    int i;

    // Now we have all the parameters
    for(i=0;i<img_num_images;i++) {

        // If the user didn't specify an image file then
        // get then use the last "gotten" image
        if(img_file[i] == null) {
            if(i == 0) {
                // Error - you must have an image for first image
                System.err.println("missing Image1");
                img_num_images = -1;
                continue;
            }
            img_nofilespec[i] = true;
        } else {
            // If the first character of the imf_file is $ then
            // get the previous image and reuse it
            if(img_file[i].charAt(0) == '$') {
                char chars[];
                int reuseval;
```

```
            int len = img_file[i].length();;
            // Get rid of leading $
            chars =  new char [len];


            img_file[i].getChars(0, len, chars, 0);

            reuseval = Integer.parseInt(new String(chars, 1, len-1));
            reuseval -= 1;
            img_reuseval[i] = reuseval;
            img_copyfrom[i] = true;
            debug("setting copyfrom to true for " + i);
        } else {
            // If the user specified an image file then get it
            img_gettr    = new ImgGetr(this);
            img[i] = img_gettr.process(getDocumentBase(),
                                img_file[i], false);

            debug("prepareImage["+i+"]\n");

            // It's essential to check the return value of
            // prepareImage, because if the image is already
            // prepared then imageUpdate will never be called
            // and that is the only other place the img_loaded
            // gets set
            img_loaded[i] = prepareImage(img[i], this);
            debug("RETURN from prepareImage["+i+"], img_loaded["+i+"] = "
                                                + img_loaded[i]);
        }
    }
    }
}


public synchronized boolean imageUpdate(Image image, int flags,
                        int x, int y, int w, int h) {
    int i;
    boolean retval = super.imageUpdate(image, flags, x, y, w, h);
    if((flags & ALLBITS) != 0) {
        for(i=0;i<img_num_images;i++) {
            if(image == img[i]) {
                img_loaded[i] = true;
                getAppletContext().showStatus("Loaded Image "
                        + (i+1) + " of " + img_num_images);
                return retval;
            }
        }
    }
    return retval;
}



public int[] doStandardTxFilters(int[] pixels, int width, int height,
```

```
                          Filter f, String filter_str, int i) {

StringTokenizer st;
String first_token;
int j;
int num_elements;

//========= INVOKE TEXT FILTERS ==============
if(filter_str != null) {
    setFont(tx_font);
    if(tx_color != null)
        setForeground(tx_color);
    else
        tx_color = Color.black;
    setForeground(tx_color);

    // Before we start the filters, see if the user specified
    // $N as the beginning filter which means to reuse a
    // previous filter output
    //
    st = new StringTokenizer(filter_str, "|");
    num_elements = st.countTokens();
    if(num_elements > 0) {
        String newfilter_str = null;

        first_token = st.nextToken();
        for(j=0;j<num_elements-1;j++) {
            if(j==0)
                newfilter_str = st.nextToken();
            else
                newfilter_str += st.nextToken();
            if(j < num_elements-2)
                newfilter_str += "|";
        }

        if(first_token.charAt(0) == '$') {
            char chars[];
            int reuseval;
            int len = first_token.length();;
            // Get rid of leading $
            chars =  new char [len];

            first_token.getChars(0, len, chars, 0);

            reuseval = Integer.parseInt(new String(chars, 1, len-1));
            reuseval -= 1;
            tx_width[i] = tx_width[reuseval];
            tx_height[i] = tx_height[reuseval];
            if(tx_bg_color == null) {
                pixels = f.invoke(this, null, newfilter_str,
                            tx_filtered_pixels[reuseval],
                            tx_width[i], tx_height[i],
                            true, app_bg_color, tx_underline);
```

```
                } else {
                    pixels = f.invoke(this, null, newfilter_str,
                                    tx_filtered_pixels[reuseval],
                                    tx_width[i], tx_height[i],
                                    false, tx_bg_color, tx_underline);
                }
                tx_width[i]  = f.getWidth();
                tx_height[i] = f.getHeight();
                return pixels;
            }
        }
        if(tx_bg_color == null) {
            pixels = f.invoke(this, tx, filter_str,
                            pixels, tx_width[i], tx_height[i],
                            true, app_bg_color, tx_underline);
        } else {
            pixels = f.invoke(this, tx, filter_str,
                            pixels, tx_width[i], tx_height[i],
                            false, tx_bg_color, tx_underline);
        }
        tx_width[i]  = f.getWidth();
        tx_height[i] = f.getHeight();
    }
    return pixels;
}

public int[] doStandardImgFilters(int[] pixels, int width, int height,
                            Filter f, String filter_str, int i) {
    String first_token;
    int j;
    StringTokenizer st;
    int num_elements;

    //========= INVOKE IMAGE FILTERS ==============
    if(filter_str != null) {

        // Before we start the filters, see if the user specified
        // $N as the beginning filter which means to reuse a
        // previous filter output
        //
        st = new StringTokenizer(filter_str, "|");
        num_elements = st.countTokens();
        if(num_elements > 0) {
            String newfilter_str = null;

            first_token = st.nextToken();
            for(j=0;j<num_elements-1;j++) {
                if(j==0)
                    newfilter_str = st.nextToken();
                else
                    newfilter_str += st.nextToken();
                if(j < num_elements-2)
                    newfilter_str += "|";
```

```
                }

        if(first_token.charAt(0) == '$') {
            char chars[];
            int reuseval;
            int len = first_token.length();;
            // Get rid of leading $
            chars =  new char [len];

            first_token.getChars(0, len, chars, 0);

            reuseval = Integer.parseInt(new String(chars, 1, len-1));
            reuseval -= 1;
            img_width[i] = img_width[reuseval];
            img_height[i] = img_height[reuseval];

            // The reuse image may not have already gotten
            // the pixels associated with it if it did
            // not explicitly specify a filter.  However,
            // the user may have specified $N to reuse
            // an image (or filter) and now the pixels
            // don't exist.  So, go get them!
            if(img_filtered_pixels[reuseval] == null) {
                img_filtered_pixels[reuseval] =
                            img_gettr.getPixels(img[reuseval], this);
            }
            pixels = f.invoke(this, null, newfilter_str,
                            img_filtered_pixels[reuseval],
                            img_width[i], img_height[i],
                            false, app_bg_color, false);
            img_width[i]  = f.getWidth();
            img_height[i] = f.getHeight();
            return pixels;
        }
    }
    pixels = f.invoke(this, null, filter_str,
                    pixels, width, height,
                    false, app_bg_color, false);
    }
    return pixels;
}

public void start() {
    if(tx_num_images > 0 && tx_animator == null) {
        tx_animator = new Thread(this, "Tx_thread");
        tx_animator.start();
    }
    if(img_num_images > 0 && img_animator == null) {
        img_animator = new Thread(this, "Img_thread");
        img_animator.start();
    }
}
```

```java
public void stop() {
    if(tx_animator != null)
        tx_animator.stop();
    tx_animator = null;
    if(img_animator != null)
        img_animator.stop();
    img_animator = null;
}

// checkImgLoadStatus is called each time through the while
// loop in the run method as long as all_images_loaded == false
// If the image number is marked as "copyfrom" or "nofilespec"
// then it is skipped. If the img_loaded[i] flag is true then
// process any filters that may have been specified
public boolean checkImgLoadStatus() {
    int i;
    boolean all_loaded = true;

    for(i=0;i<img_num_images;i++) {
        if(img_copyfrom[i] == true)
            continue;
        if(img_nofilespec[i] == true)
            continue;
        debug("img_loaded["+i+"] = " + img_loaded[i]);
        if(img_loaded[i] == true) { // flag says it's loaded
            debug("checkImgLoadStatus: img_osi["+i+"] = " + img_osi[i]);
            if(img_osi[i] == null) {        // No osi image yet
                // We found one that must have just gotten loaded
                img_width_orig[i] = img_gettr.getWidth(img[i], this);
                img_height_orig[i] = img_gettr.getHeight(img[i], this);

                // We save a lot of time by avoid the getPixels
                // step if there is no filtering going on.  The
                // problem with this is that it's possible that
                // a subsequent filter will make reference to
                // $N (where N is the current i) and the pixels
                // aren't there.  So, we'll have to deals with
                // getting the pixels on the fly if they're
                // called for (see doStandardImgFilters)
                if(img_filter_str[i].equals("noop")) {
                    img_width[i] = img_width_orig[i];
                    img_height[i] = img_height_orig[i];
                    img_osi[i] = img[i];
                    continue;
                }
                img_pixels[i] = img_gettr.getPixels(img[i], this);
                img_filtered_pixels[i] = doStandardImgFilters(
                            img_pixels[i],
                            img_width_orig[i],
                            img_height_orig[i],
                            f, img_filter_str[i], i);
                img_width[i] = f.getWidth();
                img_height[i]= f.getHeight();
```

```
                        img_osi[i] = createImage(new MemoryImageSource(
                                        img_width[i],
                                        img_height[i],
                                        ColorModel.getRGBdefault(),
                                        img_filtered_pixels[i],
                                        0, img_width[i]));
                    return false;
                }
            } else {
                debug("setting false on " + i);
                all_loaded = false;
            }
        }
        if(all_loaded == true) {
            debug("checkImgLoadStatus: ALL LOADED!!!!!");
            getAppletContext().showStatus("");
        }
        return all_loaded;
    }


    //
    // updateImageInfo gets called after all the images have been loaded
    // with getImage.  Now we go through the list of image and see if
    // there were any Image{N} parameters that did not include a
    // file specification (img_nofilespec) and if there were any
    // that were give as "$N" which means to reuse image N
    // In either case, get the appropriate pixels, widht, height,
    // and then process them with the current filter (if any) and
    // create the new image.
    //
    public void updateImageInfo() {
        int i;
        int last_img_file = 0;

        //
        // ===== First, check for images without a image specification
        //
        for(i=0;i<img_num_images;i++) {
            if(img_nofilespec[i] == true) {
                debug("nofilespec is true for " + i +
                        " last_img_file = " + last_img_file);
                //
                // If an image specification was not given then use
                // the last one that was given
                getAppletContext().showStatus("Getting Image "
                            + (i+1) + " of " + img_num_images + ": "
                            + img_filter_str[i]);
                img[i] = img[img_reuseval[i]];
                img_width[i]  = img_width[last_img_file];
                img_height[i] = img_height[last_img_file];
                img_width_orig[i] = img_width_orig[last_img_file];
                img_height_orig[i] = img_height_orig[last_img_file];
```

```
                // If no filters are specified then don't waste time
                // creating the pixels
                if(img_filter_str[i].equals("noop")) {
                    img_osi[i] = img[i];
                    continue;
                } else {
                    img_pixels[i] = img_gettr.getPixels(img[i], this);



                    img_filtered_pixels[i] = doStandardImgFilters(
                                img_pixels[i],
                                img_width_orig[i],
                                img_height_orig[i],
                                f, img_filter_str[i], i);
                    img_width[i] = f.getWidth();
                    img_height[i] = f.getHeight();
                    img_osi[i] = createImage(new MemoryImageSource(
                                    img_width[i],
                                    img_height[i],
                                    ColorModel.getRGBdefault(),
                                    img_filtered_pixels[i],
                                    0, img_width[i]));
                    Thread.yield();
                }
        } else
            last_img_file = i;


        //
        // Second, check for images with a $N image specification
        //
        // img_nofilespec and img_copyfrom should never both be true
        //
        if(img_copyfrom[i] == true) {
            //
            // The img_reuseval array contains the index of the
            // image that we should copy
            //
            img[i] = img[img_reuseval[i]];
            img_width[i] = img_width[img_reuseval[i]];
            img_height[i] = img_height[img_reuseval[i]];
            img_width_orig[i] = img_width_orig[img_reuseval[i]];
            img_height_orig[i] = img_height_orig[img_reuseval[i]];

            // If no filters are specified then don't waste time
            // creating the pixels
            if(img_filter_str[i].equals("noop")) {
                img_osi[i] = img[i];
                continue;
            } else {
                img_pixels[i] = img_gettr.getPixels(img[i], this);
                img_filtered_pixels[i] = doStandardImgFilters(
                            img_pixels[i],
```

```
                                 img_width_orig[i],
                                 img_height_orig[i],
                                 f, img_filter_str[i], i);
                    img_width[i] = f.getWidth();
                    img_height[i] = f.getHeight();
                    img_osi[i] = createImage(new MemoryImageSource(
                                         img_width[i],
                                         img_height[i],
                                         ColorModel.getRGBdefault(),
                                         img_filtered_pixels[i],
                                         0, img_width[i]));
                }
            }
        }
    }

    public int getNextTxIndex(int current, int max, int min) {
        current++;
        if(current >= max)
            current = min;
        return current;
    }

    public int getNextImgIndex(int current, int max, int min) {
        current++;
        if(current >= max)
            current = min;
        return current;
    }

    public void tx_sleep(int s_runs, int s_images,
                         int current, int max, int min) {
        try {
            if(current+1 == max)
                Thread.sleep(s_runs);
            else
                Thread.sleep(s_images);
        } catch (InterruptedException e) {}
    }

    public void img_sleep(int s_runs, int s_images,
                         int current, int max, int min) {
        tx_sleep(s_runs, s_images, current, max, min);
    }

    public void run() {
        Thread current_thread = Thread.currentThread();;

        //
        // It's important to set the priorities on these
        // threads to some value which is smaller than the
        // priority of the thread that is called to do paint
        Thread.currentThread().setPriority(Thread.MIN_PRIORITY);
```

```
tx_index = -1;
img_index = -1;

debug("entering run");
if(current_thread == img_animator) {
    loadImages();
}

if(current_thread == tx_animator) {
    doTxFilters();
}

while(true) {
    if(Thread.currentThread() == tx_animator) {
        debug("In tx_animator thread");
        // ========== Text ===============
        if(tx_index == -1)        // First time
            tx_index = tx_lower_bound;
        else
            tx_index = getNextTxIndex(tx_index, tx_num_images,
                                      tx_lower_bound);
        if(tx_pi_clip[tx_index] != null)
            tx_pi_clip[tx_index].play();
        repaint();
        tx_sleep(tx_delay_runs, tx_delay_images,
                           tx_index, tx_num_images,
                           tx_lower_bound);
    } else if(Thread.currentThread() == img_animator) {
        debug("In img_animator thread");
        // ========== Image ===============
        if(all_images_loaded == false) {
            all_images_loaded = checkImgLoadStatus();
            if(all_images_loaded == true)
                updateImageInfo();
        }
        if(all_images_loaded == true) {
            if(img_index == -1) // First time
                img_index = img_lower_bound;
            else
                img_index = getNextImgIndex(img_index, img_num_images,
                                      img_lower_bound);
            if(img_pi_clip[img_index] != null)
                img_pi_clip[img_index].play();
            repaint();
            img_sleep(img_delay_runs, img_delay_images,
                               img_index, img_num_images,
                               img_lower_bound);
        } else {
            img_index = 0;
            if(img_display_first) {
                repaint();
            } else
                img_index = -1;
```

```
                try {
                    Thread.sleep(1000);
                } catch (InterruptedException e) {
                    break;
                }
            }
        }
    }
}

public void paint(Graphics g) {

    // If this is the first time we've been in paint
    // or the applet has changed size then create
    // an image the size of the applet into which
    // we write the background image
    if(applet_width != size().width ||
       applet_height!= size().height) {
      applet_width  = size().width;
      applet_height = size().height;
      offScreen = createImage(applet_width, applet_height);
      offGC = offScreen.getGraphics();
    }
    offGC.setColor(getBackground());
    offGC.fillRect(0, 0, applet_width, applet_height);
    tilebackground(offGC);

    if(img_index >= 0) {      // No images specified
        if(img_osi[img_index] == null) {
            // do nothing
        } else if(img_index < img_num_images && img_index >= 0) {

            img_x_coord[img_index] = calcULXcoord(img_horizcenter,
                         size().width,
                         img_width[img_index],
                         img_xoffset[img_index]);
            img_y_coord[img_index] = calcULYcoord(img_vertcenter,
                         size().height,
                         img_height[img_index],
                         img_yoffset[img_index]);

            debug("drawing Image: " + img_index);
            offGC.drawImage(img_osi[img_index], img_x_coord[img_index],
                         img_y_coord[img_index], this);
            drawFrame(offGC, img_x_coord[img_index],
                         img_y_coord[img_index], img_width[img_index],
                         img_height[img_index], img_fr_type,
                         img_fr_thick,
                         img_fr_margin);
            drawBorder(offGC, img_x_coord[img_index],
                         img_y_coord[img_index],
                         img_width[img_index], img_height[img_index],
                         img_borderwidth,
```

```
                                        img_bordermargin,
                                        img_bordercolor);
                }
        }

        if(tx_index >= 0) {
                // do nothing
                if(tx_osi[tx_index] == null) {
                        // do nothing
                } else if(tx_index < tx_num_images && tx_index >= 0) {

                        tx_x_coord[tx_index] = calcULXcoord(tx_horizcenter,
                                        size().width,
                                        tx_width[tx_index],
                                        tx_xoffset[tx_index]);
                        tx_y_coord[tx_index] = calcULYcoord(tx_vertcenter,
                                        size().height,
                                        tx_height[tx_index],
                                        tx_yoffset[tx_index]);

                        debug("drawing Text: " + tx_index);
                        offGC.drawImage(tx_osi[tx_index], tx_x_coord[tx_index],
                                        tx_y_coord[tx_index], this);
                        // Draw frame for text
                        drawFrame(offGC, tx_x_coord[tx_index], tx_y_coord[tx_index],
                                        tx_width[tx_index], tx_height[tx_index],
                                        tx_fr_type, tx_fr_thick,
                                        tx_fr_margin);


                        // Draw border for text
                        drawBorder(offGC, tx_x_coord[tx_index], tx_y_coord[tx_index],
                                        tx_width[tx_index], tx_height[tx_index],
                                        tx_borderwidth, tx_bordermargin,
                                        tx_bordercolor);
                }
        }
        // Draw frame for applet
        drawFrame(offGC, 0, 0, size().width, size().height,
                        app_fr_type, app_fr_thick, 0);
        // Draw border for applet
        drawBorder(offGC, 0, 0, size().width, size().height,
                        app_borderwidth, 0, app_bordercolor);

        g.drawImage(offScreen, 0, 0, this);
}

public void debug(String s) {
        if(debugflag)
                System.err.println(s);
}

public boolean keyDown(Event evt, int key) {
```

```
int x = evt.x;
int y = evt.y;
// Handle the text next (Text takes precedence over images)
if(tx_index != -1) {
    if(x > tx_x_coord[tx_index] &&
       x < tx_x_coord[tx_index] + tx_width[tx_index] &&
       y > tx_y_coord[tx_index] &&
       y < tx_y_coord[tx_index] + tx_height[tx_index]) {
       if(key == 'f') {
           tx_delay_images *= .9;
           if(tx_delay_images < 2)
               tx_delay_images = 2;
           getAppletContext().showStatus("Setting image delay to: " +
                       tx_delay_images);
        } else if(key == 's') {
           if(tx_delay_images < 10)
               tx_delay_images++;
           else
               tx_delay_images *= 1.1;
           getAppletContext().showStatus("Setting image delay to: " +
                       tx_delay_images);
        } else if(key == 'F') {
           tx_delay_runs *= .9;
           if(tx_delay_runs < 2)
               tx_delay_runs = 2;
           getAppletContext().showStatus("Setting run delay to: " +
                       tx_delay_runs);
        } else if(key == 'S') {
           if(tx_delay_runs < 10)
               tx_delay_runs++;
           else
               tx_delay_runs *= 1.1;
           getAppletContext().showStatus("Setting run delay to: " +
                       tx_delay_runs);
        }
    }
}

if(img_index != -1) {
    if(x > img_x_coord[img_index] &&
       x < img_x_coord[img_index] + img_width[img_index] &&
       y > img_y_coord[img_index] &&
       y < img_y_coord[img_index] + img_height[img_index]) {
       if(key == 'f') {
           img_delay_images *= .9;
           if(img_delay_images < 2)
               img_delay_images = 2;
           getAppletContext().showStatus("Setting image delay to: " +
                       img_delay_images);
        } else if(key == 's')
           if(img_delay_images < 10)
               img_delay_images++;
           else
```

```
                                  img_delay_images *= 1.1;
                        getAppletContext().showStatus("Setting image delay to: " +
                                  img_delay_images);
                  if(key == 'F') {
                        img_delay_runs *= .9;
                        if(img_delay_runs < 2)
                              img_delay_runs = 2;
                        getAppletContext().showStatus("Setting run delay to: " +
                                  img_delay_runs);
                  } else if(key == 'S') {
                        if(img_delay_runs < 10)
                              img_delay_runs++;
                        else
                              img_delay_runs *= 1.1;
                        getAppletContext().showStatus("Setting run delay to: " +
                                  img_delay_runs);
                  }
            }
      }

      return true;
}


//
// If the user clicks the mouse then load the URL
// We check the text position first, so if there is
// overlapping text and image then the text URL will
// be loaded, not the imgae URL
//
public boolean mouseDown(Event evt, int x, int y) {
      int i;

      // Handle the image maps first
      for(i=0;i<num_maps;i++) {
            if(x > map_x1[i] && x < map_x2[i] &&
               y > map_y1[i] && y < map_y2[i]) {
                  if(map_url[i] != null) {
                        if(testmode) {
                              getAppletContext().showStatus("Loading URL: " +
                                        map_url[i].toString());
                        } else
                              getAppletContext().showDocument(map_url[i]);
                        return true;
                  }
            }
      }

      // Handle the text next (Text takes precedence over images)
      if(tx_index != -1) {
            if(x > tx_x_coord[tx_index] &&
               x < tx_x_coord[tx_index] + tx_width[tx_index] &&
               y > tx_y_coord[tx_index] &&
               y < tx_y_coord[tx_index] + tx_height[tx_index]) {
```

```
                    if(tx_url != null) {
                        getAppletContext().showDocument(tx_url);
                        return true;
                    }
                }
            }

        // Handle the image last
        if(img_index != -1) {
            if(x > img_x_coord[img_index] &&
               x < img_x_coord[img_index] + img_width[img_index] &&
               y > img_y_coord[img_index] &&
               y < img_y_coord[img_index] + img_height[img_index]) {
                if(img_url != null) {
                    getAppletContext().showDocument(img_url);
                    return true;
                }
            }
        }
        return true;
    }

//
// Check the x and y coordinates to see if we're actually
// inside the boundaries of the text or image or both
//
public boolean mouseMove(Event evt, int x, int y) {
    boolean tx_status_shown = false;
    boolean img_status_shown = false;
    int i;

    if(testmode) {
        getAppletContext().showStatus("X: " + x + " Y: " + y);
        return true;
    }

    //
    // If a image map url was found (hence tx_status_shown == true)
    // then return and don't bother to call the other mouseMove
    // stuff would simply display the url for the text or image.
    //
    if(tx_status_shown == true) {
        return true;
    }

    // ========== AUDIO =============
    // Process the image first
    if(img_index != -1) {
        if(x > img_x_coord[img_index] &&
           x < img_x_coord[img_index] + img_width[img_index] &&
           y > img_y_coord[img_index] &&
           y < img_y_coord[img_index] + img_height[img_index]) {
            if(!img_playing) {
```

```
                    img_playing = true;
                    if(img_clip != null)
                        img_clip.play();
                } // else it's already playing, leave it alone
            } else {
                // Since we don't get any kind of notification when the audio
                // clip has terminated (due to playing to completion) we set
                // playing to false everytime we move out of the boundaries
                // of the string
                img_playing = false;
                if(img_clip != null) {
                    img_clip.stop();
                }
            }
        }
    }


    // Process the text last
    if(tx_index != -1) {
        if(x > tx_x_coord[tx_index] &&
           x < tx_x_coord[tx_index] + tx_width[tx_index] &&
           y > tx_y_coord[tx_index] &&
           y < tx_y_coord[tx_index] + tx_height[tx_index]) {
            if(!tx_playing) {
                tx_playing = true;
                if(tx_clip != null)
                    tx_clip.play();
            } // else it's already playing, leave it alone
        } else {
            // Since we don't get any kind of notification when the audio
            // clip has terminated (due to playing to completion) we set
            // playing to false everytime we move out of the boundaries
            // of the string
            tx_playing = false;
            if(tx_clip != null) {
                tx_clip.stop();
            }
        }
    }


    // ========== IMAGE MAPS =============
    for(i=0;i<num_maps;i++) {
        if(x > map_x1[i] && x < map_x2[i] &&
           y > map_y1[i] && y < map_y2[i]) {
            if(map_url[i] != null) {
                getAppletContext().showStatus(map_url[i].toString());
                tx_status_shown = true;
            }
        }
    }


    // ========== URLs =============
    // Handle the text first
    if(tx_index != -1) {
```

```
            if(x > tx_x_coord[tx_index] &&
               x < tx_x_coord[tx_index] + tx_width[tx_index] &&
               y > tx_y_coord[tx_index] &&
               y < tx_y_coord[tx_index] + tx_height[tx_index]) {
                if(tx_url != null) {
                    getAppletContext().showStatus(tx_url.toString());
                    tx_status_shown = true;
                }
            }
        }

        // Handle the image last
        // If a Text URL is being displayed then don't
        // display the image URL
        if(img_index != -1) {
            if(x > img_x_coord[img_index] &&
               x < img_x_coord[img_index] + img_width[img_index] &&
               y > img_y_coord[img_index] &&
               y < img_y_coord[img_index] + img_height[img_index]) {
                if(img_url != null && tx_status_shown == false) {
                    getAppletContext().showStatus(img_url.toString());
                    img_status_shown = true;
                }
            }
        }
        // If we are not over either text or image that has
        // a corresponding URL then clear the status line
        if(tx_status_shown == false && img_status_shown == false)
            getAppletContext().showStatus(null);
        return true;
    }


    //
    // Just to be sure, when we exit the applet, stop the clips
    // It should already be stopped
    //
    public boolean mouseExit(Event evt, int x, int y) {
        // Just to be sure
        tx_playing = false;
        if(tx_clip != null)
            tx_clip.stop();
        img_playing = false;
        if(img_clip != null)
            img_clip.stop();
        getAppletContext().showStatus(null);
        return true;
    }
}
```

AnimateOnButtonTwoWay.java

```java
import java.awt.*;
import java.awt.image.*;
import java.applet.Applet;
import java.awt.MediaTracker;

public class AnimateOnButtonTwoWay extends Animate implements Runnable {
    boolean tx_goingup = true;
    boolean img_goingup = true;
    protected boolean   tx_runonce;
    protected boolean   img_runonce;
    protected boolean   tx_firsttime = true;
    protected boolean   img_firsttime = true;

    public void init() {
        tx_runonce      = GetParm.toBoolean(this, "TxRunOnce", false);
        img_runonce     = GetParm.toBoolean(this, "ImgRunOnce", false);
        super.init();
    }

    // getNextTxIndex() is called right before repaint
    public int getNextTxIndex(int current, int max, int min) {
        if(tx_goingup == true)
            current++;
        else
            current--;

        if(current >= max) {
            current = max - 2;
            tx_goingup = false;
        }
        if(current < min) {
            current = min + 1;
            tx_goingup = true;
        }
        return current;
    }

    // getNextImgIndex() is called right before repaint
    public int getNextImgIndex(int current, int max, int min) {
        if(img_goingup == true)
            current++;
        else
            current--;

        if(current >= max) {
            current -= 2;
            img_goingup = false;
        }
        if(current < min) {
```

```
            current = min+1;
            img_goingup = true;
        }
        return current;
    }


// tx_sleep() is called right after repaint
public void tx_sleep(int s_runs, int s_images,
                        int current, int max, int min) {
    try {
        if(((current == max-1 && tx_goingup == true) ||
            (current == min) && (tx_goingup == false))) {
            Thread.currentThread().suspend();
        } else
            Thread.sleep(s_images);
    } catch (InterruptedException e) {}
}

// img_sleep() is called right after repaint
public void img_sleep(int s_runs, int s_images,
                        int current, int max, int min) {
    try {
        if(((current == max-1 && img_goingup == true) ||
            (current == min) && (img_goingup == false))) {
            Thread.currentThread().suspend();
        } else
            Thread.sleep(s_images);
    } catch (InterruptedException e) {}
}

public boolean mouseDown(Event evt, int x, int y) {
    // Handle the text next (Text takes precedence over images)
    if(tx_index != -1) {
        if(x > tx_x_coord[tx_index] &&
           x < tx_x_coord[tx_index] + tx_width[tx_index] &&
           y > tx_y_coord[tx_index] &&
           y < tx_y_coord[tx_index] + tx_height[tx_index]) {
           if(tx_animator.isAlive()) {
                tx_animator.resume();
           }
        }
    }

    // Handle the image last
    if(img_index != -1) {
        if(x > img_x_coord[img_index] &&
           x < img_x_coord[img_index] + img_width[img_index] &&
           y > img_y_coord[img_index] &&
           y < img_y_coord[img_index] + img_height[img_index]) {
           if(img_animator.isAlive()) {
                img_animator.resume();
           }
```

```
            }
        }
        return super.mouseDown(evt, x, y);
    }

    // In order to get the RunOnce behavior, we have to override
    // the run method.  Most of what's in the run method is unchanged
    // from the parent class with the exception of the run once stuff
    //
    public void run() {
        Thread current_thread = Thread.currentThread();;

        //
        // It's important to set the priorities on these
        // threads to some value which is smaller than the
        // priority of the thread that is called to do paint
        Thread.currentThread().setPriority(Thread.MIN_PRIORITY);

        tx_index = -1;
        img_index = -1;

        debug("entering run");
        if(current_thread == img_animator) {
            loadImages();
        }

        if(current_thread == tx_animator) {
            doTxFilters();
        }

        while(true) {
            if(Thread.currentThread() == tx_animator) {
                debug("In tx_animator thread");
                // ========== Text ==============
                if(tx_index == -1)        // First time
                    tx_index = tx_lower_bound;
                else
                    tx_index = getNextTxIndex(tx_index, tx_num_images,
                                              tx_lower_bound);
                if(tx_pi_clip[tx_index] != null)
                    tx_pi_clip[tx_index].play();
                repaint();
                tx_sleep(tx_delay_runs, tx_delay_images,
                                  tx_index, tx_num_images,
                                  tx_lower_bound);
                if(tx_firsttime == true) {
                    tx_firsttime = false;
                    if(tx_runonce == false) {
                        tx_animator.suspend();
                    }
                }
            } else if(Thread.currentThread() == img_animator) {
                debug("In img_animator thread");
```

```
// ========== Image ===============
if(all_images_loaded == false) {
    all_images_loaded = checkImgLoadStatus();
    if(all_images_loaded == true)
        updateImageInfo();
}
if(all_images_loaded == true) {
    if(img_index == -1) // First time
        img_index = img_lower_bound;
    else
        img_index = getNextImgIndex(img_index, img_num_images,
                        img_lower_bound);
    if(img_pi_clip[img_index] != null)
        img_pi_clip[img_index].play();
    repaint();
    img_sleep(img_delay_runs, img_delay_images,
                    img_index, img_num_images,
                    img_lower_bound);
    if(img_firsttime == true) {
        img_firsttime = false;
        if(img_runonce == false) {
            img_animator.suspend();
        }
    }
} else {
    img_index = 0;
    if(img_display_first) {
        repaint();
    } else
        img_index = -1;
    try {
        Thread.sleep(1000);
    } catch (InterruptedException e) {
        break;
    }
}
        }
    }
  }
}
```

SAnimate.java

```java
import java.awt.*;
import java.applet.Applet;
import java.net.*;
import java.io.*;

abstract class SAnimate extends Applet implements Runnable {
    protected char          separated[];
    protected char          separateda[][];
    protected Thread        StringThread = null;
    protected int           xlocation[];
    protected int           xlocationa[][];
    protected int           xwidth[];
    protected int           xwidtha[][];
    protected boolean       threadSuspended = false;
    protected int           chardelay;
    protected int           rundelay;
    protected boolean       endofstring = false;
    protected int           total_width;
    protected int           total_widtha[];
    protected boolean       thread_running;

    // Parameters that apply to the entire applet
    protected Color         app_bg_color;          // Applet background color
    protected Image         offScreen;
    protected Graphics      offGC;
    protected int           applet_width;
    protected int           applet_height;
    protected int           app_height;
    protected int           app_width;
    protected String        bgimage_file;
    protected Image         bgimage;
    protected boolean       tile;
    protected int           bgimage_height;
    protected int           bgimage_width;
    protected Image         tiled_bgimage;
    protected Graphics      bg_g;
    protected ImgGetr       ig;

    // Parameters specific to Text
    protected String        tx;                    // Text
    protected String        txa[];                 // Text array
    protected int           xoffset;               // Text X offset
    protected int           yoffset;               // Text Y offset
    protected Color         textcolor;             // Text color
    protected boolean       horizcenter;           // Text horizontally centered
    protected boolean       vertcenter;            // Text vertically centered
    protected Font          font;                  // Text font
    protected FontMetrics   fontmetrics;           // Text font metrics
    protected boolean       underline;             // Text underline
```

```
protected int        width;          // Text width
protected int        widtha[];       // Text width array
protected int        height;         // Text height
protected int        ascent;         // Text ascent
protected int        descent;        // Text descent
protected int        txcount;        // number of texts

public void init() {
    int i, j;
    // Applet parameters
    app_bg_color    = GetParm.toColor(this,    "AppBGColor", null);

    // Text parameters
    txcount     = GetParm.toInt(this,      "TextCount", 0);
    tx          = GetParm.toString(this, "Text", "");
    xoffset     = GetParm.toInt(this,      "XOffset", 0);
    yoffset     = GetParm.toInt(this,      "YOffset", -1);
    textcolor   = GetParm.toColor(this,    "TextColor", null);
    horizcenter = GetParm.toBoolean(this, "HorizCenter", false);
    vertcenter  = GetParm.toBoolean(this, "VertCenter", false);
    font        = GetParm.toFont(this,     "Font",
                                           "Style",
                                           "PointSize");
    if(txcount > 0)
        txa = new String[txcount];
    for(i=0;i < txcount;i++)
        txa[i] = GetParm.toString(this, "Text"+(i+1), "");

    chardelay      = GetParm.toInt(this, "DelayBetweenChars", 20);
    rundelay       = GetParm.toInt(this, "DelayBetweenRuns", 3000);

    // ======== BG Image ===========
    tile           = GetParm.toBoolean(this, "AppTile",     false);
    bgimage_file   = GetParm.toString(this, "AppBGImage",  null);

    if(bgimage_file != null) {
        ig = new ImgGetr(this);
        bgimage = ig.process(getDocumentBase(), bgimage_file, false);
        ig.prepareImage(bgimage, this);
        bgimage_width = ig.getWidth(bgimage, this);
        bgimage_height = ig.getHeight(bgimage, this);
    }


    setFont(font);
    fontmetrics = getFontMetrics(font);

    width  = fontmetrics.stringWidth(tx);
    height = fontmetrics.getHeight();
    ascent = fontmetrics.getMaxAscent();
    descent = fontmetrics.getDescent();
    if(txcount > 0)
        widtha = new int[txcount];
```

```
for(i=0;i < txcount;i++)
    widtha[i]  = fontmetrics.stringWidth(txa[i]);


// Set the background and foreground colors, if specified
if(app_bg_color != null)
    setBackground(app_bg_color);
else
    app_bg_color = getBackground();
if(textcolor != null)
    setForeground(textcolor);
else
    textcolor = getForeground();

// Allocate space for array of chars, location, and width
separated =  new char [tx.length()];
xlocation =  new int  [tx.length()];
xwidth    =  new int  [tx.length()];
if(txcount > 0) {
    separateda = new char[txcount][];
    xlocationa = new int [txcount][];
    xwidtha    = new int [txcount][];
}
for(i=0;i < txcount;i++) {
    separateda[i] =  new char [txa[i].length()];
    xlocationa[i] =  new int  [txa[i].length()];
    xwidtha[i]    =  new int  [txa[i].length()];
    txa[i].getChars(0, txa[i].length(), separateda[i], 0);
}

// Put each character from the string into the separated array
tx.getChars(0,tx.length(),separated,0);


// Calculate the x locations for each character based on width
if(txcount > 0)
    total_widtha = new int[txcount];
for(i=0;i < txcount;i++)
    total_widtha[i] = 0;

for(i=0;i<txcount;i++) {
    for(j=0;j<txa[i].length();j++) {
        xwidtha[i][j] = fontmetrics.charWidth(separateda[i][j]);
        total_widtha[i] += xwidtha[i][j];
        if(j+1<txa[i].length())
            xlocationa[i][j+1] = total_widtha[i];
    }
}


total_width = 0;
for(i=0;i<tx.length();i++) {
    xwidth[i] = fontmetrics.charWidth(separated[i]);
```

```
                total_width += xwidth[i];
                if(i+1<tx.length())
                    xlocation[i+1] = total_width;
        }
        offScreen = createImage(size().width, size().height);
        offGC = offScreen.getGraphics();
        offGC.setFont(font);
    }


    //
    // Overwrite the default update method
    // This may not be necessary for this case
    // but it certainly doesn't hurt
    //
    public void update(Graphics g) {
        paint(g);
    }

    public void paint(Graphics g) {

        // If this is the first time we've been in paint
        // or the applet has changed size then create
        // an image the size of the applet into which
        // we write the background image
        if(applet_width != size().width ||
           applet_height!= size().height) {
            applet_width  = size().width;
            applet_height = size().height;
            offScreen = createImage(applet_width, applet_height);
            offGC = offScreen.getGraphics();
            offGC.setFont(font);
        }
        // We never know when the size might change so check it every time
        if(horizcenter) {
            xoffset = (size().width / 2) - (total_width / 2);
        }
        if(vertcenter) {
            yoffset = (size().height / 2) + (ascent / 3);
        } else if(yoffset == -1) {
            yoffset = height - descent;
        }
        if(tile) {
            tilebackground(offGC);
        } else {
            offGC.setColor(getBackground());
            offGC.fillRect(0, 0, applet_width, applet_height);
        }
    }

    public void start() {
        if(StringThread == null) {
            StringThread = new Thread(this);
            StringThread.start();
```

```
        }
    }

    public void stop() {
        if(StringThread != null)
            StringThread.stop();
        StringThread = null;
    }

    public boolean keyDown(Event evt, int key) {
        int x = evt.x;
        int y = evt.y;

        if(key == 'f') {
            chardelay *= .9;
            if(chardelay < 2)
                chardelay = 2;
            getAppletContext().showStatus("Setting image delay to: " +
                        chardelay);
        } else if(key == 's') {
            if(chardelay < 10)
                chardelay++;
            else
                chardelay *= 1.1;
            getAppletContext().showStatus("Setting image delay to: " +
                        chardelay);
        } else if(key == 'F') {
            rundelay *= .9;
            if(rundelay < 2)
                rundelay = 2;
            getAppletContext().showStatus("Setting run delay to: " +
                        rundelay);
        } else if(key == 'S') {
            if(rundelay < 10)
                rundelay++;
            else
                rundelay *= 1.1;
            getAppletContext().showStatus("Setting run delay to: " +
                        rundelay);
        }
        return true;
    }

    //
    // Tile the background with the specified image
    //
    protected synchronized void tilebackground(Graphics g) {
        int i, j;

        if(bgimage == null)
            return;
        if(ig.isImagePrepared(bgimage, this) == false)
            ig.loadImageAndWait(bgimage, this);
```

```
        //
        // If the applet has changed size or this is the first time
        // tilebackground has been called then create the bg image
        //
        if(app_width != size().width || app_height != size().height) {
            app_width  = size().width;
            app_height = size().height;

            tiled_bgimage = createImage(size().width, size().height);
            bg_g = tiled_bgimage.getGraphics();
            bg_g.setColor(app_bg_color);
            bg_g.fillRect(0, 0, size().width, size().height);
            if(tile) {
                for(i=-bgimage_height;i<app_height;i+=bgimage_height) {
                    for(j=-bgimage_width;j<app_width;j+=bgimage_width) {
                        bg_g.drawImage(bgimage, j+2, i+2, this);
                    }
                }
            } else {
                bg_g.drawImage(bgimage, 0, 0, this);
            }
        }

        if(tiled_bgimage != null) {
            g.drawImage(tiled_bgimage, 0, 0, this);
        }
    }
}
```

Coalesce.java

```java
import java.awt.Graphics;
import java.awt.Font;
import java.awt.FontMetrics;
import java.awt.Color;
import java.applet.Applet;
import java.awt.Event;
import java.awt.Image;

public class Coalesce extends SAnimate {

        int        Index = 0;            // Index
        int        xval[];               // X values for char position
        int        yval[];               // Y values for char position
        boolean    coalescing = true;    // Direction
        int        steps;                // Number of steps in movement

        public void init() {
            super.init();

            steps = GetParm.toInt(this, "Steps", 50);

            // tx is set up in StringAnimation
            xval =  new int [tx.length()];
            yval =  new int [tx.length()];

            // Calculate original random positions
            calc_new_random();
        }

        public void paint(Graphics g) {

            super.paint(g);

            if(Index == 0) {
                offGC.setColor(getBackground());
                offGC.fillRect(0, 0, size().width, size().height);
            }

            offGC.setColor(getBackground());
            offGC.fillRect(0, 0, size().width, size().height);
            tilebackground(offGC);
            offGC.setColor(getForeground());
            for(int i=0;i<tx.length();i++) {
                offGC.drawChars(separated, i, 1,
                    calcval(xval[i], xoffset+xlocation[i], Index, steps),
                    calcval(yval[i], yoffset, Index, steps));
            }
            g.drawImage(offScreen, 0, 0, this);
```

```
        // If the characters are not supposed to be moving then
        // we don't want an expose event to increment or decrement
        // the position of the characters
        if(StringThread != null) {
            if(coalescing) {
                Index++;
                if(Index > steps) {
                    endofstring = true;
                    Index = steps;
                    calc_new_random();
                    coalescing = false;
                }
            } else {
                Index--;
                if(Index < 0) {
                    endofstring = true;
                    Index = 0;
                    coalescing = true;
                }
            }
        }

    }

    public void run() {
        thread_running = true;
        endofstring = false;
        while (StringThread != null) {
            try {Thread.sleep(chardelay);} catch (InterruptedException e){}
            if(endofstring == true) {
                thread_running = false;
                StringThread = null;
                endofstring = false;
            } else
                repaint();
        }
    }

    public int calcval(int from, int to, int index, int range) {
        int value;
        if(from == to) {
            value = from;
        } else if(from > to) {
            value = from - ((from - to) * index / range);
        } else {
            value = from + ((to - from) * index / range);
        }
        return value;
    }

    public synchronized boolean mouseEnter(Event evt, int x, int y) {
        if(StringThread == null) {
            StringThread = new Thread(this);
```

```
            StringThread.start();
        } else {
            coalescing = true;
        }
        return true;
    }

    public synchronized boolean mouseExit(Event evt, int x, int y) {
        if(StringThread == null) {
            StringThread = new Thread(this);
            StringThread.start();
        } else {
            coalescing = false;
        }
        return true;
    }

    public boolean keyDown(Event evt, int key) {
        int x = evt.x;
        int y = evt.y;

        if(key == 'f') {
            chardelay *= .9;
            if(chardelay < 2)
                chardelay = 2;
            getAppletContext().showStatus("Setting image delay to: " +
                    chardelay);
        } else if(key == 's') {
            if(chardelay < 10)
                chardelay++;
            else
                chardelay *= 1.1;
            getAppletContext().showStatus("Setting image delay to: " +
                    chardelay);
        }
        return true;
    }


    public void start() {
        Index = 0;
    }

    public void calc_new_random() {
        for(int i=0;i<tx.length();i++) {
            xval[i] = (int)((Math.random()*1000.0) % size().width);
            yval[i] = (int)((Math.random()*1000.0) % size().height);
        }
    }
}
```

Ticker.java

```java
import java.awt.Graphics;
import java.awt.Font;
import java.awt.FontMetrics;
import java.awt.Color;
import java.applet.Applet;
import java.awt.Event;

public class Ticker extends SAnimate {

    int index = 0;
    int cur_xoffset;
    int move_dist;
    boolean thread_suspended;
    boolean forward = true;
    boolean reverse = false;

    public void init() {
        super.init();
        move_dist = GetParm.toInt(this,      "MoveDist", 20);
        reverse   = GetParm.toBoolean(this, "Reverse",  false);
        if(reverse == true)
            forward = false;
    }

    public synchronized void paint(Graphics g) {
        int i, j;

        super.paint(g);

        if(forward == true) {
            if(widtha[index] + cur_xoffset > 0) {
                cur_xoffset -= move_dist;
                offGC.setColor(getForeground());
                offGC.drawString(txa[index], cur_xoffset, yoffset);
            } else {
                endofstring = true;
            }
        } else {
            if(cur_xoffset < size().width) {
                cur_xoffset += move_dist;
                offGC.setColor(getForeground());
                offGC.drawString(txa[index], cur_xoffset, yoffset);
            } else {
                endofstring = true;
            }
        }

        g.drawImage(offScreen, 0, 0, this);
    }
```

```
public void run() {
    int i;
    endofstring = false;
    cur_xoffset = size().width;
    thread_suspended = false;
    StringThread.setPriority(1);
    while (StringThread != null) {
        try {Thread.sleep(chardelay);} catch (InterruptedException e){}
        if(endofstring == true) {
            if(forward == true) {
                index++;
                if(index == txcount)
                    index = 0;
            } else {
                index--;
                if(index < 0)
                    index = txcount - 1;
            }
            try {Thread.sleep(rundelay);} catch (InterruptedException e){}
            if(forward == true)
                cur_xoffset = size().width;
            else
                cur_xoffset = -widtha[index];
            endofstring = false;
        } else
            repaint();
    }
}

public boolean keyDown(Event evt, int key) {
    int x = evt.x;
    int y = evt.y;

    if(key == 'm') {
        move_dist += 1;
        getAppletContext().showStatus("New distance: " + move_dist);
        return true;
    } else if(key == 'l') {
        move_dist -= 1;
        if(move_dist <= 0)
            move_dist = 1;
        getAppletContext().showStatus("New distance: " + move_dist);
        return true;
    }
    return super.keyDown(evt, key);
}

public boolean mouseDown(Event evt, int x, int y) {

    if((evt.modifiers & Event.SHIFT_MASK) != 0) {
        forward = !forward;
    } else {
        if(thread_suspended == true) {
```

```
                StringThread.resume();
                thread_suspended = false;
            } else {
                StringThread.suspend();
                thread_suspended = true;
            }
        }

        return true;
    }
}
```

SlideShowFade.java

```java
import java.applet.Applet;
import java.applet.AudioClip;
import java.awt.*;
import java.awt.image.*;

public class SlideShowFade extends Applet implements Runnable {
    Image image[][];
    int imagedisplayed;
    boolean threadSuspended;
    Thread ssthread = null;
    int maxwidth, maxheight;
    boolean ImagePrepared;
    int checkImageFlags;
    int num_images = 0;
    String imagename[];
    boolean imageprepared[][];
    int width[];
    int height[];
    String soundname[];
    AudioClip sound[];
    AudioClip currentClip;
    int i, j;
    int current, next;
    Color      app_bg_color;              // Applet background color
    Panel      controlPanel;
    Panel      canvasPanel;
    ssCanvas   imageCanvas;
    boolean    controls;
    Button     nextButton, prevButton;
    boolean    autoPlay;
    int        fadesize;
    int        bg_red, bg_green, bg_blue;
    int        index;
    boolean    loaded = false;
    int        delayBetweenFades;
    int        delayBetweenImages;
    boolean    forward = true;
    Checkbox   audioCB;
    boolean    playaudio = true;

    public void init() {
        num_images  = GetParm.toInt(this,     "NumImages", 0);
        app_bg_color = GetParm.toColor(this, "AppBGColor", null);
        controls    = GetParm.toBoolean(this, "Controls", false);
        autoPlay    = GetParm.toBoolean(this, "AutoPlay", false);
        fadesize    = GetParm.toInt(this, "FadeSize", 10);
        delayBetweenFades = GetParm.toInt(this, "DelayBetweenFades", 20);
        delayBetweenImages = GetParm.toInt(this, "DelayBetweenImages", 5);
        delayBetweenImages *= 1000;
```

```
    // If autoPlay is true then force controls off
    if(autoPlay == true)
        controls = false;

    // Set the background and foreground colors, if specified
    if(app_bg_color != null)
        setBackground(app_bg_color);
    else
        app_bg_color = getBackground();

    bg_red = getBackground().getRed();
    bg_green = getBackground().getGreen();
    bg_blue = getBackground().getBlue();

    if(num_images > 0) {
        image         = new Image[num_images][fadesize];
        imagename     = new String[num_images];
        imageprepared = new boolean[num_images][fadesize];
        width         = new int[num_images];
        height        = new int[num_images];
        soundname     = new String[num_images];
        sound         = new AudioClip[num_images];
    } else {
        System.out.println(
                    "You must specify the number of images (NumImages)");
        return;
    }
    for(i=0;i<num_images;i++) {
        for(j=0;j<fadesize;j++)
            imageprepared[i][j] = false;
        imagename[i] = GetParm.toString(this, "Image" + (i+1), null);
        if(imagename == null) {
            System.out.println("Missing image " + (i+1));
            return;
        }
        image[i][0] = getImage(getDocumentBase(), imagename[i]);

        // Get the sounds
        soundname[i] = GetParm.toString(this, "Sound" + (i+1), null);
        if(soundname[i] != null) {
            sound[i] = getAudioClip(getDocumentBase(), soundname[i]);
            if(sound[i] == null) {
                soundname[i] = null;
            }
        }
    }


    // Start loading the other images
    for(i=0;i<num_images;i++)
        imageprepared[i][0] = prepareImage(image[i][0], this);
```

```
// Make sure we have the images loaded
for(i=0;i<num_images;i++) {
    if(imageprepared[i][0] == false) {
        while(((checkImageFlags =
                        checkImage(image[i][0],this))&ALLBITS) == 0) {
            try {Thread.sleep(delayBetweenFades);}
                    catch (InterruptedException e){}
        }
        imageprepared[i][0] = true;
    }
}


// Get width and height of all images
for(i=0;i<num_images;i++) {
    while((width[i] = image[i][0].getWidth(this)) == -1) {
        try {Thread.sleep(delayBetweenFades);}
                catch (InterruptedException e){}
    }
    while((height[i] = image[i][0].getHeight(this)) == -1) {
        try {Thread.sleep(delayBetweenFades);}
                catch (InterruptedException e){}
    }
}

maxwidth = Math.max(width[0], width[1]);
maxheight = Math.max(height[0], height[1]);
for(i=0;i<num_images;i++) {
    maxwidth = Math.max(maxwidth, width[i]);
    maxheight = Math.max(maxheight, height[i]);
}

for(i=0;i<num_images;i++) {
    for(j=1;j<fadesize;j++) {
        ImageFilter colorfilter = new FadeFilter(bg_red, bg_green,
                                bg_blue, fadesize, fadesize-j-1);
        image[i][j] = createImage(
            new FilteredImageSource(image[i][0].getSource(),
                        colorfilter));
        imageprepared[i][j] = prepareImage(image[i][j], this);
    }
}
// Make sure we have the images loaded
for(i=0;i<num_images;i++) {
    for(j=1;j<fadesize;j++) {
        if(imageprepared[i][j] == false) {
            while(((checkImageFlags =
                        checkImage(image[i][j],this))&ALLBITS) == 0) {
                try {Thread.sleep(delayBetweenFades);}
                        catch (InterruptedException e){}
            }
            imageprepared[i][0] = true;
        }
    }
}
```

```
        }
        loaded = true;


        imagedisplayed = 0;

        current = 0;
        setLayout(new BorderLayout());
        canvasPanel = new Panel();          // Default to Flow layout
        add("Center", canvasPanel);

        imageCanvas = new ssCanvas(this);
        canvasPanel.add(imageCanvas);
        if(controls == true) {
            controlPanel = new Panel();
            nextButton = new Button("Next");
            prevButton = new Button("Previous");
            audioCB    = new Checkbox("Audio");
            audioCB.setState(true);
            controlPanel.add(nextButton);
            controlPanel.add(prevButton);
            controlPanel.add(audioCB);
            add("South", controlPanel);
        }
    }

    public void paint(Graphics g) {

        //System.out.println("paint ("+current+","+index+")");

        imageCanvas.reshape(0, 0, width[current], height[current]);
        imageCanvas.getGraphics().setColor(getBackground());
        if(width[current] < canvasPanel.size().width)
            imageCanvas.getGraphics().fillRect(width[current], 0,
                        canvasPanel.size().width-width[current],
                        imageCanvas.size().height);
        if(height[current] < canvasPanel.size().height)
            imageCanvas.getGraphics().fillRect(0, height[current],
                        imageCanvas.size().width,
                        canvasPanel.size().height-height[current]);
        if(loaded)
            imageCanvas.getGraphics().drawImage(image[current][index],
                                                    0, 0, this);

    }

    public synchronized boolean imageUpdate(Image img,
                                            int infoflags,
                                            int x, int y,
                                            int width,
                                            int height){
        int i, j;
        int cur = -1;
        int curj = -1;
```

```
        for(i=0;i<num_images;i++) {
            for(j=0;j<fadesize;j++) {
                if(img.equals(image[i][j])) {
                    cur = i;
                    curj = j;
                    break;
                }
            }
        }
        if((infoflags & ABORT) != 0) {
            if(cur != -1)
                System.out.println("Abort image = " + imagename[cur]);
            img.flush();
            img = null;
            return false;
        }
        if((infoflags & ERROR) != 0) {
            if(cur != -1)
                System.out.println("Error getting image = " + imagename[cur]);
            img.flush();
            img = null;
            return false;
        }
        if((infoflags & ALLBITS) != 0) {
            if(cur != -1)
                imageprepared[cur][curj] = true;
            return true;
        }
        return (infoflags & (ALLBITS|ABORT)) == 0;
    }

    public void update(Graphics g) {
        paint(g);
    }

    public void run() {
        boolean first = true;
        Thread.currentThread().setPriority(Thread.MIN_PRIORITY);
        while (ssthread != null) {
            if(autoPlay) {
                if(first) {
                    first = false;
                    repaint();
                    if(playaudio && sound[current] != null)
                        sound[current].play();
                    currentClip = sound[current];
                    try {Thread.sleep(delayBetweenImages);}
                        catch (InterruptedException e){}
                }

                for(index=0;index<fadesize;index++) {
                    repaint();
                    try {Thread.sleep(delayBetweenFades);}
```

```
                        catch (InterruptedException e){}
        }
        current++;
        if(current >= num_images)
            current = 0;
        // Stop audio now since the image is no longer being displayed
        if(currentClip != null)
            currentClip.stop();
        if(playaudio && sound[current] != null)
            sound[current].play();
        currentClip = sound[current];
        for(index=fadesize-1;index>=0;index--) {
            repaint();
            try {Thread.sleep(delayBetweenFades);}
                catch (InterruptedException e){}
        }
        // Set index to 0 in case we get expose event
        index = 0;
        try {Thread.sleep(delayBetweenImages);}
                catch (InterruptedException e){}
    } else {
        if(first) {
            first = false;
            repaint();
            if(playaudio && sound[current] != null)
                sound[current].play();
            currentClip = sound[current];
            togglethread();
        }

        for(index=0;index<fadesize;index++) {
            repaint();
            try {Thread.sleep(delayBetweenFades);}
                    catch (InterruptedException e){}
        }
        if(forward) {
            current++;
            if(current >= num_images)
                current = 0;
        } else {
            current--;
            if(current < 0)
                current = num_images - 1;
        }
        if(currentClip != null)
            currentClip.stop();
        if(playaudio && sound[current] != null)
            // Stop the currently playing audio clip
            // If it has already terminated,
            // then calling stop won't hurt
            sound[current].play();
        currentClip = sound[current];
        for(index=fadesize-1;index>=0;index--) {
```

```
                    repaint();
                    try {Thread.sleep(delayBetweenFades);}
                        catch (InterruptedException e){}
                }
                // Set index to 0 in case we get expose event
                index = 0;
                togglethread();
            }
        }
        ssthread = null;
    }

    public void start() {
        if(ssthread == null) {
            threadSuspended = false;
            ssthread = new Thread(this);
            ssthread.start();
        }
        if(currentClip != null)
            currentClip.stop();
        if(sound[current] != null) {
            // Stop the currently playing audio clip
            // If it has already terminated, then calling stop won't hurt
            if(playaudio && sound[current] != null)
                sound[current].play();
            currentClip = sound[current];
        }
    }

    public void stop() {
        ssthread = null;
        if(currentClip != null)
            currentClip.stop();
    }

    public boolean mouseDown(Event evt, int x, int y) {

        if(autoPlay == true)
            return true;
        if((evt.modifiers & Event.SHIFT_MASK) != 0) {
            forward = false;
        } else {
            forward = true;
        }
        if(autoPlay == false)
            togglethread();
        return true;
    }

    public boolean action(Event evt, Object o) {
        if(autoPlay == true)
            return true;
        if(evt.target.equals(nextButton)) {
```

```
                forward = true;
        } else if(evt.target.equals(prevButton)) {
                forward = false;
        } else if(evt.target instanceof Checkbox) {
            if(audioCB.getState()) {
                playaudio = true;
                if(sound[current] != null)
                    sound[current].play();
                currentClip = sound[current];
            } else {
                playaudio = false;
                if(currentClip != null)
                    currentClip.stop();
            }
            // Return so that we don't toggle the thread for checkbox
            return true;
        }
        if(autoPlay == false)
            togglethread();
        return true;
    }

    public void togglethread() {
        if (threadSuspended == true) {
            threadSuspended = false;
            ssthread.resume();
        } else {
            threadSuspended = true;
            ssthread.suspend();
        }
    }

    public boolean keyDown(Event evt, int key) {
        int x = evt.x;
        int y = evt.y;

        if(key == 'f') {
            delayBetweenFades *= .9;
            if(delayBetweenFades < 2)
                delayBetweenFades = 2;
            getAppletContext().showStatus("Setting delay to: " +
                        delayBetweenFades);
            return true;
        } else if(key == 's') {
            if(delayBetweenFades < 10)
                delayBetweenFades++;
            else
                delayBetweenFades *= 1.1;
            getAppletContext().showStatus("Setting delay to: " +
                        delayBetweenFades);
            return true;
        } else if(key == 'F') {
            delayBetweenImages *= .9;
```

```
                if(delayBetweenImages < 2)
                    delayBetweenImages = 2;
                getAppletContext().showStatus("Setting delay to: " +
                        delayBetweenImages);
                return true;
            } else if(key == 'S') {
                if(delayBetweenImages < 10)
                    delayBetweenImages++;
                else
                    delayBetweenImages *= 1.1;
                getAppletContext().showStatus("Setting delay to: " +
                        delayBetweenImages);
                return true;
            } else if(key == 'a') {
                playaudio = !playaudio;
                if(playaudio && currentClip != null)
                    currentClip.play();
                if(!playaudio && currentClip != null)
                    currentClip.stop();
                if(controls) {
                    if(playaudio)
                        audioCB.setState(true);
                    else
                        audioCB.setState(false);
                }
            }
            return true;
        }
}

// We need this Canvas in order to get the expose event when
// our window is obscured by another, or deiconified
class ssCanvas extends Canvas {
    Applet applet;

    public ssCanvas(Applet a) {
        applet = a;
    }

    public void paint(Graphics g) {
        applet.paint(g);
    }
}

class FadeFilter extends RGBImageFilter {
    int bg_red, bg_green, bg_blue;
    int total;
    int index;

    public FadeFilter() {
        // The filter's operation does not depend on the
        // pixel's location, so IndexColorModels can be
        // filtered directly.
```

```
            canFilterIndexColorModel = true;
    }

    public FadeFilter(int r, int g, int b, int t, int i) {
        bg_red = r;
        bg_green = g;
        bg_blue = b;
        total = t;
        index = i;
        canFilterIndexColorModel = true;
    }


    int count = 0;

    public int filterRGB(int x, int y, int rgb) {
        int red, green, blue, alpha;
        count++;

        red   = (rgb & 0x00ff0000) >> 16;
        green = (rgb & 0x0000ff00) >> 8;
        blue  = rgb & 0x000000ff;
        alpha = (rgb & 0xff000000) >>> 24;
        if(red > bg_red)
            red = bg_red + (red - bg_red)*index/total;
        else
            red = bg_red - (bg_red - red)*index/total;
        if(green > bg_green)
            green = bg_green + (green - bg_green)*index/total;
        else
            green = bg_green - (bg_green - green)*index/total;
        if(blue > bg_blue)
            blue = bg_blue + (blue - bg_blue)*index/total;
        else
            blue = bg_blue - (bg_blue - blue)*index/total;


        return ((alpha << 24) | (red << 16) | (green << 8) | blue);
    }
}
```

APPENDIX B

Supported Applet Colors

Color	Value
aliceblue	f0f8ff
antiquewhite	faebd7
aquamarine	7fffd4
azure	f0ffff
beige	f5f5dc
bisque	ffe4c4
black	000000
blanchedalmond	ffebcd
blue	0000ff
blueviolet	8a2be2
brown	a52a2a
burlywood	deb887
cadetblue	5f9ea0
chartreuse	7fff00

Color	Value
chocolate	d2691e
coral	ff7f50
cornflowerblue	6495ed
cornsilk	fff8dc
cyan	00ffff
darkgoldenrod	b8860b
darkgreen	006400
darkkhaki	bdb76b
darkolivegreen	556b2f
darkorange	ff8c00
darkorchid	9932cc
darksalmon	e9967a
darkseagreen	8fbc8f
darkslateblue	483d8b

Color	Value
darkslategray	2f4f4f
darkslategrey	2f4f4f
darkturquoise	00ced1
darkviolet	9400d3
deeppink	ff1493
deepskyblue	00bfff
dimgray	696969
dimgrey	696969
dodgerblue	1e90ff
firebrick	b22222
floralwhite	fffaf0
forestgreen	228b22
green	00ff00
gainsboro	dcdcdc
ghostwhite	f8f8ff
gold	ffd700
goldenrod	daa520
gray	bebebe
honeydew	f0fff0
hotpink	ff69b4
indianred	cd5c5c
ivory	fffff0
khaki	f0e68c
lavender	e6e6fa
lavenderblush	fff0f5
lawngreen	7cfc00
lemonchiffon	fffacd

Color	Value
lightblue	add8e6
lightcoral	f08080
lightcyan	e0ffff
lightgoldenrod	eedd82
lightgray	d3d3d3
lightgrey	d3d3d3
lightpink	ffb6c1
lightsalmon	ffa07a
lightseagreen	20b2aa
lightskyblue	87cefa
lightslateblue	8470ff
lightslategray	778899
lightslategrey	778899
lightsteelblue	b0c4de
lightyellow	ffffe0
limegreen	32cd32
linen	faf0e6
magenta	ff00ff
maroon	b03060
mediumaquamarine	66cdaa
mediumblue	0000cd
mediumorchid	ba55d3
mediumpurple	9370db
mediumseagreen	3cb371
mediumslateblue	7b68ee
mediumspringgreen	00fa9a
mediumturquoise	48d1cc

Color	Value
mediumvioletred	c71585
midnightblue	191970
mintcream	f5fffa
mistyrose	ffe4e1
moccasin	ffe4b5
navajowhite	ffdead
navy	000080
navyblue	000080
oldlace	fdf5e6
olivedrab	6b8e23
orange	ffa500
orangered	ff4500
orchid	da70d6
palegoldenrod	eee8aa
palegreen	98fb98
paleturquoise	afeeee
palevioletred	db7093
papayawhip	ffefd5
peachpuff	ffdab9
peru	cd853f
pink	ffc0cb
plum	dda0dd
powderblue	b0e0e6
purple	a020f0
red	ff0000
rosybrown	bc8f8f

Color	Value
royalblue	4169e1
saddlebrown	8b4513
salmon	fa8072
sandybrown	f4a460
seagreen	2e8b57
seashell	fff5ee
sienna	a0522d
skyblue	87ceeb
slateblue	6a5acd
slategray	708090
slategrey	708090
snow	fffafa
springgreen	00ff7f
steelblue	4682b4
tan	d2b48c
thistle	d8bfd8
tomato	ff6347
turquoise	40e0d0
violet	ee82ee
violetred	d02090
wheat	f5deb3
white	ffffff
whitesmoke	f5f5f5
yellow	ffff00
yellowgreen	9acd32

APPENDIX

C

- Using the CD-ROM on Windows 95 and Windows NT

- Using the CD-ROM on Solaris 2

- Using the CD-ROM on Macintosh (System 7.5 or later)

The SunSoft Press Java Series CD-ROM

There are currently four books in the SunSoft Press Java Series: Core Java, Instant Java, Java by Example, and Just Java. The same CD-ROM is included with each book and contains examples from all of the books. The CD also contains the Java Developer's Kit (Release 1.0) for Solaris 2.x, Windows 95, and Windows NT.

A Beta version of the Macintosh Java Developer's Kit was released as this book went to press and was added to the disc. It was not possible to test all of the Java programs on the disc with the Macintosh JDK. If you experience any problems with the Beta release, check the SunSoft Press Java Series Web page for updates (http://www.prenhall.com/~java_sun).

Using the CD-ROM on Windows 95 and Windows NT

In addition to the JDK and Java applets and applications from the four books, the Win95nt directory contains Symantec's Café Lite and shareware versions of WinEdit and WinZip. **This CD-ROM does not support Windows 3.1.**

The Win95nt directory structure is as follows:

Directory/File	Contents
Booksjdk	Contains the installation program for the Java Series books and the JDK (1.0)
Cafelite	Contains the installation program for Café Lite
Readme.txt	Installation notes for Windows users
Winedit	Contains the installation program for WinEdit
Winzip	Contains the installation program for WinZip

To install the JDK or Java programs from the books:

1. Click the Start button and choose Run. (Windows NT users, Select Run from the Program Manager File menu.)
2. Type D:\WIN95NT\BOOKSJDK\Setup.exe and click the OK button. (If your CD-ROM drive is not drive D, substitute the appropriate letter.)
3. The installation program will prompt you to select the components you wish to install. You may install the JDK by itself or the JDK and any combination of files from the four books.
4. The installation program will prompt you for the drive and directory to use for each of the components you select.

(Please note that the Café Lite installation program also installs a copy of the JDK on your system.)

NOTE: On Windows 95 systems, the installation program adds the Java bin directory to the PATH statement in your AUTOEXEC.BAT file and adds a CLASSPATH assignment or modifies your existing CLASSPATH to point to the Java runtime library. You must reboot for these changes to take effect. On Windows NT systems, you will have to change the environment variables manually.

Please note that UNIX and Windows text files have slightly different conventions for end-of-line. UNIX expects a newline character (linefeed) and Windows expects a carriage return and a linefeed. Many Windows editors (including WinEdit) are able to cope with UNIX conventions and vice versa. Be aware, however, that some Windows editors will not display line breaks properly if you try to read text files that were created on a UNIX system. The Java compiler handles source files created under either convention.

Using the SunSoft Press Java Series Sample Programs

Core Java

When you have finished installing the Core Java files on your system, there should be thirteen subdirectories in the CoreJavaBook directory. The source code for the programs described in this book can be found in the 12 directories named ch2, ch3...ch13. There should also be a directory named corejava that contains java files and class files needed to run various applications.

For example, if you open up the ch10 directory, you will see 5 subdirectories:

  MessageCrackerTest
  ExceptTest
  ExceptionalTest
  DebugWinTest
  BuggyButtonTest

These directories contain the class files and java files for the programs discussed in Chapter 10.

Instant Java

The Java programs described in Instant Java are all available on the CD-ROM and can easily be customized. After installing the programs onto your system, you should have 7 subdirectories in your InstantJavaBook directory. Five of the directories correspond to chapters in the book:

fund	Chapter 2 Fundamental Applets
text	Chapter 3 Text Applets
image	Chapter 4 Image Applets
animate	Chapter 5 Animation Applets
assorted	Chapter 6 Assorted Applets

The other two directories contain images and additional source code and classes:

images	Image files (GIF and JPEG formats)
classes	Additional source code and classes

Java by Example

After copying the files for Java by Example to your system, you should have 2 subdirectories in the JavaByExampleBook directory you created. This directory contains the applications and applets from the book that are marked with a CD-ROM icon. The applications directory contains Java applications illustrating everything from interfaces to memory management to encapsulation. You should see the following subdirectories:

Calculator1

Calculator2

IO

Intro

Lisp

Parser

TreeSort

LinkedList

The applets directory contains a selection of applets that illustrate use of the Java graphics library, multiple threads, multimedia, and more.

Just Java

After installing the files for Just Java, you should have 3 subdirectories in the JustJavaBook directory you created:

examples

images

noises

The programs referred to in Just Java are contained in the examples directory. There is one directory for each chapter, containing the small example programs from that chapter.

The images directory contains half a dozen image files for you to experiment with loading and manipulating using the Java features that allow you to display and change images on screen.

The noises directory contains selected sound effects files from the Java release that illustrate how Java can be used to play audio files.

To install Café Lite:

Café Lite is a trial version of Symantec Café, the Integrated Java Development Environment. A coupon for an upgrade to the full version of Symantec Café is included at the back of this book. Please note that the Café Lite installation program also installs a copy of the JDK on your system.

1.   Click the Start button and choose Run. (Windows NT users, Select Run from the Program Manager File menu.)

2.   Type D:\WIN95NT\CAFELITE\Cafelite.exe and click the OK button. (If your CD-ROM drive is not drive D, substitute the appropriate letter.)

To install WinEdit:

1.   Click the Start button and choose Run. (Windows NT users, Select Run from the Program Manager File menu.)

2.   Type D:\WIN95NT\WINEDIT\Setup.exe and click the OK button. (If your CD-ROM drive is not drive D, substitute the appropriate letter.)

NOTE: The installation program adds the directory you specified for installing WinEdit to the PATH statement in your AUTOEXEC.BAT file.

To customize WinEdit for Java Programming

If you would like to customize WinEdit to make Java programming easier, the book Core Java describes useful modifications to the standard WinEdit configuration (See Chapter 2). This CD-ROM contains a batch file named Wepatch.bat that you can run to make these modifications.

Wepatch.bat and the other files needed to modify WinEdit are on the CD-ROM in a subdirectory of Winedit named Winedita.

To run Wepatch.bat:

1.   Install WinEdit as described above.

2.   Change to the Winedita directory on the CD-ROM.
D:\WIN95NT\WINEDIT\WINEDITA

3.   Run Wepatch <WinEdit directory> <Windows directory>

For example, if you installed WinEdit in a directory on your hard drive named C:\Programs\WinEdit and your Windows directory is C:\Windows, at the system prompt you would type:

Wepatch C:\Programs\WinEdit C:\Windows

To install WinZip:

1. Click the Start button and choose Run. (Windows NT users, Select Run from the Program Manager File menu.)

2. Type D:\WIN95NT\WINZIP\Winzip95.exe and click the OK button. (If your CD-ROM drive is not drive D, substitute the appropriate letter.)

3. The setup program will display a dialog box asking you where to install WinZip.

4. A dialog box containing information about the WinZip license agreement will also be displayed.

Using the CD-ROM on Solaris 2.x

Because this CD-ROM is a standard ISO-9660 disk that does not support long file names and other UNIX extensions, the Java programs and the Java Developer's Kit (JDK) for Solaris 2.x are stored as tar archives. Use the *more* command or *vi* to read the readme.txt file.

The solaris2 directory structure is as follows:

corejava.tar	Programs from Core Java
instjava.tar	Programs from Instant Java
javaexam.tar	Programs from Java by Example
jdk_1_0_.tar	Solaris 2.x JDK (Release 1.0)
justjava.tar	Programs from Just Java
readme.txt	Installation notes for Solaris users

To install the Java programs:

1. Make a directory on your UNIX filesystem and change to that directory. Then copy the appropriate tar file to that directory.

2. Use the command *tar -xvf* to unarchive the file. For example:

   tar -xvf corejava.tar

To install the Java Developer's Kit (Solaris 2.3 or later):

1. Make a directory on your UNIX filesystem and change to that directory. Then copy the file jdk_1_0_.tar to that directory.

2. Use the command *tar -xvf* to unarchive the file. For example:

    tar -xvf jdk_1_0_.tar

3. Add or modify the appropriate variables in your .cshrc (or whatever initialization file is appropriate for the shell you use) to put the Java bin directory in your path and to set a CLASSPATH environment variable to point to the Java runtime library, which is in the lib directory under the JDK. For example:

    setenv CLASSPATH "where-you-put-java"/lib/classes.zip.

4. Logout and login again so the new variables take effect.

Using the CD-ROM on Macintosh (System 7.5 or later)

The MAC_OS directory contains a Beta release of the Macintosh JDK. Java programs from the books have also been included. Please note, however, that these Java programs have NOT been tested using the Macintosh JDK.

You should also note that Macintosh, Windows, and UNIX text files have slightly different conventions for end-of-line. Macintosh expects a carriage return, Windows expects a carriage return and a linefeed, and UNIX expects a newline character (linefeed)

Most Macintosh editors are able to cope with UNIX and Windows conventions. Be aware, however, that some Macintosh editors will not display line breaks properly if you try to read text files that were created on a Windows or UNIX system. Even though some text files may not appear to be properly formatted, however, the Java compiler handles source files created under either convention.

The MAC_OS directory structure is as follows:

COREJAVA.SEA	Programs from Core Java
INSTJAVA.SEA	Programs from Instant Java
JAVAEXAM.SEA	Programs from Java by Example
JUSTJAVA.SEA	Programs from Just Java
MJDK10B1.SEA	Macintosh JDK (Beta)

To install the JDK or program files from the books:

Because this is an ISO-9660 CD-ROM, the JDK and the program files from each of the books are stored on the disc as self-extracting archives. Copy the files that you want to use to your hard drive and double-click to open.

Index

L

label for button 30
loadImageAndWait method 220
loadImages method 265
loading
    a filter 83
    a URL 2, 30, 31, 35, 41, 246
        with image maps 41
    an image 18, 177, 301
    the CD 4
loop
    audio 20
Loop parameter 20

M

MalformedURLException exception
    212
manipulating
    color 207, 307
manipulating an image 80, 88, 124, 127
    for animation 134
manual slide show play 193
map, image 41
Map*N* group parameters 41, 47
MemoryImageSource class 255, 265,
    272
method
    action 304
    brightenit 207
    calc_new_random 294
    CalcFade 207
    calcLLCenter 232, 249
    calcLLYcoord 237, 254
    calcULCenter 232, 249
    calcULXcoord 236, 253
    calcULYcoord 236, 253
    calcval 293
    CatchFlt 223
    checkImage method 220, 300
    checkImgLoadStatus 270
    createErrorMessageImage 220
    createImage method 224, 254, 255,
        265, 272

darkenit 207
debug 276
doStandardFilters 255
doStandardImgFilters 268
doStandardTxFilters 266
doTxFilters 265
drawBorder 233, 250
drawBottomLine 233, 250
drawFrame 234, 251
drawLeftLine 233, 250
drawRightLine 233, 250
drawText 233, 250
drawTopLine 233, 250
drawUnderline 217, 236, 253
equalsIgnoreCase method 211
Fade 208
filter 81, 127, 129, 215, 224, 226, 228,
    229
filterRGB 307
forName method 210
getAudioClip method 238, 244, 299
getDocumentBase method 212, 238
getFontMetrics method 224
getHeight 210, 215, 221
getNextImgIndex 273, 282
getNextTxIndex 273, 282
getParameter method 211, 213
getPixels 221, 222
getSource method 300
getWidth 210, 221
grabPixels method 222
imageUpdate 256, 266, 301
img_sleep 273, 283
init 230, 238, 242, 257, 258, 259, 260,
    262, 282, 287, 292, 295, 298
invoke 209
isImagePrepared 219
keyDown 276, 290, 294, 296, 305
loadImageAndWait 220
loadImages 265
mouseDown 246, 278, 283, 296, 304
mouseEnter 293
mouseExit 239, 249, 281, 294
mouseMove 238, 247, 279
newInstance method 210

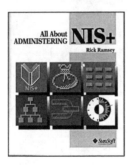

MANAGING THE NEW ENTERPRISE:

The Proof, Not The Hype
Harris Kern, Randy Johnson, Andrew Law, and Michael Hawkins with William Kennedy

In this follow-up to the best selling *Rightsizing the New Enterprise*, the authors discuss how to build and manage a heterogeneous client/ server environment. *Managing the New Enterprise* describes in detail the key technology support infrastructures, including networking, data centers, and system administration, as well as how Information Technology must change in order to manage the New Enterprise. This is an indispensable reference for anyone within Information Technology who is facing the challenges of building and managing client/server computing.

1996, 240 pp., Cloth,
0-13-231184-4 (23118-3)

INTERACTIVE UNIX OPERATING SYSTEM:

A Guide for System Administrators
Marty C. Stewart

Written for first-time system administrators and end users, this practical guide describes the common system administration menus and commands of the INTERACTIVE UNIX System V/386 Release 3.2, Version 4.0 and SVR 3.2 UNIX in general. Loaded with step-by-step instructions and examples, it discusses how to install and configure the INTERACTIVE UNIX system, including the hardware requirements. It describes the unique CUI menu interface, basic OS commands, administration of new user accounts, configuration of customized kernels, and working with the INTERACTIVE UNIX system as an end user.

1996, 320 pp., Paper,
0-13-161613-7 (16161-2)

PC HARDWARE CONFIGURATION GUIDE:

For DOS and Solaris
Ron Ledesma

This book eliminates trial-and-error methodology by presenting a simple, structured approach to PC hardware configuration. The author's time-tested approach is to configure your system in stages, verify and test at each stage, and troubleshoot and fix problems before going on to the next stage. Covers both standalone and networked machines. Discusses how to determine x86 hardware configuration requirements, how to configure hardware components (MCA, ISA, and EISA), partitioning hard disks for DOS and UNIX, and installing DOS and/or UNIX (Solaris x86). Includes configuration instructions, checklists, worksheets, diagrams of popular SCSI host bus, network, and video adapters, and basic installation troubleshooting.

1995, 352 pp., Paper, 0-13-124678-X (12467-7)

MULTIPROCESSOR SYSTEM ARCHITECTURES:

A Technical Survey of Multiprocessor / Multithreaded Systems Using SPARC, Multi-level Bus Architectures and Solaris (SunOS)
Ben Catanzaro

Written for engineers seeking to understand the problems and solutions of multiprocessor system design, this hands-on guide is the first comprehensive description of the elements involved in the design and development of Sun's multiprocessor systems. Topics covered include SPARC processor design and its implementations, an introduction to multilevel bus architectures including MBus and XBus/XDBus, an overview of the Solaris/SunOS™ multithreaded architecture and programming, and an MBus Interface Specification and Design Guide. This book can serve as a reference text for design engineers as well as a hands-on design guide to MP systems for hardware/software engineers.

1994, 528 pp., Paper, 0-13-089137-1 (08913-6)

PANIC! UNIX System Crash Dump Analysis
Chris Drake and Kimberley Brown

PANIC! is the first book to discuss in detail UNIX system panics, crashes and hangs, their causes, what to do when they occur, how to collect information about them, how to analyze that information, and how to get the problem resolved. PANIC! presents this highly technical and intricate subject in a friendly, easy style which even the novice UNIX system administrator will find readable, educational and enjoyable. It is written for systems and network administrators and technical support engineers who are responsible for maintaining and supporting UNIX computer systems and networks. Includes a CD-ROM containing several useful analysis tools, such as adb macros and C tags output from the source trees of two different UNIX systems.

1995, 496 pp., Paper, 0-13-149386-8 (14938-5) Book/CD-ROM

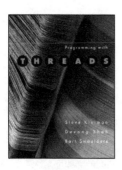

NEW!

PROGRAMMING WITH THREADS
Steve Kleiman, Devang Shah, and Bart Smaalders

Written by senior threads engineers at Sun Microsystems, Inc., this book is the definitive guide to programming with threads. It is intended for both novice and more sophisticated threads programmers, and for developers multithreading existing programs as well as for those writing new multithreaded programs. The book provides structured techniques for mastering the complexity of threads programming with an emphasis on performance issues. Included are detailed examples using the new POSIX threads (Pthreads) standard interfaces. The book also covers the other UNIX threads interface defined by UNIX International.

1996, 250 pp., Paper, 0-13-172389-8 (17238-9)

RIGHTSIZING THE NEW ENTERPRISE:
THE PROOF, NOT THE HYPE
Harris Kern and Randy Johnson

A detailed account of how Sun Microsystems implemented its rightsizing strategy going from a mainframe data center to a heterogeneous client/server distributed environment. This book covers the key infrastructures of an IT organization (the network, data center, and system administration), the rightsizing/management tools, and the training/resource issues involved in transitioning from mainframe to UNIX support. The facts contained in this book provide you with the PROOF that 'rightsizing' can be done.and has been done.

1995, 352 pp., Cloth, 0-13-490384-6 (49038-3)

NEW!

READ ME FIRST!
A Style Guide for the Computer Industry
Sun Technical Publications

A comprehensive look at documenting computer products, from style pointers to legal guidelines, from working with an editor to building a publications department — in both hard copy and electronic copy with an on line viewer, FrameMaker templates for instant page design, and a detailed guide to establishing a documentation department and its processes. Based on an internationally award-winning Sun Microsystems style guide (Award of Excellence in the STC International Technical Publications Competition, 1994)

1996, 300 pp., Paper, 0-13-455347-0 (45534-6)

Book/CD-ROM

RIGHTSIZING FOR CORPORATE SURVIVAL:
An IS Manager's Guide
Robert Massoudi, Astrid Julienne, Bob Millradt, and Reed Hornberger

This book provides IS managers with 'hands-on' guidance for developing a rightsizing strategy and plan. Based upon research conducted through customer visits with multinational corporations, it details the experiences and insights gained by IS professionals that have implemented systems in distributed, client-server environments. Topics covered include:

- Why rightsize?
- What business results can rightsizing produce?
- Key technologies critical to rightsizing
- Good starting points for rightsizing
- What is the process to rightsize an information system?
- Cost considerations and return on investment (ROI) analysis
- How to manage the transition

Throughout the book, case studies and `lessons learned' reinforce the discussion and document best practices associated with rightsizing.

1995, 272 pp., Paper,
0-13-123126-X (12312-5)

SOLARIS IMPLEMENTATION:

A Guide for System Administrators
George Becker, Mary E. S. Morris and Kathy Slattery

Written by three expert Sun system administrators, this book discusses real world, day-to-day Solaris 2 system administration for both new installations and for those migrating an installed Solaris 1 base. It presents tested procedures to help system administrators to improve and customize their networks by eliminating trial-and-error methodologies. Also includes advice for managing heterogeneous Solaris environments and provides autoinstall sample scripts and disk partitioning schemes (with recommended sizes) used at Sun. *1995, 368 pp., Paper, 0-13-353350-6 (35335- 9)*

SOLARIS INTERNATIONAL DEVELOPER'S GUIDE, Second Edtion
Bill Tuthill and David Smallberg

Written for software developers and business managers interested in creating global applications for the Solaris environment (SPARC and x86), this 2nd edition expands on the 1st edition and has updated information on international markets, standards organizations, and writing international documents. New topics in the 2nd edition include CDE/Motif, NEO (formerly project DOE)/ OpenStep, Universal codesets, global internet applications, code examples, and success stories.

1996, 250 pp., Paper,
0-13-494493-3 (49449-2)

SOLARIS PORTING GUIDE, Second Edition
SunSoft Developer Engineering

Ideal for application programmers and software developers, the Solaris Porting Guide, Second Edition, provides a comprehensive technical overview of the Solaris 2.x operating environment and its related migration strategy. The second edition is current through Solaris 2.4 (both the SPARC and x86 platforms) and provides all the information necessary to migrate from Solaris 1 (SunOS 4.x) to Solaris 2 (SunOS 5.x). Other additions include a discussion of emerging technologies such as the Common Desktop Environment (CDE), hints for application performance tuning, and extensive pointers to further information, including Internet sources.

1995, 752 pp., Paper,
0-13-443672-5 (44367-1)

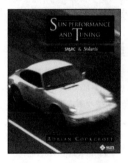

SUN PERFORMANCE AND TUNING:
SPARC and Solaris
Adrian Cockcroft

An indispensable reference for anyone working with Sun workstations running the Solaris environment, this book provides detailed performance and configuration information on all SPARC machines and peripherals, as well as on all operating system releases from SunOS 4.1 through Solaris 2.4. It includes hard-to-find tuning information and offers insights that cannot be found elsewhere. This book is written for developers who want to design for performance and for system administrators who have a system running applications on which they want to improve performance.

1995, 288 pp., Paper,
0-13-149642-5 (14964-1)

Get Café 1.0 at a Special Price

The full version of Symantec Café contains the latest Java Development Kit and many exciting new features and tools:

SYMANTEC.

✔ Debug your Java applets with the Café Visual Java Debugger

✔ Design your forms and menus with the Café Studio

✔ Navigate and edit your classes and methods with the Hierarchy Editor and Class Editor

✔ Compile your Java applets and applications 20 times faster with the Café native compiler

✔ Double the speed of your Java applications with the Café native Java virtual machine

http://www.Café.Symantec.com

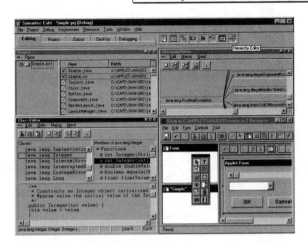

Symantec Café includes all the components found in Café Lite, plus a 2-way hierarchy editor, a class editor, a GUI multi-thread debugger, a visual menu and form designer, a native compiler which compiles the .class files up to 20 times faster, a new Java virtual machine for Windows which doubles the speed of your applications, 85 samples, a tutorial, and the API docs in help.

Get more information on Café automatically sent to you via e-mail. Send an email to **info@bedford.symantec.com** with no subject line, and an overview document will be sent to you along with a description of the other documents available and how to get them.

State Sales/Use Tax

In the following states, add sales/use tax: CO-3%; GA, LA, NY-4%; VA-4.5%; KS-4.9%; AZ, IA, IN, MA, MD, OH, SC, WI-5%; CT, FL, ME, MI, NC, NJ, PA, TN-6%; CA, IL, TX-6.25%; MN, WA-6.5%;DC-5.75%.

Please add local tax for AZ, CA, FL, GA, MO, NY, OH, SC, TN, TX, WA, WI.

Order Information:

- Please allow 2-4 weeks for processing your order.
- Please attach the order form with your payment.
- No P.O. boxes and no C.O.D.s accepted.
- Order form good in the U.S. only.
- If you are tax exempt, please include exemption certificate or letter with tax-exempt number.
- Resellers not eligible.
- Offer not valid with any other promotion.
- One copy per product, per order.

LICENSE AGREEMENT AND LIMITED WARRANTY

READ THE FOLLOWING TERMS AND CONDITIONS CAREFULLY BEFORE OPENING THIS DISK PACKAGE. THIS LEGAL DOCUMENT IS AN AGREEMENT BETWEEN YOU AND PRENTICE-HALL, INC. (THE "COMPANY"). BY OPENING THIS SEALED DISK PACKAGE, YOU ARE AGREEING TO BE BOUND BY THESE TERMS AND CONDITIONS. IF YOU DO NOT AGREE WITH THESE TERMS AND CONDITIONS, DO NOT OPEN THE DISK PACKAGE. PROMPTLY RETURN THE UNOPENED DISK PACKAGE AND ALL ACCOMPANYING ITEMS TO THE PLACE YOU OBTAINED THEM FOR A FULL REFUND OF ANY SUMS YOU HAVE PAID.

1.   **GRANT OF LICENSE:** In consideration of your payment of the license fee, which is part of the price you paid for this product, and your agreement to abide by the terms and conditions of this Agreement, the Company grants to you a nonexclusive right to use and display the copy of the enclosed software program (hereinafter the "SOFTWARE") on a single computer (i.e., with a single CPU) at a single location so long as you comply with the terms of this Agreement. The Company reserves all rights not expressly granted to you under this Agreement.

2.   **OWNERSHIP OF SOFTWARE:** You own only the magnetic or physical media (the enclosed disks) on which the SOFTWARE is recorded or fixed, but the Company retains all the rights, title, and ownership to the SOFTWARE recorded on the original disk copy(ies) and all subsequent copies of the SOFTWARE, regardless of the form or media on which the original or other copies may exist. This license is not a sale of the original SOFTWARE or any copy to you.

3.   **COPY RESTRICTIONS:** This SOFTWARE and the accompanying printed materials and user manual (the "Documentation") are the subject of copyright. You may not copy the Documentation or the SOFTWARE, except that you may make a single copy of the SOFTWARE for backup or archival purposes only. You may be held legally responsible for any copying or copyright infringement which is caused or encouraged by your failure to abide by the terms of this restriction.

4.   **USE RESTRICTIONS:** You may not network the SOFTWARE or otherwise use it on more than one computer or computer terminal at the same time. You may physically transfer the SOFTWARE from one computer to another provided that the SOFTWARE is used on only one computer at a time. You may not distribute copies of the SOFTWARE or Documentation to others. You may not reverse engineer, disassemble, decompile, modify, adapt, translate, or create derivative works based on the SOFTWARE or the Documentation without the prior written consent of the Company.

5.   **TRANSFER RESTRICTIONS:** The enclosed SOFTWARE is licensed only to you and may not be transferred to any one else without the prior written consent of the Company. Any unauthorized transfer of the SOFTWARE shall result in the immediate termination of this Agreement.

6.   **TERMINATION:** This license is effective until terminated. This license will terminate automatically without notice from the Company and become null and void if you fail to comply with any provisions or limitations of this license. Upon termination, you shall destroy the Documentation and all copies of the SOFTWARE. All provisions of this Agreement as to warranties, limitation of liability, remedies or damages, and our ownership rights shall survive termination.

7.   **MISCELLANEOUS:** This Agreement shall be construed in accordance with the laws of the United States of America and the State of New York and shall benefit the Company, its affiliates, and assignees.

8. **LIMITED WARRANTY AND DISCLAIMER OF WARRANTY:** The Company warrants that the SOFTWARE, when properly used in accordance with the Documentation, will operate in substantial conformity with the description of the SOFTWARE set forth in the Documentation. The Company does not warrant that the SOFTWARE will meet your requirements or that the operation of the SOFTWARE will be uninterrupted or error-free. The Company warrants that the media on which the SOFTWARE is delivered shall be free from defects in materials and workmanship under normal use for a period of thirty (30) days from the date of your purchase. Your only remedy and the Company's only obligation under these limited warranties is, at the Company's option, return of the warranted item for a refund of any amounts paid by you or replacement of the item. Any replacement of SOFTWARE or media under the warranties shall not extend the original warranty period. The limited warranty set forth above shall not apply to any SOFT-WARE which the Company determines in good faith has been subject to misuse, neglect, improper installation, repair, alteration, or damage by you. EXCEPT FOR THE EXPRESSED WARRANTIES SET FORTH ABOVE, THE COMPANY DISCLAIMS ALL WARRANTIES, EXPRESS OR IMPLIED, INCLUDING WITHOUT LIMITATION, THE IMPLIED WARRANTIES OF MERCHANTABILITY AND FITNESS FOR A PARTICULAR PURPOSE. EXCEPT FOR THE EXPRESS WARRANTY SET FORTH ABOVE, THE COMPANY DOES NOT WARRANT, GUARANTEE, OR MAKE ANY REPRESENTATION REGARDING THE USE OR THE RESULTS OF THE USE OF THE SOFTWARE IN TERMS OF ITS CORRECTNESS, ACCURACY, RELIABILITY, CURRENTNESS, OR OTHERWISE.

IN NO EVENT, SHALL THE COMPANY OR ITS EMPLOYEES, AGENTS, SUPPLIERS, OR CONTRACTORS BE LIABLE FOR ANY INCIDENTAL, INDIRECT, SPECIAL, OR CONSEQUENTIAL DAMAGES ARISING OUT OF OR IN CONNECTION WITH THE LICENSE GRANTED UNDER THIS AGREEMENT, OR FOR LOSS OF USE, LOSS OF DATA, LOSS OF INCOME OR PROFIT, OR OTHER LOSSES, SUSTAINED AS A RESULT OF INJURY TO ANY PERSON, OR LOSS OF OR DAMAGE TO PROPERTY, OR CLAIMS OF THIRD PARTIES, EVEN IF THE COMPANY OR AN AUTHORIZED REPRESENTATIVE OF THE COMPANY HAS BEEN ADVISED OF THE POSSIBILITY OF SUCH DAMAGES. IN NO EVENT SHALL LIABILITY OF THE COMPANY FOR DAMAGES WITH RESPECT TO THE SOFT-WARE EXCEED THE AMOUNTS ACTUALLY PAID BY YOU, IF ANY, FOR THE SOFTWARE. SOME JURISDICTIONS DO NOT ALLOW THE LIMITATION OF IMPLIED WARRANTIES OR LIABILITY FOR INCIDENTAL, INDIRECT, SPECIAL, OR CONSEQUENTIAL DAMAGES, SO THE ABOVE LIMITATIONS MAY NOT ALWAYS APPLY. THE WARRANTIES IN THIS AGREEMENT GIVE YOU SPECIFIC LEGAL RIGHTS AND YOU MAY ALSO HAVE OTHER RIGHTS WHICH VARY IN ACCORDANCE WITH LOCAL LAW.

ACKNOWLEDGMENT

YOU ACKNOWLEDGE THAT YOU HAVE READ THIS AGREEMENT, UNDERSTAND IT, AND AGREE TO BE BOUND BY ITS TERMS AND CONDITIONS. YOU ALSO AGREE THAT THIS AGREEMENT IS THE COMPLETE AND EXCLUSIVE STATEMENT OF THE AGREEMENT BETWEEN YOU AND THE COMPANY AND SUPERSEDES ALL PROPOSALS OR PRIOR AGREEMENTS, ORAL, OR WRITTEN, AND ANY OTHER COMMUNICATIONS BETWEEN YOU AND THE COMPANY OR ANY REPRESENTATIVE OF THE COMPANY RELATING TO THE SUBJECT MATTER OF THIS AGREEMENT.

Should you have any questions concerning this Agreement or if you wish to contact the Company for any reason, please contact in writing at the address below.

Robin Short
Prentice Hall PTR
One Lake Street
Upper Saddle River, New Jersey 07458

Read before
opening
CD package!

LICENSE AGREEMENT
AND LIMITED WARRANTY

BY OPENING THIS SEALED SOFTWARE CD PACKAGE, YOU ACCEPT AND AGREE TO THE TERMS AND CONDITIONS PRINTED BELOW AND IN THE FULL AGREEMENT PRINTED ON THE PAGES FOLLOWING THE INDEX. IF YOU DO NOT AGREE, DO NOT OPEN THE PACKAGE.

The software is distributed on an "AS IS" basis, without warranty. Neither the authors, the software developers nor Prentice Hall make any representation, or warranty, either express or implied, with respect to the software programs, their quality, accuracy, or fitness for a specific purpose. Therefore, neither the authors, the software developers, nor Prentice Hall shall have any liability to you or any other person or entity with respect to any liability, loss, or damage caused or alleged to have been caused directly or indirectly by the programs contained on the CD. This includes, but is not limited to, interruption of service, loss of data, loss of classroom time, loss of consulting or anticipatory profits, or consequential damages from the use of these programs. If the CD medium is defective, you may return it for a replacement CD.

The SunSoft Press Java Series CD-ROM is a standard ISO-9660 disc. Software on this CD-ROM requires Windows 95, Windows NT, Solaris 2 or Macintosh (System 7.5).

Windows 3.1 IS NOT SUPPORTED